# BEFORE
## ATLANTIS

"Making use of extensive evidence from biology, genetics, geology, archaeology, art history, cultural anthropology, and archaeoastronomy, Frank Joseph offers readers many intriguing alternative ideas about the origin of the human species, the origin of civilization, and the peopling of the Americas."

MICHAEL A. CREMO, COAUTHOR OF *THE HIDDEN HISTORY OF THE HUMAN RACE* AND AUTHOR OF *FORBIDDEN ARCHEOLOGY*

"Staggering in scope, *Before Atlantis* provides compelling evidence that there is a much richer and deeper story of our world. By setting back the clock for our civilization and species, Frank Joseph builds a foundation on which the new history of the world will be written."

STEVEN SORA, AUTHOR OF *THE LOST TREASURE OF THE KNIGHTS TEMPLAR* AND REGULAR CONTRIBUTOR TO *ATLANTIS RISING*

"Frank Joseph has come up with another tour de force about ancient seafarers and early migrations across the oceans in his new book, *Before Atlantis*."

GUNNAR THOMPSON, PH.D., AUTHOR OF *COMMANDER FRANCIS DRAKE & THE WEST COAST MYSTERIES*, *SECRET VOYAGES TO THE NEW WORLD*, AND *NU SUN: ASIAN-AMERICAN VOYAGES, 500 B.C.*

# BEFORE ATLANTIS

## 20 Million Years of Human and Pre-Human Cultures

### FRANK JOSEPH

Bear & Company
Rochester, Vermont • Toronto, Canada

Bear & Company
One Park Street
Rochester, Vermont 05767
www.BearandCompanyBooks.com

Text stock is SFI certified

Bear & Company is a division of Inner Traditions International

**Library of Congress Cataloging-in-Publication Data**
Joseph, Frank.
  Before Atlantis : 20 million years of human and pre-human cultures / Frank
Joseph.
       p. cm.
  Includes bibliographical references and index.
  Summary: "A comprehensive exploration of Earth's ancient past, the evolution of
humanity, the rise of civilization, and the effects of global catastrophe"—Provided
by publisher.
  ISBN 978-1-59143-157-2 (pbk.) — ISBN 978-1-59143-826-7 (e-book)
  1. Prehistoric peoples. 2. Civilization, Ancient. 3. Atlantis (Legendary place) I.
Title.
  GN740.J68 2013
  930—dc23

                                                                2012037131

Printed and bound in the United States by Lake Book Manufacturing, Inc.
The text stock is SFI certified. The Sustainable Forestry Initiative® program
promotes sustainable forest management.

10  9  8  7  6  5  4  3  2  1

Text design and layout by Brian Boynton
This book was typeset in Garamond Premier Pro with Gill Sans, Calligraphic, and
Legacy Sans as display typefaces

Chapter 8 is a revised, expanded version of the original article that appeared in
The Barnes Review (Washington, D.C., Volume XVII, Number 4, July/August
2011), and chapter 9 is a revised and expanded version of the original article that
appeared in The Barnes Review (Washington, D.C., Volume XVII, Number 5,
September/October 2011). Both are republished here with permission.

To send correspondence to the author of this book, mail a first-class letter to the
author c/o Inner Traditions • Bear & Company, One Park Street, Rochester, VT
05767, and we will forward the communication.

*T. E. Lee, Warren King Moorehead, Marcelino Sanz de Sautuola, Virginia Steen-McIntyre, and all those martyrs of discovery whose professional careers were destroyed by their mainstream colleagues for daring to challenge prevailing academic dogma with facts later proved correct.*

# Contents

# Godhood or Extinction?

*If you would understand anything, observe its beginning*
*and its development.*

ARISTOTLE, *METAPHYSICS*

It is impossible to determine who we are, how we got here, or where we are going unless we know from where we came. An individual ignorant of his or her own past would be utterly lost, unable to plan for the future. So too, we, as a people, cannot make sense of the social, economic, and even environmental deterioration developing around us, because the energies that molded civilization and our very bodies and brains are not properly understood.

Happily, the outline of those critical energies is beginning to emerge clearer than ever before, thanks to some very recent discoveries. These discoveries are mostly given short shrift by the purveyors of public information, but they are emphasized here in detail, because they radically revise inadequate presumptions about human origins. Among the most surprising of these discoveries is our evolution—in water.

An "aquatic phase" had been postulated as long ago as the sixth century BCE; presented here is fresh evidence to show that early humans repeatedly returned to hydrospheric environments for evolutionary development—and to such an extent that our present physical and psychological configurations were formed by these encounters. Moreover, we appear to have been neither the first nor the only humans who walked the Earth, as borne out by finds in Oklahoma, Argentina, and elsewhere, predating our evolution by millions of years.

*Before Atlantis* challenges current paleoanthropological arguments on behalf of East Africa as the birthplace of *Homo sapiens,* pointing instead to Southeast Asia, where the most terrific volcanic eruption Earth ever experienced abruptly reduced humanity from two million individuals to a few thousand, worldwide. Pushed to the very brink of extinction, our species gradually recovered to develop the first high culture—not 5,500 years ago in the Near East, as textbook archaeologists would have it, but seventy centuries earlier, in Indonesia and the Central Pacific.

*Before Atlantis* offers the most comprehensive and—so far as this author knows—the only description of Stone Age sites around the world, thereby demonstrating that the so-called megalith-builders were transoceanic seafarers who circled the globe during the mid-fifth millennium BCE to create the first global civilization. An ultimate secret locked in their immense monoliths is revealed by examining the altered states of consciousness still generated by these powerful monuments. Nor was Christopher Columbus the first overseas visitor to America from the Old World. His arrival in 1492 was preceded by ice age Europeans, as proved by an abundance of their remains newly found from the Carolinas to Brazil.

We learn the real identity of the Garden of Eden, and the location of its well-preserved ruins, as excavated by university-trained archaeologists. The profound antiquity of Atlantis herself emerges with the first Atlantean an astounding 350,000 years ago.

These latest paradigm-shattering discoveries are transforming long-established versions of the past, and together comprise the New History.

In it, we behold our true reflection as a young, civilizing species with a godlike destiny—not an old, failed primate doomed to self-destruction. The following interpretations and conclusions based squarely on fresh information accomplish for us what an appreciation of the past is meant to provide; namely, a well-defined examination of mankind's dramatic origins that shaped and continue to mold our identity and the world in which we live.

Accordingly, *Before Atlantis* is an ambitious undertaking, aimed at an expansive, comprehensive, yet close-up panorama of our beginnings as a species and subsequent course of human evolution, through our earliest cultural efforts and first civilization. As such, it endeavors to determine what made us different from all other creatures, how we arrived in our present condition, and where we are headed.

# 1

# Evolutionary Baptism

*It is hard to resist the conclusion that something must have happened to the ancestors of* Homo sapiens *which did not happen to the ancestors of gorillas and chimpanzees.*

ELAINE MORGAN, *THE AQUATIC APE*

Deeply engraved in childhood memories is one of my life's breakthrough moments—the kind of insight that drastically transformed my view of the world forever after. It occurred when I was eleven years old during a family outing to the Field Museum of Natural History, at Chicago's lakefront. I knew and revered the awesome, old institution of ancient Egyptian mummies and the far older dinosaur fossils from many previous visits, but I had never before noticed a large, glass display case containing ten or twelve mounted skeletons standing in a row. The one at the far end, to my right, seemed familiar, and my suspicions were confirmed by a small brass tablet at its feet that read, "Modern Man." Beside him stood a remarkably similar specimen, not quite as tall, but more robust. Another plaque identified it as an ape. The next nearest bones belonged to a gorilla, followed by those of a chimpanzee, then an orangutan, monkey, and perhaps five or six other sets, side by side.

Staring at these gaunt, motionless remains for the first time, a powerful sense of awareness began to dawn in my mind, until I almost cried out in recognition, "They're all related!" The natural progression of skeletons from left to right—from lowly primate to human being—seemed conspicuously obvious.[1] At the time, I was utterly ignorant of the word "evolution."* Until then, my only familiarity with human creation was the story of Adam and Eve, a version of events suddenly vaporized by my discovery. In that moment, evolution irrevocably stamped itself on my consciousness as an incontrovertible—indeed, self-evident—fact of life.

I have since learned how the mainstream view of human evolution holds that climate change deforested much of Central and East Africa about 6 million years ago, driving our apish ancestors from their former existence amid the trees into the open savannahs. They adapted to this less abundant, more perilous environment by becoming first scavengers, then hunters. A developing, upright posture allowed food to be carried away while running, and, when standing, provided a better perspective for prey or danger.

Higher temperatures on the open plains led to bodily hair loss and the introduction of sweat glands for cooling. Pressures of the hunt necessitated social cooperation, with growing emphasis on individual-to-individual communication for more successful group kills. These stimuli increased brain capacity with a consequent expanding awareness of fundamental relationships, resulting in tool use and tool making—that is, the advent of technology—which has characterized man ever since.

In the 140 years since Darwin published *The Descent of Man,* myriad anthropological discoveries confirm and elucidate our evolutionary path. There are some disturbing discrepancies in the official story, however. One primary example is that of human body hair. Modern

---

*The relationship between man and his primate relatives is much closer than anyone imagined at the time of my deduction in 1955. Early twenty-first-century genetic studies found humans shared 95 percent of their DNA with chimpanzees. We have twenty-three pairs of chromosomes; chimps, twenty-four.

humans have as much body hair as apes, but ours has become far smaller and finer. We are told that our hominid ancestors discarded their thick body hair to cool off on the hot African veldt. Yet, hair is as much an insulator against heat as it is against cold, because it traps temperate air close to the skin. No other primates put aside their hair or fur for the sake of cooling. Male hominids supposedly became overheated during the hunt, so why is it that the less physically active female became, and still remains, less hairy?

After losing their coarse body hair, our early ancestors developed layers of fat beneath the skin to keep warm, an adaptation employed by no other primate. Nonhuman primates and other mammals store fat, but in ways unlike ours; their fat wraps around their kidneys and membranes separating the viscera, acting as protection, not warmth. These creatures do have some epidermal fat—again, not against cold, but to keep the skin supple. It seems sensible that Mother Nature would have opted for retaining body hair as a much simpler alternative to a complex double mechanism—nakedness for cooling, subcutaneous fat for warmth—used by no other primate.

Mammal hair growth is so sensitive to temperature change, it thickens or thins in response to cold or heat within the lifetime on an individual. Monkeys from the tropics grow coats of thicker hair when relocated to the Moscow Zoo. A leading authority on archaeology in the Bahamas, William Donato, believes "the body hair argument is the one that seems most out of sync, since we have become less hirsute, while earlier primates were more so."[2] The loss of body hair, relative to our closest related primate cousins, suggests ancestral transition from exclusively terrestrial surroundings to an aquatic environment, just as the dolphin's land-bound predecessor discarded its fur while adapting to watery conditions. Both hair and fur are less suited to an aquatic life, as described below.

Inexplicably, man alone of all other terrestrial mammals uses perspiration to cool down, another contradiction to evolutionary development. No overriding, external stimulus compelled him to discard an effective temperature control mechanism already in place (hair) for the more cumbersome arrangement of two or three million sweat glands—far more than possessed by any other primate—alternating with subcutaneous fat.

Sweating dehydrates the body by employing excess moisture in an uneconomical cooling process, while depleting much-needed sodium. Clearly, in trying to cope with aridity and high temperatures of the African plains, hair cover is preferable to moisture loss. No other hunting mammal ever chose the clumsy heating-cooling strategy adopted by man. Those originally arboreal baboons that became predators on the open plains effected their successful transformation without discarding thick body hair.

Nor did the baboons develop verbal communication, despite intense social interaction, because visual cues are far more appropriate when hunting: silence prior to an attack is essential. Hunting cannot, therefore, have prompted early hominids to develop speech. Tool-making is sometimes cited as the inspiration for our first language. But the manufacture of tools is far better demonstrated than explained, even now. Indeed, visual communication is extraordinarily nuanced and exact in primates, particularly among anthropoid apes. Africa's !Kung Bushmen communicate via hand signals, without speaking a word, while hunting. Sounds produced by nonhuman primates are calls or cries, usually of alarm, not interactive communication. The evolutionary tendency among apes, monkeys, and chimpanzees is toward increasing visual skills.

Scientific attempts at teaching the latter to speak English produce very negligible results. While chimps can be forced to respond to specific, spoken commands, they perform far more successfully and readily to visual indications. Moreover, they are not anatomically equipped to actually speak, because their larynx is too high up in the throat. Bipedalism lengthened the hominid's resonating cavity, making the utterance of syllabic sounds possible. It was, after all, our erect posture and ability to walk upright that enabled voice communication and distinguishes us from our primate cousins. With no inclination for a chimpanzee to walk on his two legs, his larynx must remain where it is, in a position unsuited to the formation of words.

Language itself almost certainly emerged from onomatopoeia, which means the formation of words that imitate sounds associated with objects or actions to which they refer. These words include bark, cuckoo, drip, fizz, growl, hum, jangle, moo, neigh, purr, quack, rattle, screech, tinkle, twang, whack, and so on. Derived from the Greek *onoma*, "name," and *poiein*, "to make," more examples abound in traditional children's poetry, such as "Baa Baa Black Sheep," "Old MacDonald had a Farm," "Ding Dong Bell," and many others. Early hominids mimicked natural sounds, particularly those made by animals. Repetition of vocal imitations identified specific creatures or phenomena, until the sounds became names for the imitated objects or verbs describing their actions: for example, the ancient Egyptian word for "cat," *meow*, or the *Caprimulgus vociferus*, more familiar by its English name, "whipoorwill." Other avian examples include the bob-white, bobolink, curlew, and phoebe.

As an indication of their profound antiquity, alphabetical systems are likewise rooted in visual versions of onomatopoeia. The Phoenician *lamedh* began as the image of an ox, which the Romans turned into the letter L. *Mem* became Greek for water; *mu* is represented as a wavy line retained in our M. Similarly, *mu* is hieratic Egyptian for "sea," just as N, likewise a wavy line, signified "water." The Greek *ayin*, or "eye," became the Roman letter O that it physically resembled. *Ayin* was itself preceded and formed by the circular shape our lips make when the letter O is vocalized. The earliest known use of capital A, which resembles a mountain, appears in the world's oldest language, Sanskrit, which includes many A-words for mountain (Aadrika, Achala, Arjuna, etc). So too, the letter S physically resembles a snake, together with the onomatopoeian "hiss" it makes when its name is pronounced.

Thus, first the spoken and then much later the written languages began from obvious, immediate references to the sounds and appearances of animals and things. With their growing multiplicity and complexity, vocal and literary expression blossomed into more and more abstract concepts. Perhaps every word we speak might be ultimately traced to its earliest roots in the sonic description of a natural phenomenon; everything that followed was but a development or refinement.

After all, the ability possessed by average humans to vocally imitate other creatures and sounds far exceeds the range of their closest competitors in mimicry, for example parrots and lyre birds. Indigenous peoples, such as many Native American tribes, are famous for their powers of animal imitation. Even in the twentieth century, during Benito Mussolini's 1935 invasion of East Africa, Amharan warriors sowed confusion and chaos among the ranks of his soldiers by realistically mimicking Italian bugle calls. This exceptional talent suggests a stronger link between onomatopoeia and the growth of language, both spoken and written, than we suspect.

Evolutionary theorists suspect *Homo ergaster* was the first hominid to vocalize. *Homo ergaster,* perhaps the ancestor of *Homo erectus,* became extinct about 1.7 million years ago. As onomatopoeian words increased in numbers and frequency among *Homo ergaster,* they were taken over and expanded by his mentally superior successor, *Homo heidelbergensis,* until they eventually morphed into the first symbolic sounds for abstract concepts. More certainly, following the 2007 discovery of a *Homo neanderthalensis* hyoid bone, paleoanthrolpologists suspect that Neanderthals, beginning about 300,000 years ago, may have been the earliest hominids anatomically capable of producing sounds similar to modern humans. The hyoid bone, or lingual bone, situated in the anterior midline of the neck between the chin and thyroid cartilage, aids in tongue movement and swallowing, and is absent in earlier hominids.

Paleoanthropologists teach that our ancestors chose an increasingly upright posture that allowed them to carry tools, weapons, or spoils while running. Yet, baboons, chimpanzees, and gorillas are able to carry all the objects they desire in their knuckle-dragging hands with no difficulty as they scurry across open spaces on all fours. They are much faster than bipedal humans, so moving about on two legs has not granted us any speed advantage. Some baboons entirely transitioned to life on the savannah, and successfully organized as hunters without having become erect or bipedal in the process. Yet, something else happened to our ancestors that set them on a separate path to bipedalism and beyond.

There are other problems with modern theories of human evolution. When most mammals or birds relocated from an arboreal to terrestrial existence, their sense of smell intensified. Not man's. On the contrary, our sense of smell has fallen off drastically by comparison. Industrial Age pollution, perfumes, pesticides, or deodorants are not to blame, because our olfactory powers have been in decline for more than 30,000 years before the advent of civilization.

Additionally, the human female's vaginal canal is tilted forward at an angle—unlike all other anthropoids—for the accommodation of face-to-face sexual intercourse. Life on the savannah cannot explain why this manner of copulation developed in opposition to every other primate species.

Unlike any other denizen of the African plains, our eyes cry tears. Believers in the savannah as the crucible of human change are unable to identify what in the natural environment could have singled out mankind for the production of tears.

Failure to account for these and many other discrepancies in evolutionary theory began to emerge not long after Darwin's death in 1882. Forty years later, a professor of pathological anatomy at Berlin University discovered what he believed was a comprehensive solution to such disturbing inconsistencies. Dr. Max Westenhöfer's hypothesis was radical, even fantastic, and, therefore, something of a product of the times. The decades between World Wars I and II were electric with popular extremism—ideological, cultural, moral, and scientific—when fresh, often outrageous concepts were seriously entertained and almost as instantly acclaimed, no matter how farfetched.

Many of these novel ideas were absurd, but at least a few were truly visionary, and eventually came to pass in such breakthroughs as atomic power, jet propulsion, and television. Westenhöfer's view was in keeping

*Fig. 1.1. Dr. Max Westenhöfer, father of the Aquatic Ape Theory.*
*Original illustration by Kenneth Caroli.*

with this erratic Zeitgeist when he addressed his colleagues during the
international Anthropological Congress at Salzburg, Austria, in 1926. He
told them that we are separated from other primates by too many discrepancies to have followed a purely terrestrial evolutionary path. Our physical
differences result from an extended epoch when our premodern ancestors'

habitat switched from the land to the water before returning once more to the land. "Primitive, surviving features from an aquatic phase," he said, "are preserved in man's anatomy today. The postulation of an aquatic mode of life during an early stage of human evolution is a tenable hypothesis, for which further inquiry may produce additional supporting evidence."[3]

Westenhöfer took fellow scholars by surprise, but scientific opinion tended less toward condemnation than cautious consideration. His views had been somewhat preceded more than two millennia before by the father of evolutionary theory. Anaximander's nonmythic proposal in the sixth century BCE held that humankind emerged from the sea, where it had developed from more primitive forms—a position generallly accepted and elaborated upon by Greco-Roman scholars until it was lost with the fall of Classical Civilization.

*Fig. 1.2 First-century CE Roman copy of a third-century BCE Greek statue portraying Anaximander, the world's first scientist, who believed humans evolved from a watery environment.*

During subsequent centuries from the Dark Ages until Darwin's publication of *The Descent of Man,* biblical allegories alone sufficed to explain human creation, at least in Europe and the United States. Westenhöfer's own 1942 book about an "aquatic phase" in human evolution, *Das Eigenweg des Menschen* ("The Singular Way to Mankind")—

was a controversial success throughout Europe, but his research was mostly obscured by the Second World War.

In 1957, three years after Westenhöfer's death at the age of eighty-six, a distinguished marine biologist gained wider attention with a similar idea. While Westenhöfer had been lecturing in Austria about early man's watery interlude, Sir Alister Clavering Hardy (1896–1985) was chief zoologist aboard the science vessel RRS *Discovery*, studying plankton in Antarctica. His pioneering research there continues to this day with the Sir Alister Hardy Foundation for Ocean Science. Later, he became a Professor of Zoology at the University of Hull, then Professor of Natural History at the University of Aberdeen, and Linacre Professor of Zoology in Oxford. Recognized as one of Britain's extraordinary scientists of the twentieth century, he was knighted in 1957. During all these years of acclaim, he lived a double life in the pursuit of a scientific heresy, the public discussion of which would have subjected his career to a feeding frenzy of academic criticism.

As early as 1930, Hardy began to question official evolutionary theory. He had read *Man's Place Among the Mammals,* by Frederic Wood Jones, which posed the question: Why do humans, unlike all other land mammals, have fat attached to their skin? Privately sympathetic to Westenhöfer's radical hypothesis, Jones was himself a renowned naturalist, embryologist, anatomist, and anthropologist, a founder in the field of modern physical anthropology, and president of the Royal Society of South Australia. But both Jones and Hardy knew that their lofty credentials could not protect them from the fury of aroused colleagues worshipping at the feet of Darwin. Not until the sixty-four-year-old Hardy was safely retired did he go public with his thirty-year-long research into the aquatic ape hypothesis.

"It is in the gap of some ten million years or more, between Proconsul and Australopithicus," he concluded, "that I suppose Man to have been cradled in the sea."[4] *Proconsul* was an 18-million-year-old fossil species, a possible ancestor of both great and lesser apes, and of humans. Some 6 million years ago, the more advanced *Australopithecus* was an important progenitor of the *Homo* genus. "My thesis," Hardy said, "is that a branch of this primitive ape-stock was forced by competition from life in the trees to feed on the sea-shores and to hunt for food, shell-fish, sea-urchins, etc., in the shallow waters off the coast. I suppose that they were forced into the water just as we have seen happen in so many other groups of terrestrial animals. I am imagining this happening in the warmer parts of the world, in the tropical seas where Man could stand being in the water for relatively long periods, that is, several hours at a stretch."[5]

The renowned British archaeologist, Jacquetta Hawkes (1910–1996), described Man "as a basically tropical primate."[6]

The unique stimulus of a water environment was supposed to have prompted *Proconsul* to develop an erect posture and greater intelligence, characteristics that continued to evolve after it returned to the land as *Australopithecus*.

Hardy's lectures and March 17, 1960 article in *New Scientist* magazine attracted some notoriety within the academic community; however, his hypothesis was only made available to a broader audience in 1982 when *The Aquatic Ape: A Theory of Human Evolution* was published. The author was Elaine Morgan, a science writer, who couched this strange wrinkle of evolutionary theory in everyday language nontechnical readers could understand. Her book became an international bestseller, but she was often held up to ridicule in her well-attended presentations.

A reviewer of her book at Amazon.com recalls a time "when Mrs. Morgan was booed by crowds everywhere. My wife and I watched with disgust, as Science and even the lunatic fringe of pseudo-science tried laughing her off the stage. . . . So far, nothing has contravened her theory in the least. . . . And that is why scientists hate her: she's threatening to show their emperor has no clothes. . . . In other words, science persists doing to her what the Church did to Galileo. . . but Morgan's not recanting. That is bravery and integrity!"[7]

Skeptics dismissed her as nothing more than a pseudoscientist, accused her of distorting evolutionary theory for "feminist agendas,"

*Fig. 1.3. As one of the great scientists of the twentieth century, the British marine biologist Sir Alister Clavering Hardy lent important credence to the aquatic ape hypothesis. Photo courtesy of the Sir Alister Hardy Foundation for Ocean Science (SAHFOS).*

and emphasized her lack of academic credentials. They argue that "the Aquatic Ape Hypothesis is thought by some anthropologists to be accepted readily by popular audiences, students and non-specialist scholars because of its simplicity."[8]

But Elaine Morgan did not invent the aquatic ape theory; she only reintroduced it to the general public during the late twentieth century. Her predecessors, Westenhöfer, Jones, and especially Hardy, were highly respected, extraordinary scholars, whose careers still lend credibility to their heretical proposal. Nor were they alone. They have been joined by Desmond Morris, among the most famous ethnologists and zoologists from the mid-twentieth to early twenty-first centuries, best known for his popular television documentaries and books, such as *The Naked Ape* and *The Human Zoo.* "It is difficult to see how all the points assembled to back the Aquatic Theory can be explained away," he admits.[9]

Derek Ellis, a marine ecologist and professor Emeritus at the University of Victoria in British Columbia, believes "an aquatic ape is a likely ancestor of humans in terms of primate behavior, marine ecosystems and geophysical timing."[10] He has been seconded by Professor William Graham Richards, a Fellow of Brasenose College, Oxford, and the author of 300 scientific articles, plus fifteen books, including *Human Evolution.* He concludes that the aquatic ape theory "conforms to current theories of speciation better than the savannah origins model, and accounts for a number of diverse phenomena hitherto not seen as connected."[11]

Other scientific luminaries who support the aquatic ape theory include Dr. Michel Odent, founder of London's Primal Health Research Centre, and the author of eleven books in twenty-one languages; Dr. Chris Knight, Professor of Anthropology at the University of Comenius, Bratislava, Slovakia; Professor Glyn Isaac, a South African archaeologist, generally acknowledged as the most influential Africanist of the last half-century; and Michael Crawford, Professor of Ancient History at University College, London, elected a Fellow of the British Academy. Figures such as these are hardly among the "students and non-specialist scholars" who advocate the aquatic ape theory "for its simplicity."

Of particular significance is Colin Peter Groves, Professor of Biological Anthropology at the Australian National University in Canberra, and a leading evolution researcher in the world today. A spokesman for the Australian Skeptics, a nonprofit organization aimed at scrutinizing outrageous scientific claims, he has characterized the aquatic ape theory as "sophisticated" and "a possible explanation for bipedalism."[12]

# 2

# Homo Aquaticus

*The Aquatic Theory remains an open question. But such hypotheses, which at first sound so improbable, should at least serve as a stimulus for further research, on the principle that a good detective follows up on the least promising clues, as well as those that seem to point to a simple solution.*

DR. MAX WESTENHÖFER

Skeptics of the aquatic ape theory accuse its advocates of misrepresenting eleven human characteristics upon which Professor Groves and his colleagues rely to make their case: hairlessness, breath control, diet, the diving reflex, body fat, the larynx, the nose, webbing between fingers and toes (syndactyly, please see plates 1 and 2 of the color insert), the sebaceous glands, swimming, and bipedalism.

Some conventional evolutionary theorists believe that body hair was discarded, not when early humans entered the water, but more probably as a means of losing parasites. Morgan points out, however, "a great many animals occupy lairs, dens, setts [badger holes], or burrows. Most of them become infested, yet they have not attempted to delouse themselves by turning into naked wolves and naked badgers."[1]

In their mother's womb, all humans develop webbed fingers and toes—plus gills. By the final months of pregnancy, these gills close up and vanish in virtually all infants, although reports of some very rare cases of children born with clearly visible throat gill slits do occur during each generation. A baby does not breathe for oxygen in the womb, where it has no use for gills—which, in any case, are nonfunctioning—because everything the embryo and fetus needs is received through the mother's placenta.

In fact, however, the human parathyroid gland used to be our gills. Calcium levels are regulated by the parathyroid gland, which secretes a parathyroid hormone if the calcium concentration in the blood falls too low. This hormone then causes the release of calcium from bone, and increases its intake by the kidney, raising the calcium levels back to normal. Only since 2004 have scientists known that the parathyroid gland evolved from gills* when our ancestors made the transition from an aquatic to a terrestrial environment.[2] Like syndactyly and subcutaneous fat, evolution of ancestral gills into the parathyroid gland is another telltale sign of our prolonged and formative interlude in the water.

More tellingly, hair arranged along the human form, especially down the back, forms the same pattern water makes as it streams around our bodies; these tracks all meet diagonally toward the midline. While entering the sixth month in its mother's womb, the human fetus strangely—and without any discernible cause—develops lanugo. Before being entirely discarded long prior to birth, this bodysuit of fine hairs runs in tracts precisely following water as it moves over a swimming body. This pattern is found on no other primate, but typifies aquatic

---

*Writing in *Proceedings of the National Academy of Sciences*, Professor Anthony Graham and Dr. Masataka Okabe speculated that the transformation from gills to parathyroid gland occurred many millions of years ago, during life's transition from the sea to the land. But evolution concerning transition of an organ, particularly with the persistance of such visible traces of its former function and configuration, suggest a far more recent aquatic phase.

animals. Lanugo's water-ripple traits were not caused by the unborn infant swimming around in its mother's amniotic fluid, because the fetus rotates only very slowly in the womb, as do all other mammals. Other mammals, however, do not evidence the same kind of lanugo pattern.

While man's body grew naked in water, his head bobbed above the surface, where it was exposed to the bright sun. As a shield against its harmful rays, scalp hair was retained. Hair around the groin remained for sexual selection and under the armpits to cushion against skin abrasion where the torso and arm meet.

Certain factors of the aquatic ape theory are especially pertinent concerning women's biology and evolution. During their aquatic phase, women spent longer hours in and under the water, as they grew heavier with pregnancy, and were especially busy diving to retrieve nourishment for the new life growing inside their wombs. The Japanese pearl divers known as the Ama are renowned to this day, as they have been for more than 2,000 years, for their ability to free dive. They dive minus scuba gear or air tanks—and until the 1960s dressed only in loincloth—to seventy-five feet beneath the surface of the waters off southeastern Honsu. Most Ama are female, because their breath control is superior to men.

Women are also more buoyant, because they have a higher percentage of fat, which floats, as well as a lower percentage of negative-buoyancy bone mass and muscle. Their fat distribution toward the periphery of their bodies allows their legs to float higher. Subcutaneous fat makes aquatic animals buoyant in water, a decided disadvantage for any terrestrial creature, which would be slowed down by the extra weight. "Like other aquatic animals," Desmond Morris states, "but no other primates, we have a layer of blubber beneath our skin."[3]

A woman's streamlined hydrodynamic benefits permit her to exert less energy while swimming at higher speeds, as exemplified by Susie Maroney, who swam from Mexico to Cuba, the longest distance ever thus achieved without flippers in the open sea. She covered 122 miles in 38 hours, 33 minutes on June 1, 1998. The Australian's record has not been broken since. On August 6, 1926, Gertrude Ederle was the first woman to swim the English Channel, swimming 35 percent faster than the fastest male competitor before her. The year before, she swam 21 miles from the tip of Manhattan to Sandy Hook, New Jersey, in 7 hours, 11 minutes, 30 seconds, bettering the records held by men. Ederle's English Channel crossing stood for nearly a quarter of a century, until it was broken in 1950 by another woman, Florence Chadwick. Female fat not only provides better buoyancy, but improved insulation against cold.

All these attributes form a legacy modern women have received from an ancestral, aquatic phase, during which they were required to perform as superior swimmers on behalf of their children. This conclusion is underscored by a woman's hair, which grows fuller and stronger the more advanced her pregnancy becomes, providing her baby with something abundant and secure to hold; an infant's grasp is among the essential instincts with which it is born. A report in the *National Geographic* magazine described native women in Tierra del Fuego who "spend long periods in the water with the children hanging onto their hair."[4] Revealingly, after the child is about fourteen or fifteen months old, when its legs are strong enough for walking, the mother begins to lose the thickness of hair formerly characterized by pregnancy and her offspring's first year of life outside the womb. This waxing and waning of hair in relationship to birth and early infancy occurs in no other primate.

The relative disappearance of hair from the human body was occasioned not only by the development of its subcutaneous fat, but to facilitate swimming by reducing water resistance. Today, competitive swimmers shave off all their body hair just before a meet, thereby gaining a full second. Olympic athletes gain additional time by wearing full-length, skintight swimsuits that funnel water over their bodies in the same pattern followed by hair tracks running across the human torso.

It behooved early man to become more completely naked in the sea, so he could catch more food and successfully escape dangerous predators. Hairier and therefore slower aquatic hominids would have been inferior swimmers, and consequently less successful hunters, more vulnerable to sharks and other man-eaters. Only their naked betters would have survived, passing on a superior set of genetic traits to subsequent generations. Terrestrial animals need hair or fur for temperature regulation. Aquatic mammals are mostly naked, relying on subcutaneous fat instead. Otters, beavers, platypuses, and shrews have retained their fur in an aquatic habitat, trapping pockets of captured air next to the skin. This tactic works well for smaller, lighter creatures, but is impractical for an animal with the much heavier weight and greater height of a human.

Nakedness combined with subcutaneous fat is indicative of aquatic, not terrestrial animals, and certainly not of apes or chimpanzees. As such, the human body is self-evidently aquatic, unlike all our primate relatives. So too, the dolphin's progenitor was a doglike mammal that doffed its fur 50 million years ago to become a naked sea beast. A pair of small, rod-shaped pelvic bones found on skeletons of the modern dolphin are vestigial hind limbs that once belonged to the animal's terrestrial ancestor.

Critics of the aquatic ape theory believe that humans developed breath control as they became increasingly articulate. Moreover, they argue, bipedalism freed muscles around the upper torso from locomotion, thereby permitting an independent rate of breath. It was indeed the development of man's upright posture that enabled his ability to speak, because it forced him to balance his head in such a way that his larynx positioned farther down his throat. The resulting cavity made possible his ability to vocalize the kind of low-pitched sounds necessary for the utterance of spoken words.

His transformation never took place in any other apelike creature or chimpanzee, rendering them forever speechless. They also lack muscles to raise or relax the back end of the resonating cavity, an ability associated with connecting and disconnecting of our nasal passages. Such controlled breathing, essential for speech, finds no stimulus on the savannah, but is imperative for an aquatic mammal diving into water. As mentioned earlier, terrestrial mammals prefer to communicate with each other using visual signs—particularly while hunting, when stealth is of primary importance. Aquatic mammals, on the other hand, are typified by sound communication, as exemplified in whales and dolphins, whose vocalizations are far more complex than anything produced by apes or chimpanzees.

A telltale remnant of our own aquatic phase is the vellum—the soft palate of tissue constituting the back of the roof of the mouth—that closes, allowing us to hold our breath. This conscious control typical of all marine mammals is absent in terrestrials. An ape cannot submerge beneath the water's surface, because it is unable to close the large nostrils of its broad nose. Neither can man, but his nose is nevertheless proportionately longer and thinner for diving; its flesh and cartilage roof deflect water from being forced into the sinuses during a dive, an arrangement found in no other primate.

Around the openings to his nostrils are muscles (possibly vestigial) that once could have closed them, but today produce limited movement—flaring during certain emotional conditions, especially anger. They appear to have atrophied since our aquatic phase, when, like other marine mammals, we were capable of shutting our nostrils against the intrusion of water. In any case, apes and chimpanzees entirely lack our flaring nasal muscles. "We have a unique nose shape," observes Desmond Morris, "that shields our nostrils when we dive below the surface."[5]

Bernhard Hennenberg, a leading otolaryngologist (an ear-nose-throat specialist) in wartime Europe and early convert to the aquatic ape theory, concluded, as Westenhöfer paraphrased it:

that this ancestral hominid featured a contractile form of the ear muscle, with the antihelix tragus and antitragus [intrinsic muscles of the external ear] differing in shape from that of *Homo sapiens sapiens,* and that this original form was subsequently lost during the transition to life on land. It is still easily possible to reproduce the original form in children by artificial means, and the original feature has in fact been observed in one living newborn baby. In his famous work, *Physiology of Motion,* Duchenne shows that electrical stimulation of the tragus [a small pointed eminence of the external ear that collects sounds from behind] and antitragus [a small tubercle that points anteriorly] muscles in human beings is capable of closing the entrance of the ear.[*6]

"Auditory exostoses, bony swellings of the ear canal, a condition well-known to otolaryngologists, occur exclusively as a direct result of long-term exposure to relatively cold water," writes Dr. Marc Verhaegen, a physician in the Belgium town of Putte, near Brussels, who has applied his medical expertise and knowledge of human anatomy to the Aquatic Ape Theory since the 1970s.[7] He explains that "ear exostoses are only found in populations that dive, usually for shellfish. . . . We have the ear exostoses only seen in long-term cold water divers."[8] Commonly known as "surfer's ear," auditory exostosis is an abnormal bone growth within the ear canal that causes the bone surrounding the ear canal to develop lumps of new bony growth that constrict the ear canal. Surfer's ear is a human condition shared with other aquatic mammals, but with no other primate.

In this same regard, Westenhöfer mentioned "the appendix, lobulations of the kidneys, the indentation of the spleen, and formation of additional spleens. The last two characteristics are now only found in water mammals, remnants of the passage from an original aquatic way of life to terrestrial existence."[9]

The aquatic ape theory fills otherwise inexplicable gaps in our understanding of human evolution. As Ralph Waldo Emerson observed, "The value of a principle is the number of things it will explain."[10]

For example, their early aquatic phase credibly demonstrates why humans store subcutaneous fat—for warmth, conservation of energy, and buoyancy—characteristic of aquatic animals like dolphins, whales,

---

*Guillaume-Benjamin-Amand Duchenne (1806–1875) was a French neurologist who greatly advanced the science of electrophysiology, the study of the electrical properties in biological cells and tissues.

and penguins, and totally unlike all apes, who are averse to swimming. Furthermore, athletic swimmers typically experience "swimmer's fat." That is, they gain excess fat, despite normal or low caloric intake of nonfatty nutrition, even though they engage in prolonged, stressful exercise. "Elite swimmers typically undertake four thousand to twenty thousand meters per day in training," according to *Sports Science* magazine, "burning thousands of calories. However, the typical body fat levels of these athletes are significantly higher than runners or cyclists, who expend similar or even smaller amounts of energy in their training."[11]

There are no satisfactory explanations for swimmer's fat, which seems contrary to the athlete's behavior—save in his or her pedigree as marine primates. All the other formerly terrestrial animals that left the land to pursure their subsequent evolution in the sea—the whale, manatee, seal, and so forth—developed blubber. Like polar bears and beavers, which have put on additional layers of fat for life half-in and half-out of the water, the swimmer's fat humans accumulate when they spend more time beneath the surface is evidence of an ancestral aquatic phase.

Elaine Morgan observed, "if we regard Man as a terrestrial mammal, he is, in this respect, as in others, somewhat freakish. But if we regard him as aquatic or ex-aquatic, he is simply conforming to type."[12] After entering the water he took on subcutaneous fat as a better insulator against cold than his body hair—which capably regulates temperatures using free-flowing air, but fails when wet.

During early man's aquatic phase (more likely, *phases*), he experienced a broad range of constantly changing temperatures, as he moved back and forth from the water to the shore. To cool him off in what must have been the tropical environment of a seasonal existence, he developed between 2 million and 3 million sweat glands, far many more than any other primate. The act of perspiration is an imitation of the cooling process of water itself: as it evaporates from the skin, it lowers the surface temperature. Sweat glands require a great deal of moisture though, far more than was ever available on the arid African plain. The fact that humans developed sweat glands as a cooling mechanism at all implies adequate, even abundant water sources available to early man. Our closest living relatives, the chimpanzees and great apes, require much less water to survive and thrive. They derive sufficient moisture from rain, supplemented by their diet of fruits. We, by contrast, are easily dehydrated, and must drink more than all other land mammals to survive. Chimpanzees and great apes succeeded in making the change to East Africa's hot, dry climate. We never developed any of their water-economic countermeasures, as indicated by our moist urine and dung.

"The truth is," admits Desmond Morris, "we're simply not well-adapted to savannah living."[13] Verhaegen goes on to point out, "Abundant eccrine thermoactive sweating is only seen in humans and sealions on land. Humans have a normal temperature resembling that of sea mammals, lower than most terrestrial ones, and markedly lower than that of any active savannah species."[14]

Tears come naturally to man, but no other primate, even the chimpanzee. Freshwater crocodiles cannot shed tears, but oceangoing crocodiles do. Darwin himself learned that marine iguana at the Galapagos Islands shed tears, but landlocked lizards cannot. In other words, the shedding of tears is an attribute of an aquatic animal living in a saline environment, and is not found among terrestrials. Shedding tears is a vehicle to vent excess salt, thereby maintaining the proper balance of minerals in the body. Terrestrial animals and freshwater aquatic animals have no need for this, as they are not ingesting more salt than necessary.

The precipitous decline in man's sense of smell likewise conforms to the progress of a mammal from an aquatic setting to a terrestrial one. Dolphins and whales have entirely dispensed with the olfactory lobes they formerly possessed as land animals.

Unlike all other primates, preferred human copulation is face-to-face. Before *Hydrodamalis,* a kind of sea cow, went extinct, its observed mating habits were very similar to human sexual behavior. As mentioned earlier, the human female's sexual canal is tilted forward at an angle differing from all other anthropoids, but precisely the same configuration present in the vast majority of marine mammal species. A female's tilted genital canal facilitates bouyant copulation in which her head head and that of her mate are above the surface of the water, allowing them to breathe freely, because sexual union in mammals demands more oxygen than their lungs can otherwise hold.

Human posture became upright in the sea. Approaching the shore as a quadruped, our primate ancestors would have been unable to proceed very far into the water. The more frequently they did so, the more they would have been forced to stand on their hind legs. Japanese macaques walk on their hind legs while carrying potatoes down to the ocean, in which they stand upright while washing their food.

Hardy envisioned the process:

Wading about, at first paddling and toddling along the shores in the shallows, hunting for shellfish, Man gradually went further and further into deeper water, swimming for a time, but having at intervals to rest—resting with his feet on the bottom and his head out of the surface: in fact, standing erect with the water supporting his weight. He would have had to raise his head out of the water to feed; with his hands full of spoil he could do better standing than floating. It seems to me likely that Man learnt to stand erect first in the water and then, as his balance improved, he found he became better equipped for standing up on the shore when he came out, and indeed also for running. He would naturally have to return to the beach to sleep and to get water to drink; actually, I imagine him to have spent at least half his time on land.[15]

Biologist Jan Wind observed, "In animals, as in lifeless objects, the center of gravity during immersion tends to become fixed perpendicularly below the center of the upward forces. In Man, this results in a vertical or semi-vertical position."[16] In other words, buoyancy shifts a mammal's center of gravity into an upright posture, as exemplified by seals, manatees, and dolphins.

"While they are in the water," Morgan points out, "whether horizontal or vertical, the spine and the hind limbs are aligned in one, straight line quite different from the ninety-degree angle of a land-dwelling quadruped."[17]

Man alone of all other mammals walks with his spine perpendicular to the Earth. While moving vertical in water is stable and risk-free to the spine, upright locomotion on land is inherently unstable and prone to falls. It engenders numerous spinal and muscular disorders from whole categories of back ailments to prolepses and hernias, none of which occur when the body is buoyant in water. Far from being able to run faster as a biped, a human on two legs is more at risk of falling than a quadruped, slower and encumbered with additional strains.

"Our bipedal locomotion is not suited for woodland, dense bush or tall grassland," observes Algis Kuliukas, a British zoologist from Nottingham University.[18] But, as Sherwood F. Washburn (1911–2000), a pioneer in the field of primatology, emphasized, "bipedalism, by freeing the hands, led a ground-dwelling primate of this kind almost immediately to habitual use of tools as a matter of survival. This, in turn, promoted far-reaching changes in intelligence, anatomy and social behavior."[19]

Another telling difference between ourselves and our next nearest primate cousins is our vastly superior sense of balance, something we have far more in common with other marine mammals. Otters, seals, and dolphins possess flexible spines that allow them to balance an inflated beach ball on the tips of their noses, a feat beyond any ape or chimp. Another significant connection with our aquatic past: our bodies are streamlined, a design wholly unnecessary for life on the savannah, but appropriate for swimming. Hardy noticed, "all the curves of the human body have the beauty of a well-designed boat. . . . Native boys diving for coins in a foreign port do indeed look as if they were truly aquatic animals!"[20]

It is perhaps not without cause that human physiognomy and maximum general physical performance attain their ideal in the champion swimmer. Athletic heroes and heroines such as Michael Phelps, Ester Williams, Buster Crabbe, Dawn Fraser, or Johnny Weismueller epitomize a degree of combined endurance and elasticity other athletes do not possess. So too, the best overall exercise is swimming, which strengthens more muscles than any other comparable physical regimen, and is the most total body work-out possible. Nearly every major human muscle group is used during swimming. It improves cardiovascular health, lowers blood pressure, maintains ideal weight, and aids in the healing of joint injuries. Swimming is used for treating arthritis, spinal cord injuries, low back pain, and recuperation from stroke. "We have more flexible spines than other apes," observes Desmond Morris, "enabling us to swim more rapidly."[21]

We are also equipped for feats in the water totally beyond all other primates, but typical for sea mammals. As recently as 2010, William Trubridge set a new world record for the deepest free immersion dive. At Dean's Hole in the Bahamas, the twenty-nine-year-old New Zealander—strictly on lung power—descended 380 feet and returned to the surface in 4 minutes, 9 seconds.[22] Such an achievement has nothing whatsoever to do with apes, even our closest chimpanzee relatives, but is characteristic of dolphins or whales.

This special relationship between water and ourselves is not baseless, but could only have resulted from those evolutionary forces that formed the human body. The soles of our feet feature 72,000 nerve endings, providing us with a high sensitivity unneeded and detrimental to existence on the African plains, but very useful for beachcombers feeling about for morsels of food just beneath the wet sand. To facilitate swimming, our big toe is joined to the others, making our feet more flipperlike, unlike the ape's foot, the big toe of which is separate from the others.

Westenhöfer himself noted:

The shape of the human foot, broadening towards the front, could indicate a paludine [marshy] habitat, especially when we note the observations of Mr. O. Abel in his Palaeobiology, where he discusses the secondary plantigradism [walking with the entire sole of the foot on the ground, as humans do] of certain fossilized bog animals, for instance, the Coryphodon [among the first, large, browsing, semiaquatic mammals that flourished from 56 million to 34 million years ago], whose footprint shows a remarkable similarity to that of humans. For such a mammal, moreover, a move to an aquatic environment would mean that powerful teeth would become unnecessary due to the relative softness of the available food resources.[23]

Webs of skin between the toes—known medically as syndactyly—still occur among 7 percent of humans, occurring in approximately one in every 2,000 to 3,000 live births. The Canadian comedian, Dan Aykroyd, and Communist tyrant, Joseph Stalin, were both born with webbed toes. An early twentieth-century examination of 1,000 school children found webbing between the second and third toes in 9 percent of boys and nearly 7 percent of girls. Webbing between all toes took place, but was represented by smaller percentages.[24] These webs are vestigial evidence for our ancestors' adaptation to a watery environment. They are seen less often between the fingers of the human hand, with a notable exception: a triangle of thin skin separating our thumb and forefinger, a connection missing from all other primates. The appearance of this triangle cannot be accounted for on the plains of Africa, but could only have developed in response to the singular pressures of an aquatic environment.

The intricate dexterity of the human hand itself suggests its real origins in such a setting, where improved manual finesse would have been more and more called upon to extricate shellfish and crabs, breaking open clams and overturning stones for additional nourishment. The constant pressure of these activities related to survival nourishment would have engendered behavior-modifying forces for evolutionary adaptation into what became the human hand. These same forces produced similar development in the hands of raccoons and macaques, animals that likewise feel about for and manipulate food in water.

Sebaceous glands secrete a waxy substance that lubricates a mammal's skin or hair. This oily, fragrant sebum first appears in humans during puberty, and far more abundantly among males, implying that the purpose of these microscopic glands is to attract a mate, a conclusion reinforced by the female's superior scent receptors. But today's role on behalf of sexual selection was not an original function of the glands, which adapted instead to different challenges associated with a return to the land. The body oil's only known purpose is to waterproof the fur or skin of aquatic animals. Like the seal, sebum completely covers our head, face, and torso. By contrast with our nearest relative, the chimpanzee, which has virtually no sebaceous glands, we have millions of them.

The presence of these sebaceous glands, like the webbed fingers and toes some of us still possess, could mean that human anatomy was becoming progressively aquatic, when our evolution in that direction was interrupted and redirected toward a land-based existence. Or it may signify that at one time we, in fact, were more aquatic than presently suspected, but surviving details in our syndactyly, vellum, diving reflex, and all the rest are vestigial traces of a former existence in the water, just as the cetaceans still evidence atrophied limbs as useless souvenirs of their terrestrial past.

These considerations prompt us to wonder what might have become of us had we not left that liquid environment, but pursued our evolutionary destiny there. By now, we might bear more physical resemblence to dolphins than apes. If, in the future, some major environmental change we cannot now imagine should compel us back into aquatic surroundings for a sufficiently prolonged period, our descendants could resume our ancestral path toward sea-mammalhood by accelerating the development of those vestigial aquatic characteristics we still possess, while adding yet more, transforming humankind into a new species.

# 3

# The Cradle of Life

*Speculation is the fuel of scientific progress; it drives forward to discovery only if it is continually being burnt in a fire of constructive criticism. Let the critics open fire!*

SIR ALISTER HARDY,
"WAS MAN MORE AQUATIC IN THE PAST?"

Man is by no means the only land animal that went into the sea. Ancestors of today's penguin, hippopotamus, platypus, manatee, water shrew, whale, and seal were all formerly terrestrials. Perhaps nowhere else do our aquatic roots show more self-evidently than in the circumstances of our birth. As delivery approaches, the human infant, unlike any other primate fetus, increases the weight of its subcutaneous fat, a decided liability for any tree-dwelling or savannah-bound mother. By contrast, human newborns are plump for buoyancy in water at birth, a conclusion powerfully underscored by an inborn diving reflex: our heart beat slows down when our face is under water. Humans are additionally equipped at birth with a swimming reflex.

Desmond Morris shows how "Newborn babies, under careful supervision, can swim without any training. Placed in a prone position in warm water, they show no panic, keep their eyes wide open, and automatically hold their breath."[1]

Both reflexes fade during the baby's first year, but the diving reflex lasts a lifetime. This diving reflex—common among all aquatic mammals—is utterly absent from apes and chimps, who, as we know, are unable to hold their heads beneath the surface of the water for any period of time.

After a marine mammal gives birth in water, the placenta is ignored, as it sinks away. Land animals—not excepting nonhuman primates—devour the placenta, behavior even the most cannibalistic human societies avoid.

Starting in the 1960s—perhaps influenced by Hardy's article published in *New Scientist*—growing numbers of women began giving birth in water, because a liquid medium afforded less pain and stress. Surprisingly, their newborns experienced neither difficulties nor fears, properly held their breath, and swam naturally.[2] They normally popped to the surface of their own accord, but a midwife stood nearby to assist them in the event they untypically preferred staying underwater too long. When dolphin mothers give birth, they too are assisted by another female that acts as a kind of midwife, gently assisting the newborn to the surface. In the decades since these mid-twentieth-century human water-babies were born, they mostly matured with superior intelligence and health, and are more independent and self-confident than average.[3]

Swimming at birth may not be the only inherited aquatic behavior exhibited by newborn humans. Throughout recorded history, in every culture around the world, crying babies have been and still are soothed by being rocked back and forth, although developmental psychologists and pediatricians do not know why. "Gentle rocking helps settle a baby who is already upset and could even relax a baby enough to prevent the onset of crying in some cases," observes Bridget Coila, a parenting specialist writing for the online magazine *Livestrong*.

The benefits of rocking a baby don't just involve its ability to calm a fussy infant, either. Rocking your child can affect a baby's body, as well as her brain. In research published in *The Canadian Medical Association Journal* . . . the study looked at babies between six to eight weeks old, and noted that the breathing changed from an irregular, shallow pattern to a more regular, deep one. The babies also exhibited less crying when rocked, typically halting a crying episode within four minutes of the start of rocking. Another study, in the journal *Pediatrics,* found that rocked babies experienced fewer episodes of sleep apnea, providing them with better sleep.[4]

A cause may lie in the first few moments of contact a *Homo erectus* water-baby enjoyed with its mother, as she floated on the surface, cradling her newborn, while gently rocking to and fro in the sea. Today, being rocked by either parent could be a genetic memory common to infants from their evolutionary legacy, a vague recollection that persists even into adulthood. Witness the lyrics of that popular song from the late nineteenth century, "Rocked in the cradle of the deep, I lay me down in peace to sleep. Secure I rest upon the wave, and calm and peaceful shall I sleep. Rocked in the cradle of the deep, I calmly rest and soundly sleep."[5] Coila may have said more than she meant when she stated, "Rocking a baby to sleep is instinctual for many new parents."[6] It might be among the inborn skills all newborns inherit at the moment of birth, such as finding, grabbing, and sucking the hitherto unseen mother's breast.

Aquatic-oriented behavior exhibited by infants seems to echo the very deepest recesses of our evolutionary past, which still resonate even in adulthood. "Humans are the only primates I know of that have an inborn fear of heights," observed recreational tree-climber, Richard Preston. "Other primates, when they are frightened, instinctively run up a tree, where they feel safe and at home."[7] This, one among numerous points of difference between us and all other primates, is a carryover of our pre-human transition from an arboreal to a terrestrial existence, some 6 million years ago.

But the most decisive feature distinguishing us from our primate predecessors is the larger size of our brain. The braincases of aquatic mammals are more capacious than those of their relatives on land, as exampled by the talapoin. This swimming monkey from Gabon, in west-central Africa, owns a braincase much larger than its entirely terrestrial counterparts, due mostly to his superior diet of abundant shellfish.

According to Morgan, "Man's brain size now deviates from the mammalian norm to an extent that is shared only by the bottle-nosed dolphin."[8]

Intelligence far superior to all other creatures on Earth is the foremost aspect of our evolution. But this unique quality was not altogether brought about by the singular challenges our ancestors encountered in an aquatic environment. Previously, as entirely terrestrial mammals, they were first scavengers then hunters, whose irregular diet did not significantly contribute to brain growth. Saturated fat from meat goes largely unused by the brain, which is itself mostly composed of fats and water, the chief components of cell membranes and of specialized tissues enclosing the nerves. Instead, our brains thrive and grow on polyunsaturated fats, especially the long-chain omega-3 fatty acids found in fish.

During their aquatic phase, our ancestors were surrounded with an abundance of seafood, which would have made a profound impact on successive generations. During 2007, three independent international studies determined that traditional characterizations of fish as "brain food" are correct after all. Their findings, as described in the November issue of the *American Journal of Clinical Nutrition,* demonstrated that omega-3 fatty acids in fish improve cognitive performance.[9]

According to Gorton's, Inc., website:

A Norwegian study of more than two thousand elderly people found that those who ate more than ten grams per day of fish had markedly better test scores and a lower prevalence of poor cognitive performance than those who ate less than ten grams of fish a day. The more fish a person ate, the greater the effect. People who ate about seventy-five grams a day of fish had the best test scores. A Dutch study of four hundred four people, ages fifty to seventy, found that higher plasma concentrations of omega-three fatty acid at baseline were associated with a lower decline in several cognitive measures over three years. Finally, a New Zealand study of more than twenty-four hundred people found a strong and consistent association between circulating concentrations of the omega-three fatty acid and physical health and a less compelling link between omega-three fatty acids and mental health.[10]

These finds were supported two years later by British nutritionists at the University of Manchester. According to *Science Daily:*

> The study, published in *The Journal of Neurology, Neurosurgery and Psychiatry,* compared the cognitive performance of more than three thousand men aged forty to seventy-nine years at eight test centers across Europe. Subjects who received higher levels of vitamin D as processed from oily fish performed consistently better in a simple and sensitive neuropsychological test that assesses an individual's attention and speed of information processing.[11]

Feasting on abundant "brain food" made available to our ancestors by a watery environment would have given them a significant intellectual edge over their terrestrial contemporaries and set them irrevocably on the road to becoming *Homo sapiens sapiens.* Desmond Morris added that "a switch to an aquatic life style would have suddenly made available high protein diet that would have reduced the amount of time they had to have finding food. This would have given more opportunities for other activities, activities that could have led them to develop important, new skills."[12]

Human evolution was propelled by its diet, beginning with our arboreal stage as placid vegetarians, until our tree-dwelling ancestors were expelled by deforestation into the savannah. There, we were compelled to become scavengers, developed a taste for meat, and became hunters. But natural forces again intervened, marooning some of our forerunners in an islandlike environment, where fish were more bountiful and easier to catch than prey on the African plains. If, as meat-eaters, we became aggressive predators, consuming seafood made us more intelligent.

So much so, we first mastered the earliest forms of technology on shore, Hardy believed.[13] He speculated that our ancestors learned the basics of tool use from observing other aquatic mammals. While surfaced and floating on their back, California sea otters balance sea urchins retrieved from the ocean bottom on their chest, using a stone to break open a hard shell. Hardy speculated that early man, like any good primate, duplicated the practice in a "monkey see, monkey do" fashion after having brought his own captured urchins and crustaceans back to shore. Repeated pounding of stones and the chance, yet eventual, introduction of flints struck the first spark that led to the discovery of fire—made all the more convenient by an abundance of dried seaweed at hand. If so, then an aquatic phase was among the very most crucial episodes in our evolution, because it provided us with the polyunsaturated fats that made all the difference between the brains of an ape and a human.

Echoes of our aquatic and even earlier arboreal past still resonate in modern man. Waterfront properties are the preferential and most expensive real estate. Donato points out the obvious: "Humans love to play in water."[14] We also find recreation in forest preserves. Something deeply profound in our nature responds to riverbanks, lakeshores and seacoasts, or draws us into the magnetic embrace of woodlands and forests. We instinctually recognize rather than consciously understand a genetic memory of life long ago in the water and even earlier among the trees.

"If we regard the ancestral primate as an aquatic ape," writes Elaine Morgan, "he ceases to be a mysterious zoological aberration evolving unique and inexplicable features of no use to himself and highly deleterious to his children. Put him among the aquatic mammals and he becomes a conformer, obeying the laws of evolution instead of running contrary to them."[15]

Although Man was by no means the only terrestrial animal to undergo a sea interlude, few others executed an evolutionary U-turn from land to shore and back again to land. Among the best known exceptions is the modern elephant, whose evolutionary path is worth considering because his aquatic episode resulted in some changes that similarly occurred in humans. These changes convinced Elaine Morgan that a terrestrial ancestor ventured into a prolonged period of development in a watery environment before it returned entirely to the land

In 1989, when she published *The Aquatic Ape,* she was universally ridiculed by the entire life-science community for her deduction regarding the elephant. Nineteen years later, scientists at Oxford University and New York's Stony Brook University reported in *Proceedings of the National Academy of Sciences* that the modern elephant did indeed have an aquatic predecessor. Their announcement followed the discovery of well-preserved teeth from a protopachyderm, the Moeritherium, a hoofed mammal not unlike a tapir that inhabited the Lower Nile Valley in northern Egypt about 37 million years ago.

"It has often been assumed that elephants have evolved from fully terrestrial ancestors and have always had this kind of a lifestyle," Dr. Erik R. Seiffert, a specialist in the early evolution of placental mammals and coauthor of the study, told BBC News. "Now we can really start to think about how their lifestyle and behavior might have been shaped by a very different kind of existence in the distant past."

DNA research of its dentition demonstrated that the Moeritherium was related to seagoing manatees and dugongs. When analyzed, chemical signatures preserved in the extinct creature's fossilized teeth showed it grazed on aquatic plants. "The isotopic pattern preserved in their teeth is very similar to that of living aquatic mammals," Seiffert explained. "It supports the hypothesis that, at some point early in the evolution of elephants, these animals were very dedicated to either a fully aquatic or amphibious lifestyle. They probably spent most of their life in water."[16]

Cooling at the close of the Eocene Epoch, around 34 million years ago, dried up Egypt's broad swamps and rivers, forcing the elephant's ancestors to return to the land. Like us, he emerged virtually hairless, save for a tuft on his tail and occasional patch atop his head. He has retained webbing between his toes, as some of us still do—an otherwise anomalous trait for a land mammal.

As a legacy from his aquatic phase, today's elephant is a natural-born swimmer, known to cross, without coercion, 300 miles or more of open water at a stretch, from one island to the next. And his diaphragm is oblique, as occurs in the dugongs, his seagoing relatives. Again like us, his entire body is covered with a subcutaneous layer of fat. All these traits we share with the modern elephant were inherited from water-friendly ancestors.

Moeritherium's discovery is particularly important to our discussion because Morgan postulated an aquatic phase for pachyderm evolution based solely on the modern elephant's marine characteristics—the same traits found in ourselves. As she correctly points out, subcutaneous fat and hairlessness characterize marine mammals, not terrestrial animals. Modern man's own body testifies to a decisive, aquatic phase his formative evolution underwent in the deep past.

Just where and when his transformation took place is less certain, however. Leon P. La Lumiere Jr., at the United States Naval Research Laboratory on the Potomac River in Washington, D.C., postulated that a population of apes driven onto the savannah by the deforestation of their previous arboreal habitat became isolated from their fellows by massive flooding that cut off the Ethiopian Highlands—otherwise known as East Africa's Danakil Alps—from the rest of the continent.[17] Suddenly restricted to this radically dissimilar environment—and all the different challenges and opportunities it afforded—the apes were forced to adapt to and eventually exploit their new surroundings. Thus stimulated, successive generations trod the path toward mankind—until the seas that had marooned them for several million years gradually retreated, and the developed hominids migrated down the exposed Rift Valley throughout Africa, where they fulfilled their evolutionary destiny.

Hardy theorized that the transition was fulfilled by *Australopithicus* in East Africa, sometime after 4 million years ago. He was proved correct as recently as early 2011 with the discovery of an arched fossilized foot bone belonging to *Australopithecus afarensis,* a human ancestor that walked upright in Ethiopia 3.2 million years ago. "This fourth metatarsal is the only one known of A. afarensis," said Professor

William H. Kimbel, Institute of Human Origins Director at Kent State University (Ohio), "and is a key piece of evidence for the early evolution of the uniquely human way of walking."[18]

Modern man's aquatic characteristics—acquired during Lumiere's proposed sea interlude—cannot rightly be expected to have endured after so prolonged a period following the debut of *Australopithecus*. Surviving traits would be more likely muted, vestigial or, more probably, expunged. It seems unlikely that so many connections with our species' former aquatic existence could not only still linger in our bodies but also be preserved in such operable condition, after 4 million years. The retention of our diving or swimming reflex, strengthening scalp hairs, or subcutaneous fat following a permanent return to terrestrial life for so long a stretch of time would not have made evolutionary sense.

This is not to deny that the Danakil episode ever happened. On the contrary, Lumiere's arguments on its behalf are persuasive. He capably correlates the geological facts with current evidence for human evolution in Africa to show that a broad-spreading deluge did indeed isolate part of that continent at a time and place where humanlike apes made the transition to apelike humans.

However, that single period of change at such a remote stage in hominid beginnings cannot account for the persistence of our physical and instinctual connections to a watery environment. The temporal and evolutionary gulf separating *Australopithecus* from *Homo sapiens sapiens* is far too deep and wide. Although *Australopithecus* walked in our direction, he was very far removed from any of our more immediate, evolutionary ancestors. Instead, our ancestors must have experienced more than one aquatic phase. And, given the variety of distinct marine characteristics we still possess, our hominid predecessors underwent several—perhaps many—such watery interludes throughout their evolutionary history, right up to the brink of modern times.

As Donato observes, "We seem to have more aquatic characteristics, as we become more 'sapien,' suggesting some recent developments."[19]

A most significant aquatic stage involved the advent of *Homo erectus*, when it began to differ importantly from its australopithecine forerunners. Perhaps this single, most crucial aquatic phase represented a quantum leap forward in brainpower and improved body type. *Homo erectus'* cranial capacity was 820 cc for the 440 cc of *Australopithicus.*[20] The former was the first hominid fully adapted to walking upright, and possessed the earliest projected nose, an adaptation associated with diving.

Darwin had postulated an African homeland for early man, but a Dutch anatomist and medical doctor believed it lay in Southeast Asia. Following that supposition, Eugene Dubois undertook a personal quest for physical evidence in 1887. Four years later, on the banks of the Solo River in East Java, he found a skullcap, femur, and several teeth belonging to a creature he called *Pithecanthropus erectus,* the "upright ape-man," known today as *Homo erectus,* or, specifying the Indonesian case, Java Man. Another set of more complete skeletal remains was unearthed less than twelve miles to the north, in the Central Javanese village of Sangrian. Many additional *Homo erectus* finds were subsequently made in Java and throughout Indonesia. Their recurrence in Southeast Asia seemed to confirm human origins in this part of the world, until other specimens surfaced in East Africa. Most paleoanthropologists maintain that *Homo erectus* arose there first, migrating almost at once into Indonesia on behalf of causes unknown.

But Dubois' discoveries and those made after him are at least contemporaneous with, possibly somewhat anterior to, the earliest evidence for *Homo erectus* in East Africa. Java seems a less likely location for the evolution of *Homo erectus* due to its setting as an island. But it was not always so. The Sunda Shelf on which it sits is a shallow, sunken platform susceptible to fluctuations in sea levels. During the mid-Pliocene Period, prior to the appearance of *Homo erectus,* they were much lower than they are today—exposing the entire Sunda Shelf as a single, immense landmass connecting Indonesia with Sumatra, Borneo, the Philippines, the Celebes, and Java. Onto this dry land wandered *Australopithecus* about 3 million years ago. With rising sea levels that followed in the early Pleistocene, the manlike apes found themselves stranded on Java and its neighboring islands, where the stimuli of aquatic challenges and opportunities were factors for evolutionary change.

Archaic *Homo sapiens* appeared in Southeast Asia some 300,000 years ago, about 100,000 years after he arose in Africa and Europe. As a progressively skilled hunter, he was well on his way to becoming Earth's dominant predator, when his entire species virtually died out in a single instant. At the same moment, almost all orangutans in Borneo, macaques in Central India, East African chimpanzees, and tigers everywhere were liquidated by one of the most epic natural catastrophes of all time. The mass killer was an Indonesian volcano. At 2,000 megatons, it was 3,000 times greater than North America's Mount Saint Helens' eruption of 1980, or 150,000 times more potent than America's atomic bomb that destroyed the Japanese city of Hiroshima in 1945.

During a summer 75,000 years ago, over a span of between nine and fourteen days, 8 million metric tons of superheated rock and ash were disgorged every second—vomiting altogether some 670 cubic miles of debris material. Blown sky-high into the atmosphere were 6 billion tons of sulphur dioxide. Molten lava amassing 1,000 cubic kilometers, between 50 meters and 400 meters thick, surged over 30,000 square kilometers of Sumatra from coast to coast. There were 800 cubic kilometers of pyroclastic ashfall, composed chiefly of rock fragments, that rained an average thickness of ten centimeters around the entire Earth—although areas close to the eruption naturally suffered much greater deposition. Central India was buried under more than eight feet of ash, and twenty-seven feet smothered parts of Malaysia, while a fifteen-centimeter carpet of ash utterly deforested all of South Asia.

For the next six to ten years, global temperatures plummeted between ten and fifteen degrees Centigrade. The planet's rainforest belt was devastated by prolonged drought, and vegetation worldwide perished.

These extraordinary events clearly impacted the evolution and survival of our early human ancestors. Just how these global changes shaped us into the humans we are today demonstrated how periously close we came to the edge of extinction.

# 4

# Genes Don't Lie

*. . . the forest canopy from which we had arisen became as
remote from us as the depths of the sea.*

RICHARD PRESTON, *THE WILD TREES*

While the incomprehensively cataclysmic scope of Mount Toba's super eruption was known to geologists for some time, its role in a so-called bottleneck of human evolution went unsuspected. Not until the early 1990s could the new science of mitochondrial DNA analysis reveal a profound genetic decline and divergence contemporaneous with this singular volcanic event. It excavated a depression more than sixty-two miles across, resulting in the largest crater of its kind on Earth, known today as Lake Toba, in Sumatra.

Tracing female-to-female descent, the DNA researchers found an anomalously broad diversity of human types going back at least 1.2 million years before the eruption. That species diversity was almost utterly wiped out by Mount Toba. From a world population of approximately 2 million individuals, humanity had been suddenly reduced to perhaps as few as 1,000 breeding couples. High estimates put the total number of adults and children at around 20,000 survivors.[1]

Instead of the horrific holocaust this mass die-off may seem from an early-twenty-first-century perspective, it was—in the long run—the most beneficial occurrence our kind has so far experienced. Until then, there was little to distinguish man from any other mammal.

"Tool kits" of quartzite flaked into unifacial and bifacial points recovered from Gona, Ethipoia date to 2.6 million years ago. These earliest known implements have been associated with *Australopithecus garhi,* a species ancestral to humans, and the final so-called missing link connecting *Australopithecus* to the human genus, *Homo.* Thereafter, he kept making the same kind of "tools"—actually, just slightly modified rocks—for almost a million years. Only with the advent of *Homo erectus* around 1.7 million years ago did some innovations appear, and these too went mostly unchanged for another 1.6 million years.

Until then, our ancestors' manufacturing ability was not much better than a chimpanzee's talent for cutting and fashioning selected twigs to ferret out tasty termites. As such, hominids had been riding an evolutionary merry-go-round, coming into existence and leaving it, succeeded by other, hardly less capable variants since their predecessors climbed down out of the trees more than 4 million years earlier. Their dead-end stasis inhibited possibilities for an evolutionary breakthrough and threatened the very development of any higher type. Continued interbreeding would have inevitably merged *Homo sapiens*—the lone specimen that stood out from the rest for its intellectual superiority— into just another lackluster hominid, like all other indistinguishable versions.

Mount Toba virtually exterminated these evolutionary nonentities, leaving only the most tough, adaptable, and clever individuals of the most advanced type to face and triumph over continuous generations of the harshest survival conditions. Friedrich Nietzsche's declaration, "What does not destroy me, makes me stronger," applied to *Homo sapiens,* whose ability to master severe challenges posed seventy-five centuries ago we have inherited directly as a genetic legacy in the resilient strengths of our physical and intellectual being.[2] So much so, we would not have become the ingenious, robust mammal we are today had

Mount Toba never intervened in our evolution. And civilization would not have been invented.

When date correlations between its eruption and our ancestral bottleneck were first publicized in the mid-1990s, critics expressed serious doubts concerning real possibilities for such a numerical downsizing. But after the turn of the last century, further DNA research, plus the discovery of contemporaneous near-extinction that overwhelmed other plant and animal species around the world, affirmed the effective magnitude of the eruption.[3] It signified a line drawn in the sand, after which *Homo sapiens'* diversity terminated and his racial diversity began, as mass migrations in search of better living conditions moved northward out of Africa. It was there, in Europe, that the so-called Great Leap Forward much later took place, as preserved in the magnificent cave paintings and stone sculpture of Paleolithic art. For all of its near-genocidal fury, Toba made possible the advent of modern man.

Although recollection of Mount Toba's eruption seems impossibly beyond the reach of even the most tenacious folk traditions, human memory nonetheless appears to have enshrined it in surviving myth. For nowhere on Earth do as many indigenous versions of Garden of Eden-like accounts exist as among the native peoples of Indonesia and the Pacific realm. They are all cultural inflections on a common theme; namely, the birth of the first humans on a paradisiacal island and florescence there until their expulsion and subsequent dispersal throughout the world by a fiery catastrophe. So too, the biblical Adam and Eve were expelled by an angel bearing a torch on high. Despite fundamental similarities to the Old Testament rendition in Genesis, there were Southeast Asian, Melanesian, Micronesian, Macronesian, and Polynesian versions handed down from generation to generation time out of mind before Christian missionaries began proselytizing indigenous peoples throughout the Pacific in the eighteenth century.

For example, the Dyak natives of Sarawak, the larger of two Malaysian states situated in northwest Borneo, recall that the first man and woman were born on a garden-island, at the center of which was a holy tree guarded by a dragon. Upon her request, her husband stole one of its forbidden fruits, precipitating a terrible natural catastrophe. H. Ling Roth's late nineteenth-century monograph on the Dyaks—cited by British geneticist Stephen Oppenheimer of Green Templeton College, Oxford—demonstrated how the Dyak account predated missionary contacts.[4] So too, pre-Christian Polynesian oral tradition tells of Pali-uli, literally, the "Garden of Paradise," where the earliest humans were created. The name of the first woman in Hawaiian myth was Iwi, literally, "the bone." In Samoa and at Rotumah, she was remembered as Iwa.

These and numerous other traditions seem inescapably paralleled with the Old Testament's Eve and indigenous accounts of a sunken island-kingdom more famously known as Mu or Lemuria, described in a series of early twentieth-century books by the British Army Colonel and engineer, James Churchward. While directing Indian famine relief during the 1870s, he assisted in the translation of secret Hindu monastery tablets inscribed with the history of an early paradise in the Pacific, where humankind supposedly originated and eventually prospered for many centuries. After its inhabitants raised the world's first civilization, an unspecified natural calamity—about twelve thousand years ago—obliterated the Motherland. Some of its inhabitants allegedly perished, but enough survivors migrated to influence the subsequent development of high cultures as far removed from each other as India, Tibet, Southeast Asia, China, Japan, Polynesia, British Columbia, Mexico, and South America.

Released in 1926, Churchward's *The Lost Continent of Mu* was mostly ignored, though occasionally dismissed as a ludicrous fantasy by mainstream scholars for the rest of the twentieth century. But seventy-five years later—as recently as 2001—their laughter stopped abruptly when the first of literally hundreds of cultural artifacts were dredged up from the bottom of the Gulf of Cambay, or Khambhat, off the coast of Gujarat in northwestern India. The objects were accidentally discovered by oceanographers from India's National Institute of Ocean Technology while conducting a survey of pollution levels in the Arabian Sea. After the Indian government's Minister of Science and Technology ordered a professional investigation, underwater researchers plotted out the parameters of a submerged city five miles long by two miles wide, 120 feet down. Streets and boulevards were laid out in grid patterns similar to those of Indus Valley ceremonial centers at Harappa and Mohenjo Daro.

An abundance of retrieved physical evidence included stone tools and pottery shards, plus fossilized wood and even human bones. These organic materials yielded a generally consistent radiocarbon date of about 9,500 Years Before Present (YBP). The C-14 age-range was independently supported by geological tables, which showed that sea levels in the area were more than 120 feet lower circa 7500 BCE than at present. While this period demonstrates when the city was inhabited, it is not synonymous with its founding, which may have occurred long before. The natural catastrophe that overwhelmed the site most likely took place 1,300 years later—circa 6200 BCE—during an epoch of global flooding known as "The 8.2 Kiloyear Event," as described in chapter 8.

According to textbook historians, India's first cities were not built for another forty-seven centuries after 7500 BCE. In fact, the first urban centers are not supposed to have arisen anywhere until the mid-fourth millennium BCE at the earliest, and not in the Indian Subcontinent, but in the Near East, in Mesopotamia. Although archaeologists everywhere acknowledged their Indian colleagues' correct procedures and testing results, the rather momentous Gulf of Cambay discovery carried out by university-trained professionals using state-of-the-art research technologies has been given a low profile in the Western World; no textbook revisions of old, invalidated information about humankind's earliest urban centers have been properly annotated in light of this new data; and certainly no word about James Churchward in connection with the 2001 find has been uttered by mainstream scholars, who, in the name of their academic predecessors, at the very least, owe his memory an apology.

Doubtless, the "Mu" he translated from original Hindu sources was the sunken city found after the turn of the twenty-first century. But the Colonel himself wrote how it was destroyed 4,500 years before, and that the monastary documents to which he was given access were only parts of a much larger, crumbling library recording even earlier events. These appeared to have referred to the presently underwater Sunda Shelf, which was dry land when *Australopithecus* arrived there 10 million years ago. We have already suggested Indonesia as the likely setting for his aquatic transformation into *Homo erectus.*

Since he was under no compulsion to leave this Southeast Asian Garden of Eden, he undoubtedly continued to evolve in place toward *Homo sapiens,* and probably arose to achieve higher intellectual and physical levels than his African counterparts, because Indonesia was blessed with lush vegetation and an inexhaustible abundance of "brain food." Sated on a mixed diet of fish, crustaceans, and fruit, while mentally and physically stimulated by the challenges of an aquatic environment, man would have developed higher and faster than terrestrial *Homo sapiens* in East Africa, where food was comparatively scarce and the local ecology less nourishing. As such, the Mu of which Churchward wrote was the highest and final manifestation of human development from *Homo erectus* beginnings in Indonesia. The Gulf of Cambay site was only part of a much broader Lemurian civilization stretching across island-chains from the Arabian Sea into the Indian Ocean and throughout the Central Pacific.

On several of the Brahaputra monastery baked-clay tablets that the Colonel examined appeared representations for the lost land of Mu in the form of a flat-topped T, or *tau*, encompassed at its base by lapping waves and surmounted by a blooming lotus, flanked on either side by a smaller bush. To the left of the *tau* stood a deer on its hind legs, as though about to spring upon the glyph. Churchward was informed by the monastery *rishi,* or chief priest, that the deer signified "Man's advent in the Land of Mu."[5] The lotus suggested spiritual enlightenment, while the twin bushes stood for material abundance. The *tau* was the sacred Tree of Life, Mu itself, in the midst of the sea. Such imagery could hardly have been invented by the Hindu holy man or British Army Colonel. Invariably at the center of these Edens was a Tree of Life, a motif recurring in cave art, bronze drums, and murals throughout Southeast Asia—such as the ceremonial cloths, called *tampan,* from Lampung, in southern Sumatra.

Kings and high priests in the Marquesas Islands of French Polynesia carry a T-shaped baton known as the "Cross of God," used, according to Hawiian historian Leinani Melville, "on state occasions or in religious processions when officiating at temple rituals. A *tau* was hewn from a flawless piece of hard wood that had been carefully chosen and blessed by a high priest. It was usually between two and four feet long, two or three inches wide, and an inch or two in thickness."[6] The Cross of Gold and carefully chosen wood from which it was made signified the Hawaiians' own Tree of Life, the Puka-tala, the fruits of which were alleged to have bestowed immortality on the first humans. Pohutukawa, a Maori variant, was a sacred tree growing at the center of Limu's sunken palace, "from which the spirits dropped down into the chasm that led under the sea to spirit land," according to the twentieth-century mythologist, Jan Knappert.[7]

Both Hawaiian and Maori accounts describe the land in which this tree was venerated as the paradisiacal birthplace of mankind, from which humans spread throughout the world. They were not driven out by divine wrath, but forced to leave when Kahiki-homnua-kele, Kapakapaua-a-Kane, Pali-ilu, or any of the many other descriptive titles by which the Pacific Eden was known, disappeared beneath the sea to become the realm of the dead. Numerous Polynesian creation accounts describe Te tumu o te pohoe as literally the "Tree of Life" that nurtured the first human beings in Haiviki.

Oppenheimer demonstrated that the Tree of Life myth originated in the Moluccas, an Indonesian archipelago, and spread outward as far as the Near East in a disbursement that uncannily paralleled a genetic outflow of migrating human populations. With the loss of that earthly paradise, they moved throughout Polynesia and Southeast Asia, across the Indian Ocean, up the Persian Gulf and into Iraq, leaving traces of their myth among various peoples along the way. They finally resettled between the Tigris and Euphrates Rivers, where their tradition was preserved but distorted over the millennia by local influences in Sumerian, Babylonian, and, ultimately, biblical accounts.

Tracing their long trek, Oppenheimer followed specific Eurasian genetic marker lines, both nuclear and mitochondrial, spreading from an area of ocean south of Thailand, across India and into Mesopotamia, beyond to Central Europe.[8] Among the Sumerians, the Garden of Eden became Dilmun. Much later, authors of the Old Testament transformed it into a moral fable to explain the origin of sin and downfall of man. The Hebrew "Eden," for example, clearly derives from the Sumerian *edin* for a "fertile plain."[9]

"In Egypt," the late-nineteenth-century explorer and pioneer archaeology photographer, Augustus Le Plongeon, pointed out, "the eating of a quince [a relative of the apple and pear] by two young people together constituted betrothal. . . . In this custom, we find a natural explanation of the first seven verses of the third chapter of Genesis."[10]

Interestingly, the Polynesian Tree of Life was almost always associated with the realm of the dead believed to lie at the bottom of the sea, and guarded, as mentioned above, by Limu. The name reappears in an island among the Ha'apai Group still known as Limu. Many thousands of miles away, the indigenous Chumash of southern California's Pacific coast originally knew the offshore island of Santa Cruz as Limu, or "In the Sea."[11] A pre-Hindu people remembered as the Redin by natives of the Maldives in the Indian Ocean named one of the islands Laamu, referred to locally as the "first land sighted," because it was initially glimpsed by the Redin on their long-distance arrival from the east in large, fast, oar-driven ships. Laamu features the largest *hawitta*—a pyramidal stone-and-earth mound—in the Maldives. It is surrounded by a cluster of other islands, all of them populated by ruins, said to have been the Redin's earliest settlement.[12]

These and so many additional variants on a place-name spanning the Indian and Pacific Oceans are echoes of a profound past. They suggest that the ascent of early man and his evolutionary coming of age as *Homo sapiens sapiens* both occurred on the Indonesian landmasses prior to their inundation. If so, then Mu or Lemuria certainly lived up to its title as "the Motherland."[13]

The Japanese Ama mentioned in chapter 2 are as much a tribal people as members of a profession, and claim their ancestors were taught the art of pearl diving by foreigners, like the Redin, from a lost civilization. The ancient visitors preached a solar religion, and one of its symbols, a rising sun, became the national emblem of Japan. It also signified the direction from which the culture-bearers came; namely, the eastern Pacific Ocean. Their island-kingdom, Nirai-Kanai, was eventually overwhelmed by a great flood, which sent it to the bottom of the sea. To commemorate these events, the Ama still conduct an annual ceremony on the eastern shores of Honsu, held in early April or October. The celebrants gather on the beach to face the dawn and pray for the souls of their antediluvian ancestors. After purification with seawater, a designated leader walks into the ocean up to his neck, bearing a small tree branch in his hand. After a pause, he turns to face the shore. Emerging from the sea, he is greeted with the wild beating of drums and joyful chanting, as though just having survived some terrible catastrophe. The branch he carries is an obvious reference to Lemuria as the "Tree of Life."

That anything more than such ritual evidence is lacking after so many millennia should hardly surprise anyone. What few trace elements able to survive a volcanic eruption of the magnitude produced by Mount Toba would have been mostly lost when Sumatra was buried under colossal lava flows, while Malaya, Borneo, and Java were carpeted by no less monumental ashfall. The last sticks of the original Mu or Lemuria herself vanished, as the Sunda Shelf on which she perched was enveloped by the South China Sea. But at least some indirect proofs for the arrival of immigrants from the Toba catastrophe in East Africa came to light as recently as 2004.

Physical evidence appeared in the form of shell globules discovered at Blombos Cave, located in the De Hoop Nature Preserve on the east coast of South Africa's Cape peninsula, outside Cape Town. Found in clusters of up to seventeen and crafted from *Nassarius kraussianus*—a tiny, scavenging mollusk—all forty-one had been identically perforated for stringing into necklaces and showed similar marks left from wear, indicating the adornments were actually used during the deeply ancient past. But, it was just how deeply ancient these artifacts were that made them a singularly valuable discovery: removed from a layer of sediment deposited 75,000 years ago, they are the world's oldest known example of human culture.

According to Chris Henshilwood, the site's chief excavator and professor from the Center for Developmental Studies at Norway's University of Bergen, "the Blombos Cave beads present absolute evidence for perhaps the earliest storage of information outside the human brain."[14] They more certainly represent the oldest such specimens on the continent, although their real origins are open to question. Nothing like them existed in Africa before, but their manufacture occurs at the same time a seventieth millennium BCE factory on the other side of the Indian Ocean was in operation. As testimony to this center's size and significance, approximately 50,000 lithic pieces were worked into pebble tools by early *Homo sapiens* laborers using such surprisingly advanced implements as hammer stones and anvils at Kota Tampan in the Lenggong Valley of Ulu Perak, in peninsular Malaysia. Both the South African and Malaysian sites are contemporaneous with Mount Toba's epic eruption, from which survivors apparently fled Kota Tampan by sea, landing near Cape Town, where the Blombos Cave find was made.

Just two years after Henshilwood's discovery, not far to the south, in the Tsodilo Hills of Botswana, Shelia Coulson from the University of Oslo stumbled upon a relevant location. Inside another cave she found about 13,000 artifacts, all dating yet again to that common volcanic cataclysm. Many of the weapons she uncovered there are unlike other spearheads from the same area or time in that they are made from stone originating hundreds of kilometers away, and are more carefully carved and more colorful.[15] Some of them appear to have been deliberately broken, which led Coulson to wonder if their condition resulted from ritual activity of some kind, a speculation underscored by the additional presence of powdered red ochre—used for its blood-color in funeral services by many primitive cultures—and collected quartz crystals. If so, then Python Cave is the oldest known ceremonial center on Earth.

The site derives its name from a six-foot wide, eighteen-foot tall rock at the entrance shaped by natural forces to resemble a serpent. The simulacrum did not go unnoticed by seventieth millennium BCE artists, who etched between 300 and 400 markings to suggest eyes and scales. Python Cave and related, nearby finds outside Cape Town imply the arrival of Indonesian refugees from the far-flung terror spawned by Mount Toba.

Just months after the Blombos necklaces came to light, similar beads found decades before at what is now Israel and Algeria were dated to the same period. Specimens, respectively, from the Skul collection at London's Natural History Museum and Oued Djebbana at the Musee de l'Homme, in Paris, show perforations and wear very similar to the Blombos' globules. The simultaneous appearance of all these anomalous objects without precedent or equal in South Africa, Israel, or Algeria, appearing just when Mount Toba was active, suggests their technology was not indigenous, but imported with various populations of seafaring survivors from ravaged Southeast Asia.

There, previous to the natural catastrophe, *Homo sapiens* had risen culturally higher than anywhere else due to the lush abundance and ecological stimuli of his surroundings. The very existence of contemporaneous shell beads at locations separated by thousands of miles during such a critical moment for humankind suggests influences coming from outside, not normal trade between the bottom of the African Continent and the Mediterranean area.

Indeed, the Lemurian origins of these finds are suggested by local myth. The supreme deity of Buganda was Mu-kasa. His oracular shrine, forbidden to all but the tribal chief, was set up on Lake Victoria's sacred island of Bubembe in imitation of the god's original homeland, over-whelmed during the deep past by a Great Flood. Another Ugandan god with watery associations, Mu-gizi, was the Bunyoro guardian of Lake Albert. His fellow immortal, Mu-nume, was invoked during periods of drought or, appropriately enough, deluge. Elsewhere in East Africa, Mu-lungu was the Swahili god from which all creation spread around the world.

In South Africa, Mu-jaji is still the goddess of destructive tempests, recalling the catastrophic annihilation of her distant homeland. She has been long represented by a lineage of mortal queens, high guardians of Mu-jaji's secret of eternal life. It was upon her cult that the writer Rider Haggard based his famous novel, *She*. Even the Pygmies of Central Africa tell of Mu-gasa (the Ugandan Mu-kasa), who, in the ancient past, presided over a paradise in the distant east where the first man and woman were created. Due to their disobedience, a great tempest arose, and Mu-gasa departed before his homeland was utterly destroyed, eventually settling—unseen—among the pygmies.

Mount Toba's impact on the course of human evolution simultane-ously suggests the solution to an important question: When and where did the first civilization arise? If, as implied by South Africa's Blombos and Python Cave sites, some survivors of the eruption fled westward across the Indian Ocean, others may have escaped into the east, reset-tling among the islands of Micronesia and the Carolines. Over time, stimuli favorable to population growth (a temperate climate plus abun-dant food provided by the surrounding sea) combined with impetus for social cooperation and technological development spurred on by, respec-tively, limited living space and challenges derived from the ocean. Thus were laid the foundations for man's premiere civilization with roots in a global cataclysm of 75,000 years ago. It was an awesomely venerable heritage for the Motherland, which had been reborn through its refu-gees in the West-Central Pacific after the Sunda Shelf's inundation by the South China Sea.

*Fig. 4.1. Finely engraved and crafted bifacial points, with engraved ochre and bone tools; 75,000 years old, from South Africa's Blombos cave. Photo by Chenshilwood.*

Successive generations of islanders continued or resumed their aquatic existence, as suggested by the *chog rabs,* or "origin myths," of Tibet. They record the late second millennium BCE arrival of a spiritually gifted foreigner, who introduced the tenets of Boen, a pre-Buddhist mystery-religion of shamanic ecstasy. According to Tibetan historian Namkhai Norbu, Shenrab Miwoche's appearance was so vital to his country, it signified "the beginning of Tibetan history."[16]

That this seminally important personage belonged to a people identified in the chog rabs as the "Mu" is revealing enough. But both his hands were said to have had webs of skin between each finger and thumb. Unless the ancient authors of this origin myth intended some allegory since missed by modern readers, they appear to have described Shenrab Miwoche as the representative of a race that developed physical characteristics associated with marine mammals—they never left the aquatic phase of their evolution, which continued uninterrupted over the previous 71,000 years and unhindered by the eruption of Mount Toba.

Outside of references such as the chog rabs, the Mu have long ceased to exist. We are unable to determine whether or not Miwoche's people—unlike the dynastic Egyptians, who were his contemporaries on the other side of the world—actually possessed syndactyly fingers, because no mummified remains exist for archaeologists to examine. Two hundred eighty-nine years after he visited Tibet during 1917 BCE, his Motherland was finally and utterly obliterated by a series of killer waves many times larger and more devastating than the Indonesian or Japanese tsunamis of 2004 and 2011, respectively.

Geologists know that the South Pacific island of Rabaul erupted with extraordinary violence in 1628 BCE, but was surpassed at the same moment by more massive outgassing from the Hawaiian Mauna Kea. Meanwhile, in the distant north, Alaska's Akiachak volcano suddenly disgorged fifty cubic miles of ash, as Mount Sanbe, far to the west in southern Honsu, Japan, exploded. But even these cataclysms were eclipsed by the simultaneous detonation of New Zealand's Taupo Valley Center volcanoes, which shot a 200-foot-high wall of water at speeds more than 500 miles per hour. It joined a relay of tsunamis generated by the Polynesian, Alaskan, and Japanese eruptions, traveling over the entire face of the Pacific Ocean, scouring every vestige of life across islands and coastal regions. The archipelagoes over which the civilization Mu had spread by the late seventeenth century BCE were violently depopulated and culturally erased.

Most survivors drifted eastward to the Americas and westward to Asia, where they were assimilated on both sides of the Pacific, and vanished forever among native populations—which retain folk memories of the Lemurian refugee experience, after the passage of forty centuries. Fewer survivors lingered in the Pacific at places such as Hawaii, where the Polynesians still remember them as the Menehune, or "Mu," before driving them to extinction, the same fate that befell the Easter Islanders, who endeavored to transplant the lost Motherland's culture in the East Central Pacific.

Lemuria died of the the same cause that had given her birth, some 71,300 years before. Due to the wide radius of devastation wrought by Mount Toba's far more catastrophic eruption, the migration of premodern human survivors over land from Southeast Asia through India and the Middle East, then down the East African coast to the southern part of the continent was not possible. An only escape route led directly westward in an open-water crossing, an alternative deemed preposterously out of the question by mainstream paleoanthropologists, because they believed *Homo erectus* simply did not possess the intellectual ability to envision, let alone build and operate, a vessel of any kind.

The earliest, firm evidence for human navigation dated back just 11,000 years ago in the Eastern Mediterranean, although archaeological suggestions for voyages across open water nearly 50,000 years earlier have recently become the focus of renewed attention. During an archaeological survey of caves and rock shelters on the south coast of the Aegean island of Crete in late 2010, near the village of Plakias, scientists from the American School of Classical Studies at Athens and the Greek Ministry of Culture found a cache of Paleolithic tools. In an Associated Press announcement, senior ministry archaeologist, Maria Vlazaki, stated that a recovered stone ax was at least 130,000 years old. Related implements appear to date back as far as 700,000 years.

"The results of the survey not only provide evidence of sea voyages in the Mediterranean tens of thousands of years earlier than we were aware of so far," she said, "but also change our understanding of early hominids' cognitive abilities."[17]

Since Crete has been separated from the mainland by at least forty miles for the last 5 million years, the tools unearthed at Plakias could only have been brought across the Eastern Mediterranean Sea by boat. The perishable materials with which these first, crudely primitive but sufficiently adequate vessels—probably rafts—were constructed cannot rightly be expected to have escaped deterioration over the last 75,000 years. But other proof, in the form of anomalous Old Stone Age tools on an otherwise inaccessible island, has established the maritime skills of *Homo erectus*—or, at any rate, very early versions of *Homo sapiens*.

These abilities were doubtless not confined to Europe, as demonstrated by islands between the Malay Peninsula, Sumatra, Borneo, Java, Bali, Australia, and New Guinea. Collectively known as "Wallacea," they have always been surrounded by deep water, which forever cut them off from the nearest mainland, even when sea levels were at their lowest during the height of glacial epochs. Wallacea's isolation is characterized by its few terrestrial mammals, birds, and freshwater fish from continental Asia.

Yet, the remains of *Homo erectus* and his artifacts have been recovered throughout these islands, which are now—as they have always been—accessible only via a sea-route. Flores, for example, is separated from the nearest landfall by more than eighteen miles of open ocean, although it was colonized by early humans during the late Lower Pleistocene, some 850,000 years ago. Lombok and Sumbawa, the two major Indonesian islands between Flores and Bali, were inhabited earlier still. Flores is midway between Wallacea and Sahul, where the oldest *Homo erectus* remains were discovered.

"Stone tools similar to those on Flores," writes Bennett Blumenberg, a naturalist and environmental educator in Maui, Hawaii:

> have been found on other deep-water islands in Wallacea: central Timor, western Timor, Roti and Sulawesi. The finds from Timor and Roti have been identified in Middle Pleistocene deposits. . . . *H. erectus* eventually journeyed from Alor to Timor, a distance of sixty to one hundred km [thirty-eight to sixty-two miles] of open water. Fossil deposits in the volcanic strata of the Soa Basin of Flores have many remains of the [now extinct] Stegdon elephant, and there are typical, Lower Paleolithic, human-made tools in the Ola Bula Formation, central Flores. At the Mata Menge site, nineteen paleomagnetic samples produced age estimates for the sediment-bearing tools of seven hundred eighty thousand BP [Before Present]. Fission track analysis of the same sediments produced an age of eight hundred thousand to seven hundred twenty thousand BP.[18]

The maritime origins of *Homo erectus* remains and artifacts found on these isolated islands were demonstrated in January 2000, when a primitive raft built with replicas of Paleolithic tools successfully carried fourteen men equipped only with Stone Age-like objects from Bali and Lombok. The *Nale Tasih 4* was one of six similar vessels as part of the First Mariners Project directed by Australian archaeologist Robert G. Bednarik. "Nusa Tenggara, the islands east of Bali," he stated, "have never been connected to either Asia or Australia, but they were found to have been occupied by *Homo erectus,* as well as by several endemic species of Stegodonts,* early in the Ice Age."[19]

In 2004, participation of the National Geographic organization helped the First Mariners Project replicate a Lower Paleolithic voyage from Sumbawa to Komodo, a distance of some thirty-five miles. Additional assistance from the British Broadcasting Corporation four years later enabled eight men on a raft to reach Sumbawa from Lombok. These voyages, according to Bednarik, represent "the largest endeavor ever undertaken in replicative archaeology."[20] They were conducted over sometimes prodigious stretches of open sea—commonly more than fifty miles at a time—indicating that *Homo erectus* did indeed possess the maritime technology and courage to traverse the broad waters separating the islands of Indonesia, where his otherwise unaccountable remains are found.

As discussed, the appearance of culturally similar shell beads, first in Blombos Cave, then very shortly thereafter at Skul, in Israel, and the Algerian Oued Djebbana, suggest that the human survivors fled their Indonesian homelands westward over the Indian Ocean from the contemporaneous eruption of Mount Toba, landing near Cape Town. This supposition is underscored by the total absense of any similar contemporaneous human remains between *Homo erectus* in East Africa and Java man in Indonesia. For the sake of comparison, such remains abundantly connect Neanderthals and Cro-Magnons. But conditions in the new continent were not much better; so the newly arrived refugees migrated far into the north, as the related shell beads discovered in Algeria and Israel indicate. This interpretation is supported by recent analyses of mitochondrial DNA, which identified mankind's major migration out of Africa around 75,000 years ago.[21]

---

*Stegodonts were elephants that lived from 11.6 million to 4,100 years ago.

Having found refuge on the shores of the Mediterranean Sea, our ancestors experienced their most recent aquatic phase. Previously, in Africa, they had emerged into primary races from the genetic bottleneck afforded by Mount Toba's species-cleansing ferocity. These races do not include Melanesian natives—known as Negritos—nor Australian Aborigines. Both sets are later developments of pre-Toba hominids, descended from remnant populations of survivors in the immediate vicinity of the natural catastrophe. Negritos and Australoids—along with numerically less significant indigenous populations scattered throughout New Guinea, Borneo, Sumatra, and Java—are examples of premodern *Homo sapiens*.

Bouncing back from near-extinction, several generations of population regrowth underwent racial diversification. Groups that chose to remain in sub-Saharan regions readapted to a predominantly terrestrial lifestyle, minus any aquatic stimulus. Consequently, their hair no longer grew long for the anchoring clutches of newborn children. Instead, it shortened, became denser, kinky, and coarse to protect the scalp from the hot equatorial sun. The inherited adaptations of earlier hominid ancestors were retained in dark skin, which grew blacker over generations to shield against ultraviolet rays, the cause of epidermal cancer. Their longer noses were no longer needed for diving, so were of no use on the African plains. Now, a broad nose with flaring nostrils evolved with larger sinus cavities for the more efficient processing of scant moisture—thereby aiding in the cooling process—enabling hunters to run in the heat. Their powerful, prothaganous jaw and strong teeth likewise carried over from preaquatic times for the mastication of tougher-skinned prey.

*Homo sapiens* populations in Southeast Asia likewise abandoned aquatic environments when they recoiled inland from the broad destruction caused by Mount Toba. Their torso became squatter, shorter, and stockier for the better preservation of body heat against steeply declining temperatures, and the eye developed an epicanthic fold in response to windblown, dusty conditions.

Other human groups inhabiting Mediterranean shores continued to pursue a maritime existence. After more than 20,000 years of dieting on intelligence-enhancing seafood and dealing with the unique challenges of an aqueous lifestyle, their burgeoning population spread throughout the European continent. It was here that the most recent evolutionary changes to emerge from this latest aquatic phase occurred. For example, Caucasians grow fuller, thicker facial hair than the males of any other race, because they spent more recent time in an hydrospheric environment, where beards developed to aid in raising children. While the mother took turns searching for food in the sea or resting upon it, the floating infant clung to its father's strong facial hairs, which concurrently became an identifying aspect of sexual dimorphism: the onset of facial hair growth signaled the emergence of a male's developing reproductive capacity.

Asian beards are not profuse; sub-Sahara African facial hair is yet more sparse; and American Indians do not grow beards at all, because these races are much further removed in time from their last aquatic phase. Accordingly, the hair follicles of modern Caucasians are oily, a typical adaptation against cold water temperatures, while sub-Sahara African hair follicles are dry: oily hair follicles would only speed up and increase heating in equatorial conditions, resulting in sunstroke.

Skeptics may argue that some two dozen millennia would have been insufficient for such aquatic changes to have taken place, given the gradual pace of evolution. But not all genetic mutations occur at the same, steady rate—they can be accelerated by stimuli. A case in point is a recent study (2006) that showed how, just 8,000 years ago, all adult human beings, like those of every mammal species, were lactose intolerant.

"Most mammals lose their ability to digest milk after being weaned," explained James Owen, a science writer for *National Geographic News*. His report concerns a study led by Joachim Burger of Germany's Institute of Archaeology at Mainz University that compared the DNA of mature European skeletal remains from the Neolithic Period (circa

5800 BCE to 5300 BCE) with those of the Late Renaissance (1500 CE) and today.[22] Results showed the following: the Neolithic specimens evidenced total lactose intolerance, Renaissance intolerance dropped by 40 percent, and 5 percent of today's populations of European descent are lactose intolerant.

These findings mean that

some humans can continue to benefit from the calcium-rich, high-energy liquid. This is because they carry a mutation that lets them continue producing lactase, the gut enzyme needed to break down the milk sugar lactose, in adulthood. Early farming communities that could digest milk could consume the liquid during otherwise poor harvests. . . . The team says it found no trace of the lactase gene [in Neolithic specimens], indicating that people from the period weren't yet able to drink milk. The study suggests that the lactase gene spread rapidly in the human population only after dairy livestock were introduced to Europe about eight thousand years ago, the gene suddenly became useful, and its presence in the population quickly grew through natural selection.[23]

Europeans—together with some surviving remnants of ancient, farming communities in North Africa—are the only lactose-tolerant groups in the world, because their ancestors alone developed dairy farming. "People who had cows, goats, or sheep and were lactose resistant had more children, and those children survived infant mortality and years of poor harvests," according to Burger. The legacy of this evolutionary process is very apparent in the DNA of modern northern and central Europeans.

"All over the world, most people can't drink milk when they're adults," he said. "It's only some populations in northern Africa and Europeans that can."[24] Today, 98 percent of Southeast Asian adults, 79 percent of African Americans, 73.8 percent of Mexicans, and 68.8 percent of North American Jews are lactose intolerant.[25] The development of a lactose-tolerant gene in just 7,000 years proves that human evolutionary change does not always need far greater blocks of time, but can move very quickly under environmental duress.

The Great Leap Forward from basic survival characterized the previous 2 million years of human evolution. However, the onset of glacial conditions 50,000 years ago triggered an entirely different set of evolutionary leaps in humans, at that point in their Mediterranean interlude. Skin, eye and hair color lightened in response to dimmer ultraviolet light conditions. And from the terrible hardships imposed by a full-blown ice age emerged modern man. Incredible as it may seem, a memory of that transformation appears to have been preserved in ancient myth.

Westenhöfer himself believed that "human tradition reaches very far back, and perennial tradition certainly cannot invent something that has never existed; even the boldest minds cannot do that. Somewhere, reality connects to the thread of every story."[26]

Such may apply to Iceland's *Prose Edda*, an early-thirteenth-century collection of far older Norse myths that tells of a time long ago, when the world was barren of most life because it was locked in ice. One of the few living creatures was a cosmic cow named Audhumbla. "She licked the ice-blocks, which were salty," reads the Edda. "And the first day that she licked the blocks, there came forth from the blocks in the evening a man's hair; the second day, a man's head; the third day, the whole man was there."[27] His name was Búri, for "maker," or the "son" of "fate" (Audhumbla). Thus, the first fully evolved human stepped forth from the last glacial epoch.

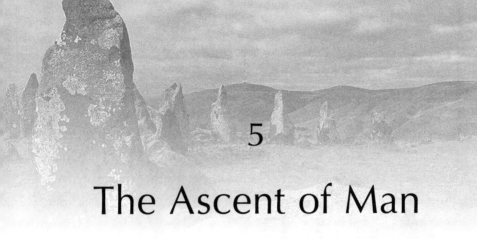

# 5

# The Ascent of Man

*After Altamira, all is decadence.*

As indicated by the earliest human cultural artifacts at Blombos Cave, Skul, and Oued Djebbana, refugee *Homo sapiens* escaped Indonesia's Mount Toba to arrive in South Africa 75,000 years ago, shortly thereafter migrating to Palestinian and Algerian shores. It was here, in this far more supportive Mediterranean environment, that our ancestors underwent their final, most recent aquatic phase—which allowed for the ongoing evolution of those traits still evident in our physical and instinctual being. This extended period, probably the longest golden age in all human history, came to an abrupt end after 25,000 years. Human mass migrations left North Africa for the European Continent via the Middle East at the same moment *Homo sapiens sapiens* discarded the primitive behavior characteristic of all his hominid forerunners to become modern man.

The cause of this sudden shift eluded paleoanthropologists until spring 2010, when global data modeling revealed climate footprints for drastic ecological change during the Upper Paleolithic Era. Worldwide, the environment rapidly deteriorated into plummeting temperatures and excessively dry conditions, as discovered by an international team of scientists at Denmark's Center for Macroecology, Evolution and Climate at the University of Copenhagen.[1] North Africa was rendered virtually uninhabitable by massive flooding that transformed the southern coastal Mediterranean regions into vast lakes and swamps today occupied by the Sahara Desert. What they refer to as the "Mousterian Pluvial" was a southward displacement of the Northern Hemisphere's temperate climatic zone by immense ice sheets, as they advanced over the northern half of Europe.

The result was prolonged, cataclysmic flooding that struck the paradisiacal shores of the Mediterranean Sea with 10,000 Hurricane Katrinas. For what may have been decades or even centuries, unremitting typhoon-force winds battered the region; entire animal species were wiped out; immense lakes and mighty rivers suddenly appeared where today the Sahara Desert spreads in every direction from horizon to horizon, overflowing their banks in one catastrophic deluge after another to drown millions of creatures. Humans fled for their lives into the Middle East, but conditions there were the precise opposite of North Africa's furious catastrophe. A deteriorating climate of dry air progressively transfigured the formerly broad grasslands and abundant forests into lifeless deserts.

Food became increasingly scarce, existence grew more and more tenuous, until game animals began migrating out of the Arabian Peninsula into the Black Sea area. They were followed by hunter populations traveling only on foot through the Danubian corridor into Ice Age Europe, where environmental conditions resembled those of Siberia on a bad day. Winds were strong, and winter temperatures averaged from -20 to -30 degrees Centigrade. Fuel and shelter were difficult to find. There was another factor at play as well: the newcomers were not alone.

The European continent was already occupied by another human species. It was known to science as *Homo neanderthalensis* since 1856, when remains were discovered in a cave above Germany's Neander Valley, near Düsseldorf. Predecessors resided in Europe 350,000 years, when they crossbred with *Homo erectus*. From this union with a much earlier, more primitive hominid type emerged Neanderthal man, a retrograde species. Writers for the Columbia Encyclopedia observed, "When placed in an evolutionary perspective, Neanderthal anatomy gives the impression of a large and somewhat 'primitive' hominid, as though the evolutionary trajectory of Homo sapiens had somehow reversed itself."[2]

The Neanderthal head featured pronounced brow ridges; long, low, and wide braincases, flattened behind; prothagenous jaw; small cheekbones; a low, sloping forehead; a chinless and heavy, forward-jutting jaw, with extremely large front teeth. The shoulders and pelvis were wider, the rib cage more conical in shape, the forearms and lower legs shorter and heavier. The Neanderthals' build was thick, robust, squat, and barrel-chested. Their large hands were much stronger than those of *Homo sapiens sapiens*. They had big feet with flat, wide toes, and walked in a lumbering, more irregular, side-to-side gait. Their skin was universally pale; their hair, sometimes red.[3]

In 2008, a study employing three-dimensional computer-assisted reconstructions of Neanderthal infants based on fossils recovered from Russia and Syria revealed that their brains were as large as those of modern humans at birth and larger than today's adults.[4] Neanderthal brains were less structurally convoluted, however, and more primitive. Based on data from forty-five long bones from fourteen males and seven females, Neanderthal men averaged five feet nine inches in height; their women were shorter by four inches.

As such, they were in stark contrast to the strangers who first appeared in the Balkans about 45,000 years ago. These were displaced persons driven from the Mediterranean area and the Middle East by a deteriorating climate afflicting the entire Northern Hemisphere. Referred to by scholars as Cro-Magnons, they were the first fully fledged modern humans, both anatomically and culturally. Their predecessors had been distinguished by prothaganous browridges resulting from muscular jaws meant to bite and masticate terrestrial prey and hard-shelled fruits and nuts. These cranial features become progressively distinct the earlier back we trace man's evolutionary path, leading into the more powerful jaws and heavy browridges of gorillas, baboons, chimpanzees, and monkeys. These primates also have much stronger dentition. But after forty-five millennia of eating the soft-bodied shellfish of the Mediterranean, *Homo sapiens'* jaw grew weaker and less pronounced, while his teeth became more delicate to form our present facial profile.

Abri de Crô-Magnon—a rock shelter in southwest France—gave its name to the first specimen of its kind, found there in 1868. Prior to their arrival in Europe, humans had changed little since *Homo erectus.* True, early *Homo sapiens* crafted shell pendants and even built oceangoing rafts after Mount Toba erupted, but virtually nothing more in the 25,000 years since.

"For something like half-a-million years, his cultural development had been so slow," Jacquetta Hawkes pointed out, "that a hundred generations might live and die without making any perceptible progress. There had, it is true, been some acceleration during the warmer interval before the last advance of the ice. But, at the end of this interval, a time when the somewhat brutal-looking and culturally uninventive Neanderthal breed was dominant in Europe, there were few signs of the great things soon to come."[5]

The emergence of human culture in the form of toolmaking, sophisticated weaponry, sculpture, cave painting, body ornaments, long-distance trade, and the invention of baked bread did not appear until their sudden profusion in the hands of Cro-Magnon man. Their creation had been instigated by the life-or-death challenges confronting him after 50,000 BCE, and resulted in the Great Leap Forward from mere hominid to culture-builder. Glacial conditions compelled social cooperation, the advancement of language skills, and communication. All these the Neanderthals lacked, but they gradually, partially absorbed from their new neighbors, with whom they lived in peace for perhaps 2,000 years or more. They learned how to manage fire, make stone tools, wooden spears, and animal-hide clothes, care for the sick, and conduct rituals on behalf of their dead.

Evidence from Neanderthal funerals includes flower wreaths, suggesting spiritual concepts of some kind. Although very limited interbreeding occurred between Cro-Magnon and Neanderthal groups (not in Europe, according to DNA studies, but almost entirely in the Near East, as Neanderthals neared extinction), both preserved their distinct identities across the millennia, while sharing the same continent.[6] But population growth inevitably led to conflict over territorial imperatives and food resources. The Neanderthals, being the resident people, were more numerous than their opponents, and physically stronger. The Cro-Magnons could only hope to prevail by applying their superior intelligence to advanced weapons technology and better social cooperation. Their struggle for sole possession of Europe raged over 18,000 years.

Another factor may have contributed to the ferocity of genocidal conflict. Around the turn of the twenty-first century, researchers began finding the cannibalized skeletons of Neanderthal occupants inside Cueva de El Sidrón, a 1,800-foot-long cave in northwestern Spain. By 2010, a dozen or so remains had been identified, all of them dated to approximately 43,000 years ago, long before Cro-Magnons arrived in continental Europe. Similar although not as definitive discoveries going back 100,000 years were made at Moula-Guercy, in south-central France, during 1991; and Krapina, in northern Croatia. Less certain—if more numerous—indications of cannibalism have surfaced from time to time across continental Europe since the late 1800s, although no physical evidence connecting Cro-Magnons with the practice has ever been found, leading some investigators to speculate that it might have contributed to Neanderthal extermination. In any case, by 22,000 Years Before Present, at the height of ice age conditions, the Neanderthals were wiped out.

Their disappearance coincided with an easing of glacial severity and the first golden age of painting and sculpture. Until then, the Cro-Magnons had been preoccupied with incessant warfare and basic survival in virtually unrelieved wintery surroundings. Now, a moderated climate of milder temperatures sparked an extended, cultural surge resulting in such outstanding achievements as the famous Venus of Willendorf. Carved from limestone not native to the area of its discovery in Lower Austria, the 4.3-inch-high statuette represents a Mother Earth figure, an artifact of modern man's earliest spiritual concepts. It was in his subterranean art, however, that he particularly excelled. "They invented drawing, engraving, stenciling, painting, modeling in relief and in the round," Hawkes said, "almost every process known to us today."[7]

The first and among the most outstanding examples were found near the town of Santillana del Mar in Cantabria, Spain, nineteen miles west of the city of Santander. In 1879, the nine-year-old daughter of Marcelino Sanz de Sautuola told him of an obscure cave with "strange drawings" she saw while playing on a hill locally known as Altamira, the "high view." Returning with her father, they beheld the walls and ceiling of the underground location alive with an extensive series of vibrant images depicting a herd of bison in different poses, two horses, a large doe and wild boar, goats, and human handprints. All were masterfully executed in charcoal and ochre or hematite, which had been occasionally diluted to achieve variations in intensity. Many of the representations were etched into the naked rock face, the natural contours of which had been skillfully and realistically incorporated into a portrayed animal's anatomy and muscleture, thereby producing a three-dimensional effect.

For almost a year, de Sautuola explored Altamira's 971 feet of interconnecting chambers and twisting passages, all of them decorated with brilliant figures, without disclosing their existence to the outside world. Only in spring 1880, after meticulous note-taking of the complex interior, did he make his daughter's discovery public. But professional scholars unanimously dismissed his "Stone Age art gallery" as a hoax, because mainstream scientific opinion held that prehistoric man lacked the intellectual capacity to produce any kind of aesthetic expression. Their chouses of ridicule were led by the leading antiquarian of the time, Emile Cartailhac (1845–1921), curator of the Académie des

Jeux Floraux, and one of the founders of the Institut de Paléontologie Humaine in Paris, during Lisbon's Prehistorical Congress. He dismissed de Sautuola as "an amateur archeologist" who had "forged" the images, given their exceptionally high quality and very good state of preservation.

"They all look as though they were completed by a hired artist just a few months ago," the influential Cartailhac asserted, "as they most certainly were."[8]

Throughout the rest of the 1800s and into the twentieth century, Altamira became synonymous for "fraud" in the public mind—a transparent attempt to dupe the official guardians of scientific truth. In 1902, however, university-trained anthropologists found several other, subterranean paintings of self-evident Paleolithic origins in Cantabria. These discoveries forced a reexamination of Altamira's main passage, which varies from six to thirty-six feet in height. Excavating the floor, they uncovered rich cultural deposits from 18,500 years ago dating to the Palaeolithic, or Old Stone Age. Investigators determined that, prior to its modern discovery, the cave had not been visited since 13,000 BCE, when a landslide had sealed its mouth, thereby perfectly preserving the paintings and artifacts inside—until a large tree fell on the buried entrance, dislodging enough rocky debris to partially expose the opening sometime during the late nineteenth century.

Abashed by these revelations, Cartailhac recanted his rejection of the site in a famous article, "Mea Culpa d'un Sceptique" (The apology of a skeptic), for a prestigious scientific journal, *L'Anthropologie*. Alas, his contrition came too late for the disgraced de Sautuola; his reputation ruined, he died fourteen years earlier. Long after, in 2008, scientists using Uranium-thorium dating determined that at least sections of the rock art had been painted between 25,000 and 35,000 years ago.

The story of discovery was a pattern that preceded Altamira and continues to repeat itself onto the present day: The greatest archaeological finds are made by lowly "amateurs" unfettered by conventional blinders, their documentation dismissed as fraudulent and they themselves castigated as swindlers by mainstream academics, who rarely give more than a cursory glance at the new evidence—which is later authenticated, typically, long after all persons originally concerned have passed away in disgrace. Visionaries of every kind are invariably despised, because their fresh perspectives undermine the faulty foundations of prevailing doctrine and the careers invested in that paradigm. The only difference between Cartailhac and today's scientific dogmatists is that they are emotionally incapable of writing a *Mea culpa d'un sceptique*, because their professional pride prevents them from admitting they were wrong.

With official admission that Paleolithic man was, in fact, capable of artistic achievement, other related locations came to light. In all, some 100 Old Stone Age caves, containing humankind's earliest representational art, would be found throughout the twentieth century. Most occur in France (mainly the southwest, in the Périgord and Pyrenees), then Iberia, with one in Russia.

In almost all cases, local limestone deposits supplied cave artists with iron-oxide for red, brown, yellow, and orange paints, and manganese oxide for purple and black. All were applied with fingertips, brushes of hair or plant fiber, and blow-tubes; these allowed for shading and low relief. More than twenty different species of animals were dynamically portrayed, with emphasis on red deer, ibex, ox, mammoths, and reindeer. Some, like bison and horses, were often paired, while particular symbols appeared only in the caves' most remote sections. Although numerous and widely separated, all Upper Paleolithic cave art was executed in prescribed patterns, thereby demonstrating the cultural uniformity of a single people spread over the European continent.

During 1922, André David and Henri Dutertre found a cave 840 feet up the eastern side a hill in the Midi-Pyrénées region of southern France. Known as Pech Merle, or "Blackbird Hill" in the local Occitan language, the entrance had been only recently opened by excessive rains washing away millennia of deposition. Returning to their nearby village of Cabrerets, the teenage discoverers directed a local priest to the cave. Father Amédée Lemozi descended more than a mile into the subterranean site, some 900 feet of which were covered with dramatic murals, fresh in appearance, of woolly mammoth, bovids, reindeer, and spotted horses. Altogether, he counted sixty representations of animals, fifty outlines of hands, and three images of humans. Curiously, of the two levels inside Pech Merle, paintings occur only on the first level. Seven of the chambers have been decorated, while galleries average thirty feet across, rising to ceilings fifteen to thirty feet high. More than half-a-mile inside the cave, Lomozi noticed the footprints of children, preserved in what was once clay.

Using Pech Merle as a reference point, archaeologists have since discovered ten other underground art complexes from the Upper Paleolithic period within a six-mile radius. The most spectacular find of its kind to date was made eighteen years later by four more teenagers at Lascaux, outside the village of Montignac, in the Dordogne département of southwestern France. On a late summer's morning, their dog, "Robot," pursued a hare down into a hole, through which the boys, following close behind, tumbled into something more than a rabbit warren. The subterranean location contained nearly 2,000 paintings: most of them applied directly to the walls with mineral pigments of red, yellow, black, brown, and violet; others were incised into the rock face.

Of the more than 900 animals portrayed, 605 have been positively identified; equines predominate with 364 examples—just one short for the number of days in a solar year. The walls and ceilings are adorned with ninety lifelike representations of stags, while cattle and bison comprise 4 percent to 5 percent of the images. Others include seven felines, a bird, and one each of a bear and rhinoceros. A section referred to as "The Great Hall of the Bulls" features thirty-six animals dominated by four black bulls, a seventeen-foot-long specimen of which is the largest animal discovered so far in cave art anywhere. The hind legs of an animal in another painting, "The Crossed Bison," demonstrate its skillful use of perspective—a technique subsequently lost long before the official advent of civilization in Mesopotamia, and not rediscovered until the European Renaissance during the fifteenth century. No less remarkably, all the bulls were portrayed in realistic motion.

The Paleolithic art gallery was found three months after France had been defeated in World War II, although German forces did not occupy the Dordogne at the time of the cave's discovery on September 12, 1940. Instead, it came under the jurisdiction of pro-Axis Vichy Government officials. On October 24, they investigated the site with Abbé Henri Édouard Prosper Breuil, one of the great names in twentieth-century science. A Catholic priest, draftsman, archaeologist, anthropologist, ethnologist and geologist; professor of prehistoric ethnology in Paris and at the Collège de France, he was the world's foremost authority on the Stone Age, and still regarded as one of the most important scholars of the past century—notable for his faithful renderings of Paleolithic art. At Abbé Breuil's instigation, the first photographic documentation of Lascaux's artwork was completed, followed by closure of the location as a protective measure.

His actions undoubtedly saved its Old Stone Age masterpieces, because the cave has been troubled ever since it was reopened after the war. Carbon dioxide exhaled by 1,200 visitors per day so badly damaged its paintings that public access was terminated by 1963 for all but a few individuals willing to pay high admission fees. When the presence of even these privileged persons caused a fungus to grow on the walls, entry was restricted to anthropologists in 1998. Ten years later, they too, were banned from the premises, because a new, black mold threatened the interior. Only a single curator was allowed to monitor conditions once a week for twenty minutes. Today, three or five preservationists and scientists at a time are permitted to visit the underground site no more than as many days each month. Unfortunately, their attempts to remove the mold have caused some damage to the 17,300-year-old artwork.

What these images signified to their Paleolithic creators continues to be a source of debate since mainstream scholars acknowledged the Old Stone Age provenance of Altamira. Taking the paintings at face value, early theorists concluded that they illustrated successful hunting scenes. But of the many thousands of depicted animals, none are represented as prey. A badly wounded bison portrayed at Lascaux seems to have been gored by a passing rhinoceros. Moreover, human figures appear infrequently among the murals, where their execution is invariably far inferior to that of the beasts—as though deliberately so—and never in the heroic guise of mighty hunters. "The question of human representation in this art is of great interest," Hawkes wondered. "The contrast between the match-stick man at Lascaux and the noble realism of the dying bison is representative. With the exception of the Angles-sur-l'Anglin portrait [in western France], almost all representations of men are either schematic or childishly crude."[9]

The subterranean sites themselves are difficult and dangerous to reach, some only by climbing down narrow shafts. Most of the paintings do not occur in accessible chambers, but were hidden away amid hard-to-reach nooks and crannies. As such, the galleries suggest less a series of vainglorious billboards than places of initiation for arcane rites of passage. This interpretation is seconded by children's footprints occurring deep inside several Paleolithic caves, and the outlines of juvenile hands more deliberately made on the walls by blowing pigment through a tube around the spread fingers—color-stained, hollowed-out bones for the purpose have been recovered nearby.

Abbé Breuil's first impression of Lascaux convinced him that its paintings belonged to a shrine or temple for the enactment of magical ceremonies. Because his views were stated under the Vichy regime, they were considered politically undesirable by postwar French authorities, who reverted to the hunting scene hypothesis, an official interpretation that prevailed for the rest of the twentieth century.

In March 2000, however, a German archaeoastronomer at the University of Munich demonstrated that Lascaux's cave art was part of a prehistoric sky-chart. Dr. Michael Rappenglueck was able to show how the illustrations of a rhinoceros, bird-headed man, and bird on a stick (a scepter?) corresponded to three prominent stars: Vega, Deneb, and Altair. They form the Summer Triangle, and are among the brightest objects in the heavens throughout the middle months of the northern summer. During the Old Stone Age, these stars were especially prominent at the onset of spring, and would never have set below the

*Fig. 5.1. Stone Age constellations portrayed on the
ceiling of Lascaux. Photo by Professor Saxx.*

horizon—suggesting eternal life to Paleolithic observers. He found evidence of other stellar clusters duplicated at Lascaux, including the Pleiades. But his most remarkable find was a correlation between spots inside the rendering of a bull with stars in the Constellation Taurus.

His discovery means that they have been associated with the likeness of a bull long before the historical advent of astrological symbolism in Mesopotamia 5,000 years ago. It is nothing short of astounding that such an identification should have been consistently carried over fourteen millennia through cultures as different from each other as they were innumerable—from Old Stone Age artists to the first farmers and earliest civilizers in the Near East. Dr. Rappenglueck's conclusions were underscored by French archaeologist, Chantal Jègues-Wolkiewiez, whose extensive survey of prehistoric cave sites in the Vallée des Merveilles revealed that most of them had been specifically selected for orientation with the sun as it sets on the winter solstice to illuminate the murals.

Ceremonial implications of this deliberate association between subterranean sites and sky prompted James David Lewis-Williams to compare geometric images in Lascaux and related locations with virtually identical examples found at the oldest sacred areas still visited by South African natives. A professor emeritus of cognitive archaeology at the University of the Witwatersrand in Johannesburg, he is the leading authority on the San or Bushmen, who use the same abstract designs as aids in ritualistic dancing to achieve altered states of consciousness.

The trances entered or visions they experience as a consequence "are a function of the human brain and so are independent of geographical location."[10] These parallels were likewise noticed by Nigel Spivey, a professor of classic art and archaeology at the University of Cambridge, who pointed out that "dot and lattice patterns overlapping the representational images of animals are very similar to hallucinations provoked by sensory-deprivation."[11]

The Paleolithic caves were sanctuaries for a mystery cult that brought its initiates deep under ground, as though entering Death itself, where they participated in spectacular dramatizations of the life-associated constellations, emerging with a sense of rebirth from Mother Earth. The ancient Hermetic principle of "As Above, So Below" appears to have had its origins in the subterranean temples of Old Stone Age Europe.

The most recent such discovery is also among the most bizarre. Although diver Henri Cosquer found the cave in 1985, its existence not far from Marseille was only made known to the outside world five years later, when three scuba divers exploring the site became disoriented in its sunken passages and drowned. The entrance itself at Cap Margiou is about 115 feet beneath the surface of the Mediterranean; sea levels were much lower during Upper Paleolithic (Pleistocene) times, so the shore was just a few miles away. The 574-foot-long tunnel visitors now use to access the site is itself under water. A gallery slopes up for about 360 feet beneath the surface before reaching a huge chamber, where many prehistoric paintings and engravings are preserved on its walls, together with Stone Age remains on the ground: charcoal from fires and torches, a few flint tools, a calcite lamp.

The only illustrated cave in the world with an entrance below present-day sea level, its rock art has been preserved from flooding that occurred when the seas rose after the end of the last glaciation. Over the postglacial millennia since their creation, four-fifths of the murals in

Cosquer Cave were obliterated by the rising waters, leaving 150 paintings and carvings. The remaining art consists of sixty-five stenciled handprints and 177 depictions of animals, containing eleven different animal species including bison, ibexes, horses, seals, auks, aurochs, red deer, megaloceros deer, stags, does, one feline, jellyfish, and chamois, a goat-antelope species native to the mountains of Central Europe. Juvenile handprints appear eight feet over the floor, two feet above lines of fully mature handprints, suggesting that children were hoisted onto the shoulders of adults, as ladders were not practical in the rocky environment.

At least a few of the 216 geometric designs appear to be sexual symbols; these imply the staging of coming-of-age ceremonies or initiation rituals for pubescent and late prepubescent youth into society, or perhaps a mystery cult. The latter possibility is emphasized by a general uniformity of subject matter occurring at the approximately 350 caves illustrated during the Old Stone Age, so far discovered from the southern tip of the Iberian Peninsula to the Ural Mountains. Nearly half of these sites—about 160—have been found in France, loosely clustering around Périgord, in the Dordogne, which comprises more than sixty such locations painted over 20,000 years. The European southwest was favored because it possessed more caves—apparently, a vital setting for the Paleolithic artists—than elsewhere.

Even in the Dordogne, selectivity is evident in the many, otherwise perfectly suitable, caves that were deliberately ignored because they lacked another integral quality; namely, water. Most, perhaps all, caves adorned by Old Stone Age illustrators were adjacent to rivers, or near the seacoast, like Cosquer Cave. Affirming its ritualistic character, this site displays some composite figures, most notably a human body surmounted with the head of a seal. Based on the number of surviving specimens not lost to rising sea levels, archaeologists estimate they originally totaled perhaps as many as 800 illustrations.

They also found proof of large-scale mining in Cosquer Cave during Upper Paleolithic times. Substantial quantities of stalactites, stalagmites, and mondmilch (a soft, milky-white limestone) were removed and pounded into powder for medicinal purposes; specifically, the treatment of fevers (to encourage sweating), heart conditions, to stop bleeding, for curbing diarrhea, the relief of cough, strengthening broken bones, drying up abscesses, ulcers and wounds, or aiding in the production of milk for wet-nurses. Today, calcium carbonate ($CaCo_3$) is widely prescribed for osteoporosis, bone regeneration, and ailments related to growth.

Its earliest assumed use went back to China in the fourth century BCE, when late Zhou Dynasty pharmacists prescribed identically powdered stalactites, stalagmites, and mondmilch for the same treatment. But the evidence at Cosquer Cave shows that the merits of calcium carbonate were appreciated by Old Stone Age Europeans some 25,000 years before ancient Chinese pharmacists discovered it. Far more significantly, the French location belongs to the first known manufacture of medicine in the history of mankind. These disclosures reveal an advanced mentality previously unassociated with Stone Age humans, still popularly portrayed as grunting, club-wielding cave-dwellers. Instead, our Paleolithic ancestors found expression for their medicinal and artistic genius—all without precedent—within the context of severe glacial conditions that we twenty-first-century moderns would find challenging in the extreme. As such, their re-emerging greatness appears all the more innovative, tough, and glorious.

# 6

# Discovery as Heresy

*History will die if not irritated. The only service I can do
to my profession is to serve as a flea.*

HENRY ADAMS (1838–1918),
AMERICAN HISTORIAN

Twenty-seven radiocarbon dates obtained from Cosquer Cave clustered
into two distinct periods of habitation or visitation: 27,000 Years Before
Present and 19,000 YBP. These time frames coincide, respectfully, with
the Gravettian (its very end) and Solutrean cultures distinguished from
each other by their different approaches to toolmaking. Named after
the type site of Crôt du Charnier in eastern France at Solutré, the latter
was decidedly more advanced, as evidenced by remarkable rock art at
the subterranean ceremonial center and other related sites, such as the
Dordogne's Pech Merle.

The walls of its seven chambers are adorned with the lifelike imagery of spotted horses, a woolly mammoth, other local fauna, and some
humans. Footprints of children, preserved in what was once clay, may
still be seen more than half a mile underground. Lascaux, the greatest Upper Paleolithic gallery of its kind, may have been entirely, if not
mostly, painted by these Solutrean illustrators. Their foremost artifacts

include an ibex-headed spear-thrower from Ariege's Le Mas d'Azil (now at Musee de la Prehistoire, Le Mas d'Azil), and a lamp with ibex design found in the Dordogne's La Mouthe cave (displayed at the Musee des Antiquites Nationales, St. Germain-en-Laye).

During 1965, a farmer excavating his celler in a central Ukranian village unearthed an immense jawbone. Later digs undertaken in his basement by University of Kaniv archaeologists found four huts constructed of 149 mammoth bones, which may have been used to build other structures, forming a Solutrean village. In any case, the Mezhirich remains comprise the earliest known dwelling site made by humans. Among the bones were found component parts of a drum—the world's oldest percussion instrument—made of a mammoth skull painted with a red pattern; personal ornaments of amber; and a bone inscribed with a map of the vicinity—again, the oldest example so far discovered.

These objects bespeak a discernable technological edge over Gravettian predecessors, particularly in a greater finesse demonstrated by bifacial points (stone spearheads, saws, knives, scrapers, and various blades) finely worked by the Solutreans. They introduced lithic reduction percussion and pressure flaking, instead of cruder flint-knapping, using antler or hardwood batons, and soft stone hammers. This improved technique made possible the crafting of delicate slivers of flint for the innovative production of light projectiles, including elaborately barbed and tanged arrowheads. Writing in *World Archaeology* magazine, Smithsonian Institution paleoanthropologists Bruce Bradley and Dennis Stanford stated that "Solutrean tool-making employed techniques not seen before and not rediscovered for millennia."[1]

The abrupt termination of this advanced culture produced a double mystery—still in the process of being understood. Only late-twentieth-century advances in paleoclimatology revealed an epoch of falling temperatures known to environmental scientists as the Late Glacial Maximum. Glaciers marched across Middle Europe, reducing most of the remaining continental landmass to virtually uninhabitable tundra. Burgeoning ice caps sucked up and locked in thousands of cubic miles of ocean water. Worldwide sea levels dropped by as much as 400 feet to make subterranean art galleries such as Cosquer Cave possible. Britain was joined by dry land with the European continent, while the Atlantic shores of New York, France, and Spain expanded outward by more than 100 miles. Onto these vast tracks of newly exposed territories, the Solutreans migrated and adapted maritime ways to exploit the coastal setting.

Some of their surviving artifacts from this late period were barbed harpoons designed to hunt deep-water prey—such as whales—proof that their makers and users were the first seafarers who ventured beyond the relative safety of a nearby shore. In defiance of a deteriorating climate, the Solutreans flourished until even their ice age hardihood broke 15,000 years ago under a violent surge of cold air. The so-called Keg Mountain Oscillation set in when the polar jet stream dipped over the Northern Hemisphere, causing fierce winds and blizzards to blast the world for the next two-and-a-half centuries. Then, just as abruptly as these frigid conditions arrived, they reversed themselves.

Expansion of the Laurentide ice sheet moved the jet stream southward, but later, the ice sheet's reduction in area allowed the jet stream to return north. The ice sheet covered hundreds of thousands of square miles, including much of North America, all of Canada, and as far south as New York City and Chicago, almost exactly bordered in the west by the Missouri River. With its contraction, the jet stream snapped back above the Arctic Circle, followed by great masses of warm air. Their higher temperatures melted the Late Glacial Maximum's immense ice cover to generate a truly cataclysmic deluge.

Over the next 200 years, thousands of miles of previously exposed coastal regions were engulfed by a series of floods far above biblical proportions. Archaeogeophysicists studying effects of the Keg Mountain Oscillation in the American Southwest referred to them as components of the "catastrophic Bonneville Flood . . . when the climate dropped Utah's lake below its spillway to under four thousand nine hundred fifty feet and the two hundred years when it rose back up again."[2] Paleoclimatologists agree with geologists that seas rose over littorals in Europe, obliterating or covering all signs of Solutrean habitation, about 14,880 years ago. Cosquer Cave—unlike what must have been similar examples located further west—barely escaped total inundation only because it happened to stand on the verge of higher, newly created shorelines.

Most human survivors fled inland, where they were subsumed and replaced by bearers of another culture—the Magdalenians—who, dwelling far from the sea, had not been directly affected by such natural catastrophes. Fewer took to their boats, and some, it would appear, actually crossed the North Atlantic to make landfall in America, more than 14,000 years before Columbus. Nor were these the first transoceanic voyages. Solutrean Europeans navigating from the ice age Deluge were already long familiar with the world on the opposite side of the ocean. During the Late Glacial Maximum, before the Keg Mountain Oscillation began, Western Europe was almost contiguous with Labrador by extensive, connecting sheets of pack ice, the edges of which harbored an abundance of rich marine life.

Experienced fishermen and hunters—the latter armed with their barbed harpoons—would have found an endless supply of food to sustain them throughout any waterborne travels westward. Indications for these voyages were first noticed in 1999 by Stanford and Bradley. They were shocked to discover that Solutrean stone tools were virtually identical to those made by the earliest known inhabitants of America, who were believed to have crossed a land bridge from Siberia to Alaska, supposedly no earlier than just prior to the close of the last glacial epoch. This mainstream time frame appeared confirmed during early 2009, when the Mahaffey Cache was found in Boulder, Colorado.

Traces of horse and cameloid protein residues were recovered from its eighty-three stone tools, enabling them to be dated from 13,000 to 13,500 years ago. Artifacts such as these are referred to as "Clovis points": thin, characteristically-fluted projectile heads, each with a distinctly concave base, and named after the city of Clovis, New Mexico, where the first examples were collected in 1929. Percussion hammered from flint, chert, jasper, chalcedony, and other, similarly fractural stone, the points were hafted onto wooden shafts by grooves at their base for use as spears, or socketed onto shorter lengths as knives. They were a genuine innovation, a technological leap forward, because their sharp, serrated edge meant superior cutting power over all previous designs, while fluting allowed hunters to rapidly load and reload their blades onto spear shafts.

"It's a very distinctive type of artifact," Stanford explains, "it has a flake that's been taken out of the base and there's also a flake on the other side removed from the base, and these are called flutes. And beyond that the projectile point is flaked on both sides."[3]

The Clovis Culture identified by such weapons or tools became so entrenched as America's first human society in the minds of paleoanthropologists that its status calcified into a scientific hard-line resistant to consideration of any contrary information—becoming, in effect, a textbook explanation for the peopling of our continent. "No scientific falsehood is more difficult to expunge," stated the famous historian of science, Stephen Jay Gould (1941–2002), "than textbook dogma endlessly repeated in tabular epitome without the original data."[4]

Comparisons with Solutrean look-alikes made by Stanford and Bradley were dismissed out of hand as entirely circumstantial. However, resemblances were not only remarkably close, but otherwise unique in the world. Such points are found only in Paleolithic Europe and prehistoric America. None occur in northeast Asia, the supposed place of origin for the Clovis people. The points bearing the Clovis name do not resemble their Asian counterparts, which were made from small, razor-like flints inserted into a bone handle.

Stanford described this Siberian technique as "a totally different philosophy, entirely, than using the bifacial projectile point. . . . It's just a total different mindset."[5] This critical observation is underscored by a growing body of physical evidence that not only predates their first alleged appearance some 13,000 years ago, but argues for the arrival of Old Stone Age Europeans at least two millennia before the ancestors of the American Indians.

Fig. 6.1. From American Discovery magazine, by Gunnar Thompson, Ph.D.

Dr. Cyclone Covey, history professor emeritus at Wake Forest College in North Carolina recounts how Edwin Wilmsen, a researcher at the Smithsonian Institution during the mid-1960s, "minutely measured one hundred eleven unmodified flakes from . . . Solutrean levels at Laugerie-Haute [in the French Dordogne], confirming negligable differences" from points unearthed in Colorado, and "therefore essentially identical tool production. Even during the previous century, European resemblance of projectile points found in the Delaware Valley near Trenton led C.C. Abbott to propound a European connection across the Atlantic, in 1877."[6]

The manufacture of Clovis points was a messy affair, with large scraps left over as part of their flaking process. So common was the association of this oversized debris with prehistoric blade production it became diagnostic of Clovis sites. Wondering if this identifiable residue might occur at contemporaneous Western European locations, Bradley visited Les Eyzies, France. The town museum displayed literally hundreds of Solutrean points virtually identical to Clovis examples. More decisively, the little institution also featured drawers filled with even more large flakes recovered in situ with the French blades. The American and European points were not only reverse mirror images of each other, but both had been produced by the same, distinctive technique.

Long prior to Bradley's exciting discovery, supporting evidence had already surfaced thirty-six miles from the Pacific Ocean, in south-central Chile. During 1977, Tom A. Dillehay, the anthropology department chair at Nashville, Tennessee's Vanderbilt University—then teaching at the Universidad Austral de Chile, in Valdivia—was excavating a prehistoric habitation site on the banks of a tributary of the Maullín River. The hamlet comprising about a dozen buildings had been fortuitously preserved when the Chinchihuapi Creek, on the banks of which it stood, flooded while ancient Monte Verde was still occupied, covering its 1,350 square feet with a peat bog that inhibited the bacterial decay of organic material by depriving it of oxygen. Still in surprisingly discernible condition was a twenty-foot-long, tentlike structure framed with logs and planks staked in the ground.

Inside, animal hides fastened with ropes made of local reeds separated different living quarters, each one with its own clay-lined brazier pit, around which were scattered numerous stone tools, together with spilled seeds, nuts, berries, a *Solanum maglia* (wild potato), and human coprolites (fossilized human excrement). Outside, a pair of large hearths had been used by the building's twenty or thirty tenants for making implements discovered nearby. Dillehay and his team found remains of forty-five different edible plant species in the immediate vicinity. More than a fifth of them had come from as far as 150 miles away, indicating the original inhabitants operated a trade route and/or ranged far afield themselves for specific kinds of food.

The rich abundance of carbon-datable materials at Monte Verde easily afforded a reliable time-frame for its occupation, which began 14,880 Years Before Present. This date not only greatly preceded the earliest Clovis site—which was 1,700 airline miles to the north, in New Mexico—but coincided with a proposed Solutrean dispersal from Iberia and transatlantic arrival in America just when the Keg Mountain Oscillation melted vast ice sheets, submerging the coastlines of Western Europe.

Announcement of Dillehay's find was met with predictable disdain from his academic colleagues in the United States. For the next twenty years, they ignored his invitation to visit the site themselves, until those few, hard-line skeptics who finally did pay him a visit in 1997 came away convinced his date parameters were inescapably correct after all. Their conversion was not sufficient to officially invalidate the Clovis First party line, however. Some conventional anthropologists, while conceding Monte Verde's antiquity, believed it changed nothing, because the site was obviously a fluke, not part of any real migration of peoples, but more likely the unique, accidental remnant of shipwrecked (raft-wrecked?) castaways from some unknown point of origin. This dismissive interpretation was subsequently invalidated by other southern Chilean sites—Cueva del Milodon, Tagua-Tagua, and the Pali Aike Crater lava tube—where artifacts likewise from 14,800 to 13,000 YBP have been found.

Mainstream critics in the early twenty-first century continue to question Dillehay's chronology, which was nevertheless reinforced by a May 9, 2008 issue of *Science* magazine reporting that samples of nine species of seaweed and marine algae recovered from hearths and other areas at Monte Verde were handily and positively dated between 14,220 to 13,980 years ago.[7] Still other U.S. anthropologists simply ignore the site altogether, while repeating the Clovis First Doctrine in newly published books, television documentaries, and feature articles for official journals or popular science periodicals. They have been particularly resistant to even consideration of additional sites that threaten to undermine their obsolete paradigm.

A case in point is Toca do Boqueira de Pedra Furada, located in the São Raimundo Nonato region of northeastern Brazil, where more than 1,150 prehistoric images cover the walls of a fifty-five-foot-deep rock shelter sheltering under a 300-foot-high sandstone cliff, and abounding with literally thousands of stone implements. Although the location was professionally excavated in 1978 by one of the most widely renowned and respected anthropologists in the world, most of her colleagues in the U.S. have insulted Nième Guidon's high-level expertise by accusing her of mistaking natural rocks, or "geofacts," for human artifacts. French palaeolithic archaeologist, Jacques Pelegrin, assured them that although Nature is quite capable of making stones that resemble artificial tools, the Pedra Furada objects are undoubtedly man-made.

Physicist William R. Corliss (1926–2011) went on to explain, "Critics of the site have suggested that the specimens classified as artifacts could have been flaked naturally in a high-energy depositional environment. But no such environment existed within the sheltered area where the specimens were found, as the sediments are mainly derived from the weathering of the sandstone overhang." He adds that approximately 6,000 objects were "deemed of human manufacture, even when the most stringent criteria are applied." They were found along with "some fifty Pleistocene 'structures' consisting of artificial arrangements of stones, some burned, some accompanied by charcoal."[8]

Guidon's critics were mostly upset by her discovery that human activity at the rock shelter went back further into the past than orthodox scholars deemed acceptable: "A date of 17,000 +/- 400 B.P., obtained from charcoal found in a level with fragments of a pictograph fallen from the walls, testifies to the antiquity of rupestral (rock) art in the region of Brazil."[9] A quarter of a century after her time parameters were obtained in 1986, she told *Athena Review,* "These dates are holding well. Once we learned that the Department of Earth Sciences of the Australian National University had developed a new chemical technique to decontaminate small quantities of charcoal to be dated by AMS (accelerator mass spectrometry), we sent samples to Canberra from the same charcoal dated in 1988/91 by the Gif laboratory in France."[10]

Her colleague, Fabio Parenti, commented, "The radiocarbon dates at the site of Pedra Furada, totaling fifty-two in my final report, are fully confirmed by new AMS techniques."[11]

The Brazilian rock shelter's "rupestral art" simultaneously demolished one objection to overseas' influences here during prehistory: skeptics had previously pointed out the apparent lack of cave paintings associated with the supposed presence of Solutreans in America. However, other South American sites yielding comparable dates are Peru's Pikimachay Cave, near Ayacucho, southeast of Lima, together with Muaco (on the shores of the Caribbean, appropriate for landfall made by a seafaring people) and nearby Taima-Taima. Both are located in Venezuela, where the southernmost Clovis points have been found so far.

Their distribution extends through Mexico and much of the United States, into Canada, where University of Alberta archaeologists "excavated a stone blade, a projectile point, and an engraving tool from a soil layer dated at 14,500 Y.B.P."[12] At least eight pre-Clovis sites have been discovered in the continental United States, including Saltville, in Virginia; Chesrow, Wisconsin; Smith Creek Cave, in Nevada; Danger Cave, Utah; the Meadowcroft Rockshelter, in southwestern Pennsylvania; and Connley Cave Number 5, Oregon. All of them are dated to periods commensurate with the arrival of Solutreans, particularly after their culture's abrupt decline in Western Europe and depredations engendered by the Keg Mountain Oscillation.

Their sudden disappearance 15,000 years ago and the rise of Clovis man some two millennia later represented far too great a gap in time for the Old Stone Age Europeans to have had any impact on the latter, skeptics argued. In 2000, however, archaeologists excavating Cactus Hill on sand dunes above the Nottoway River, about forty-five miles south of Richmond, Virginia, dug nine inches beneath a previously uncovered Clovis level to find bifacial stone tools. The presence of white-pine charcoal from a hearth in context with the artifacts dated them to a heretical 15,070 radiocarbon YBP.

Thermoluminescent testing came to the same conclusion. Improved dating procedures (optically stimulated luminescence) six years later confirmed not only the original time-frame, but expanded it to circa 18,000 years ago. Conventional anthropologists reacted by insisting that these dates had been skewed by vertical mixing of sandy soil. "Thorough analysis of the soil with its plant and animal remains," observes Corliss, "indicated that little if any mixing occurred over the years."[12]

Referring to Cactus Hill, Stanford stated, "Here we have a projectile point from a feature that dates right at fifteen thousand nine hundred years or sixteen thousand years ago, which is clearly right in the middle between Clovis and Solutrean. And what's really exciting about it is that the technology here is very similar to Solutrean. In fact, it's closer to Solutrean than Clovis, where you can see that it's in a progression between Solutrean and Clovis, so you have Solutrean, Cactus Hill and Clovis."[13]

Valuable as Cactus Hill may be to the proposal of Paleolithic Europeans in America, it is not the only prehistoric site bridging the gap between Solutrean and Clovis. A similar location had already come to light near Allendale, South Carolina, during 1981, when a local man, David Topper, suspected a prehistoric presence along the Savannah River. He had the good sense to contact Albert C. Goodyear III, a professor at the South Carolina Institute of Archaeology and Anthropology, a branch of the University of South Carolina, whose chief field of expertise was the Clovis Culture. Excavations at the "Topper Site," as it was thereafter known, did indeed yield the bifacial points identified with early human habitation going back between 11,200 and 10,800 years ago.

According to the prevailing academic protocol of the day, Goodyear terminated his investigations, having reached the accepted temporal limits of archaeology in North America. But when, more than ten years later, he learned of the controversy surrounding Monte Verde's alleged pre-Clovis discovery in Chile, he renewed his dig at the Topper Site. At first, predictably, he found nothing to undermine the ivory tower's old foundations. At a level far beneath his 1980s' strata, however, he unearthed more than a thousand stone flakes that had been first knapped, then discarded for their imperfections. Among them were twenty chert pebbles, fifteen microtools (most of them blades), and four hammerstones made of quartz. These artifacts were debris from a tool factory operating 16,000 years ago.

A final seal of proof was set on this material evidence by Douglas C. Wallace, the geneticist who pioneered human mtDNA as a molecular marker, and founder of the Mitochondrial Eve Research to Establish Molecular and Mitochondrial Medicine Center at the University of California at Irvine, where he became Professor of Biological Sciences and Molecular Medicine in 2002. Around that time, he examined the mitochondrial DNA of a North American tribal people, the Ojibwa Indians, because DNA is the molecule of human genetic descent. He did not concentrate on DNA found in the nucleus of the human cell, which contains a random mix of genes from both parents, confusing an individual's lineage.

Instead, Wallace studied the mitochodria—the human energy factories outside the cell's nucleus—because here mtDNA is inherited only from the mother and passed down to her descendants intact over the generations. In time, very small mutations arise along specific stretches of DNA, and variation between any two lineages shows how long ago they shared a common ancestor. Pursuing this line of research, he found four primary lines of descent that confirmed ultimate Ojibwa origins in northeast Asia, which mainstream scientists had always insisted was the original homeland of all American Indian tribes. But Wallace also discovered a fifth source of DNA he dubbed "X," because it did not appear anywhere among native populations of Siberia or eastern Asia.

It did, however, belong to present-day population groups in Western Europe, the result, he initially assumed, of interracial sexual relations with Europeans since the official discovery of the New World. Colonial and nineteenth-century white women taken captive by Ojibwa males were known to have given birth to mixed offspring, and some white men occasionally took aboriginal girls as wives. To be sure, the Indians absorbed not only modern whites of European descent, but other races as well over the last five centuries, and with growing frequency from the late twentieth through early twenty-first centuries. But a closer look at the amount of variation in the X lineage revealed that its origins went back long before Columbus landed on the beach at San Salvador in 1492.

"Well," Wallace concluded, "what it says is that a mitochondrial lineage that is predominantly found in Europe somehow got to the Great Lakes region of the Americas, fourteen thousand to fifteen thousand years ago."[14]

Tribal maternal ancestry, now genetically expressed as "haplogroup X," demonstrates that at least some individuals among the Ojibwa are distantly related to ice age Europeans. The unequivocal testimony of genetics combines with an abundance of archaeological evidence to confirm the arrival of Old Stone Age Europeans in America. Their story has been made clear: More than eighteen millennia ago, members of the Solutrean culture, dwelling in what are now the Atlantic coastal regions of France (since submerged under 400 feet of ocean) paddled in large kayaks made of animal hides along ice sheets virtually contiguous with the eastern seaboard of North America. According to marine anthropologist Jon Erlandson, the oldest known seagoing vessel is a 20,00-year-old open boat from Japan.[15]

In April 2008, the Clovis barrier was irretrieveably broached with announcement of the "Oldest Human DNA Found in the Americas."[16] For the previous six years of summer fieldwork, archaeologist Dennis

Jenkins and colleagues from the University of Oregon collected half a dozen coprolites at Paisley Five Mile Point Cave, in the south-central area of the state, on the eastern side of the Cascade mountain range. Radiocarbon dating placed the fossilized excrement at upward of 14,290 years old, some thirty-three centuries before the first humans were supposed to have arrived in the American Northwest.

Orthodox scholars were additionally vexed by heretical suggestions posed by the discovery site itself, because Paisley Five Mile Point Cave is located along the Klamath River, upriver from the Pacific Ocean, from which the ice age visitors appear to have come. Consensus anthropology not only holds that no one reached the continental United States before 11,000 years ago, but that the earliest explorers walked all the way from Siberia. Paisley Five Mile Point Cave proves they arrived long before, and probably by sea, along the Pacific coast.

A dramatic illustration of this maritime implication occurs in another cave occupied by the Solutreans themselves around 17,000 years ago. On a wall of the Grotte de la Mouthe, in the Perigord region of southwestern France, appears what paleoanthropologists describe as a *tectiform,* a roof-shaped image supposed to represent a man-made structure or dwelling. The image strikes most observers innocent of mainstream bias against possibilities for prehistoric seafaring, however, as that of a large ship!

Closer examination seems to actually confirm first impressions. Clearly portrayed is a large, vertically striped sail, trailing ropes, known as brails, for simultaneously drawing it in or up from both edges. The lower part of a thick mast may be seen jutting from beneath the sail, just where such a feature would be expected to show, descending into a hull with a serpentlike or avian figurehead, lending the vessel an ancient Old World—even a Viking—appearance.[17]

Like other examples of Paleolithic cave paintings, the Solutrean artist incorporated uneven moldings of la Mouthe's natural rock face into his illustration, thereby highlighting certain features to lend the entire work an almost three-dimensional quality, a technique used in depicting the powerful hull cresting through choppy seas. The foregoing is by no means a fanciful interpretation, as most nonpartisan examiners would probably agree. Indeed, the so-called tectiform makes for a far more credible seagoing vessel under sail than "a hut," as it is invariably defined in official sources. An unstable dwelling like the one supposedly portrayed at the Grotte de la Mouthe could not have stood up five minutes against the ice age gusts that swept Western Europe.

Indiana prehistorian Rick Osmon states that magnified scrutiny of the la Mouthe wall artwork shows what appears to be a rudder at the "stern" of the depicted vessel.[18] If this observation is correct, Solutrean use of the steering device predated its official invention in dynastic Egypt by 14,000 years.

The Périgord region's anomalous illustration is, unfortunately, among many examples of Academia's emperor's-new-clothes syndrome, wherein the obvious is unthinkable and impossible, because it is officially unacceptable: It does not exist, because it cannot exist. Yet, even the most hidebound skeptic admits that few Paleolithic artifacts are available for study, and these are mostly either made of stone or buried in caves. Everything else—particularly items fashioned from perishable materials, such as wooden-hull vessels with leather sails—has not survived the passage of tens of thousands of years. And while absence of evidence is not necessarily evidence of absence, it is hasty to conclude that a people who attained profound levels of material greatness in one important aspect of their society failed everywhere else, simply because physical proof has been erased by the passage of time.

On the contrary, art is a barometer of the epoch that produces it. The golden ages of Classical Greece and Renaissance Italy were typified not only by architecture, painting, sculpture, literature, and all the rest, but by scientific progress and far-flung voyages of exploration that translated into the attainment of a high culture. Advancement or decline in art, science, and a way of life are all simultaneously shared in common, because developments in one lead to and depend on advancements in others.

Given these historical parallels, we may assume that everything else during the Old Stone Age was on a kindred level of lofty greatness illustrated by its cave paintings. As such, a contemporaneous, ocean-going ship able to make transatlantic voyages is entirely acceptable and even likely, in view of the Solutreans' undoubted, large-scale impact on prehistoric America. Doubtless, could we travel back to their times, we would be amazed by the totality of their achievements—most of them utterly lost to time—because modern generations have been conditioned to erroneously envision our Paleolithic ancestors as grunting, club-wielding brutes not far removed from apes.

Actually, the Grotte de la Mouthe ship was a latecomer. The textbook view long held by paleoanthropologists was that vessels able to venture from shore were first launched seven millennia after the la Mouthe image was engraved, because the earliest known boats from France and the Netherlands are no more than 10,000 years old. But contradictory evidence was found as recently as late 2011, when archaeologist Sue O'Connor and her colleagues at Canberra's Australian National University dug through deposits at a shallow cave, called Jerimalai, on East Timor, an island nation just north of Australia. They discovered 38,000 fish bones from twenty-three different taxa, including tuna, sharks, and parrotfish.

These were deep water catch, radiocarbon-dated to 42,000 Years Before Present. O'Connor's team also found the earliest definite evidence for line fishing at Jerimalai: a 23,000-year-old, mollusk-shell fishhook. These finds "certainly suggest that people had advanced maritime skills" by 42,000 years ago, she said, at least "in terms of fishing technology." Her work was supported by University of Utah (Salt Lake City) archaeologist James O'Connell, who stated that the East Timor discovery belongs to "a broad range of evidence" that "solidifies the case" for deep-sea fishing and oceanic voyages between 45,000 and 50,000 years ago.[19]

The much-later vessel depicted at Grotte de la Mouthe may have illustrated just one version the Solutreans used to skirt food-rich pack ice, following migrating animal herds all the way to the New World. There, they introduced a very specific type of blade that enabled them to range throughout the continents hunting megafauna, such as giant sloths, short-faced bears, camelids (an extinct form of llama-like ungulate), bison, mammoths, and mastodons at least as far south as Venezuela for the next 1,500 years.

As the glaciers retreated and sea levels lowered, a land bridge connecting Siberia with Alaska at the Bering Straits allowed peoples migrating out of northeast Asia to make their way southward via an ice-free passage east of the Rocky Mountains in present-day western Canada. Through this so-called Mackenzie Corridor, the invaders inundated the Americas all the way down to Tierra del Fuego, exterminating most of the Paleolithic Europeans as they went, interbreeding with survivors—thereby leaving genetic traces for Douglas Wallace to find fifteen millennia later—and adopting their definitive bifacial blade, which came to be known as the Clovis point.

Had this genocidal confrontation never occurred, the subsequent prehistory of our continent would have emerged into an entirely different form. How much greatness was thus lost by the bloody curtailment of Old Stone Age European development in America is as incalculable as it was tragic. But despite the apparent finality wrought by such an early human catastrophe, other culture-bearers would eventually cross the same seas to renew the powerful impact made by their Solutrean predecessors.

# 7

# Stone Age Sophistication

*We cannot escape the fact that we are the product of propitious circumstances molded by the laws of natural selection.*

RICHARD E. LEAKEY, *ORIGINS*

At the climax of the Keg Mountain Oscillation sea levels surged to 400 feet, obliterating any coastal Solutreans who did not escape either inland to Europe or across the Atlantic Ocean to North America. The Solutreans were immediately superseded on the European continent by the Magdalenians—a people named after La Madeleine, a rock shelter located in the French Dordogne—and possessors of the last, perhaps most advanced ice age culture. Across the walls and floors of a western French cave at the bottom of a small valley bordered by the Petit Moulin River, they scattered 155 lifelike depictions of men and women. Engraved profiles are more finely executed and complex than examples found at other Paleolithic sites, where the human form is infrequently portrayed—invariably as a primitive stick figure.

The facial features of La Marche's profiles are realistic and singular enough for modern investigators to differentiate between individuals depicted—so much so, the sex of each one may be determined. No less surprising, they appear clad in hats, robes, capes, and boots—tailored clothing less utilitarian than fashionable, made from the pelts of fur-bearing animals. If earlier Old Stone Age peoples were similarly attired, they left no such representations on any other rock art. The well-dressed Magdalenians suggest a more sophisticated mentality in all surviving features of their culture.

Among the persons depicted on the floor at La Marche are curious pits laid out in a deliberate pattern. Residue of burnt animal fat scraped from inside the depressions show that they long ago glowed with small flames to collectively mimic a group of identifiable stars in the night sky, the Pleiades. Remarkably, this arrangement seems duplicated today throughout the Far East in traditional candlelight festivals dedicated to the same constellation. If so, then they signify a continuous connection going back over 13,000 years—a direct, living link from our time to the Old Stone Age.

In any case, descending through the cave's black depths to come upon its floor flaming with a recreation of the Pleiades, while illuminating the engraved portraits of several dozen men and women, must have been a particularly dramatic encounter for Magdalenian visitors, and was certainly part of a deliberate spiritual experience. Hawkes observed how "the drawings of men come near to pictogarphic writing."[1] In this regard, La Marche offers another clue to Magdalenian innovation on an engraved reindeer antler. For Francesco d'Errico, an archaeologist at the Centre National de la Recherche (University of Bordeaux), designs covering it were proof of an "artificial memory system,"[2] a precursor to writing.

Similar abstract symbols were discovered in another cave on the north-central coast of Spain, in Cantabria. These ideomorphs at Cueva de La Pasiega correspond to a binary system of arranged animal illustrations suggesting male and female groupings. At least some of the depicted beasts appear to have been marked with identifying signs: bison, for example, with a linear design. A series of rodlike symbols at the entrances to a pair of galleries appear in relation to topographical changes within the cave. In the lightless conditions, Old Stone Age visitors felt for these engraved ideomorphs as tactile symbols guiding them along their way past dangerous clefts, just as modern investigators observed that these same glyphs actually assisted their negotiation through Cueva de La Pasiega's more difficult areas.

For the Magdalenians who adorned and used caves such as this one, a subterranean environment was, in fact, the Underworld, where paintings symbolizing the mysterious energies of life were backdrops for and components of profound mystical experiences. Impenetrable darkness, real danger, and total isolation within the deep recesses contributed to an altered state of consciousness for the inducement of hypnotic trances or mystical visions, with the additional input of hallucinogenic plants. Initiates were thereby psychologically primed for high spiritual drama involving great galleries of polychrome illustrations animated by flickering torchlight, around which weirdly costumed shamans performed their ceremonial magic. Ritual graphic art excelled at the Cave of Trois-Frères in southwestern France, where a large wall painting portrays a shaman or god.

The controversial Lithuanian archaeologist Marija Gimbutas observed, "The thrilling hybrid figure of a man with antlered head, round eyes, a long beard, animal [lion?] paws instead of hands, the tail of a wild horse, and his sexual organ placed beneath the tail seems to be a more important personage than a 'sorcerer,' as he is called."[3] If, as appears likely, the famous figure she succinctly described is dancing, then its shamanic identification is more probable. According to Richard Leakey, the sorcerer of Trois-Frères is a therianthrope, a synthesis of animal and human forms encountered by southern Africa's San shamans during the final stages of their ritually induced hallucinations. "In the second stage of trance," he reports, "people begin to see these images as real objects."[4] Yet again, the Old Stone Age lives on in our modern world.

The Magdalenians were the last and perhaps greatest of the Paleolithic cave dwellers. At Cro des Cluzeau, situated about three miles south of Rouffignac, on the slope of a hill along the La Binche River, occurs the most extensive underground system in the Périgord. This "Cave of the Hundred Mammoths," as it is sometimes called, lives up to its name in more than five miles of underground passageways, much of their wall space covered with vibrant Magdalenian artwork depicting contemporaneous megafauna. But it was among the last subterranean Stone Age art gallery ever made.

Toward the close of their era, the Magdalenians were a people in transition, gradually moving out of the caves and into tents, like those preserved in clays and silts deposited by the river Seine, in north-central France. Here, at Pincevent, they formed the first known village inhabited by as many as 600 residents. They had enough foresight to preserve food for the first time by digging ice cellars into the permafrost for storing meat. They also built hearths using bones as fuel. These innovations on behalf of settled domesticity sparked a Lower Paleolithic population explosion. Approximately 15,000 individuals had resided in Europe during Solutrean times compared to about 50,000 by the late Magdalenian period. Such growth was made possible by higher levels of general prosperity; for example, abundant food supplies via particularly good hunting.

Glacial conditions gradually moderated somewhat after the Keg Mountain Oscillation had passed, allowing the appearance of broader grazing regions for increased numbers of big game, such as bison, mammoth, and auroch. Their population increased, and, as a consequence, so did that of humans. These beasts figured prominently in the cave art of numerous Old Stone Age peoples, but the Magdalenians favored the horse above all, not without cause. They devoted their highest artistic skills in depicting this animal, as exampled by superb horse-head carvings from Mas d'Azil and Ariège, and inside Les Combarelles, on the left bank of the Beune River, little more than one mile outside the village of Les Eyzies.

Four representations at this cave establish that the Magdalenians had tamed the horse some 5,000 years before its domestication was believed to have taken place. Two depicted horses have covers draped over their backs, one has a band for a simple bridle around its snout, and another wears a cheek guard. A diamond shape circumscribed by two strokes may be seen on the side of a Les Combarelles horse, while three signs resembling letters occur on the rump of another horse. Amazingly, the latter glyphlike configuration is found almost identically, and on the same section of anatomy, among archaic Greek vase depictions of horses. Once more, an important Paleolithic influence reverberated millennia beyond its own time to affect another society far removed in the future.

A Magdalenian ideomorph associated with the horse was the *claviform,* a key-shaped symbol whose literal meaning is unknown. The claviform's almost common appearance near or on cave paintings of the animal nonetheless joins other Magdalenian symbols to demonstrate the abstract thought processes of their Upper Paleolithic inventors, who were clearly on their way to developing a written language.

The Magdalenians apparently excelled at animal husbandry, because they were recognized by early French anthropologists for their domestication of reindeer—so much so, that the Late Upper Paleolithic was at first referred to as L'âge du renne, "the Age of the Reindeer." Those animals the Magdalenians could not tame, they either hunted or defended themselves against. Even the auroch, bison, and mammoth that humans depended upon for food were dangerous and doubtless inflicted casualties on their pursuers.

They shared the grassy plains with far more formidable creatures, such as the cave bear. It had a broad, domed skull with steep forehead—unlike the more gradual, sloping forehead featured in the skulls of modern bears—and adult males averaged more than 1,300 pounds. The occurrence of a single black contour drawing depicting *Ursus spelaeus* among the more than 250 engravings and wall paintings at Cro des Cluzeau may have been inspired by some confrontation with the great beast: claw marks gouged on the face of the rock walls and a huge, undisturbed bear nest were left inside the cave. Such creatures could have been overcome only through very close social cooperation, and even then at terrible risk to every participant.

The woolly rhinoceros presented a yet more hazardous challenge. At fourteen feet long and six feet tall at the shoulder, it was larger and more muscular than the modern white rhino, and it had thick, long fur; small, sensitive ears; immense, elongated head; and stocky body. A three-foot-long horn projected forward and upward like a drawn saber from its massive skull above the snout, accompanied by another horn shorter by two feet jutting from between beady, alert eyes. Both horns were not bone, but keratin, composed of the same fibrous structural proteins that produce hair and nails. Despite its adult male weight of three tons, the powerfully built woolly rhinoceros was quick and agile on its short, thick legs, and, if anything like its modern descendants, temperamental and aggressive. No evidence suggests that men ever hunted *Coelodonta antiquitatis,* which was undoubtedly avoided at all costs.

Hardly less mordacious was the cave lion with which they shared ice age Europe. A head-and-body length of ten feet and weight in excess of 880 pounds made *Panthera leo fossilis* about 33 percent larger than today's largest cat, the Siberian tiger. A virtually complete cave lion skull excavated at the town of Mauer, outside Heidelberg, Germany, was found in the same sediment with just the lower jaw of its human victim.

Challenges to Paleolithic Man's survival presented by these very dangerous animals stimulated technological development, resulting in the first long-range weapon. Previously, hunters possessed only hand-held daggers and thrown spears with which to defend themselves or take down prey. Although effective, these arms placed operators in jeopardy by requiring close proximity to the target. To create a safer distance, while simultaneously increasing applied force, the Magdalenians took up the *atlatl,* an extension of the throwing arm that uses leverage to achieve greater velocity for hurling a projectile.

Praised by that great Scottish Atlantologist, Lewis Spence (1874–1955), as "the first actual machine invented by Man," the atlatl is held in one hand, gripped near the end, then, by action of the forelimb and wrist, the dart is thrown with powerful force through increased angular momentum.[5]

Upper Paleolithic darts resembled four-foot-long arrows or thin spears propelled at speeds of up to 100 miles per hour over 300 feet; maximum accuracy was achieved inside sixty feet. The atlatl thus provided a 43 percent greater range than a hand-thrown spear, and a 127 percent increase in range over a hand-thrown dart. Modern reproductions compared against Eskimo designs demonstrated that the Old Stone Age versions offered a superior performance. Although the earliest known example is a 17,500-year-old Solutrean specimen found in the Dordogne at Combe Saunière, the atlatl became the Magdalenians' weapon of choice, which, as some indication of their pride of ownership, they commonly fashioned into various animal forms.

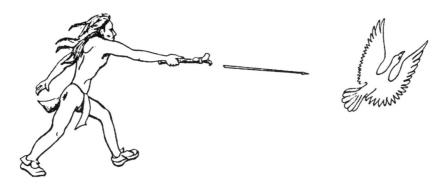

*Fig. 7.1. An atlatl, a throwing stick used to launch small spears or arrows. From* American Discovery *magazine, by Gunnar Thompson, Ph.D.*

Construction typically consisted of an eight-inch reindeer horn with a joint at one end forming a T or Y shape. Archaeologists were initially puzzled by such an object, assuming it was a *bâton de commandement,* a kind of scepter signifying the owner's political power, or perhaps a magic wand wielded by a shaman. Only extensive testing as a spear-thrower revealed its original function.

Other Magdalenian technological advances included the fishhook, rope, and the eyed needle for sewing their fancy clothes. Toolmaking produced finer blades instead of simpler, shorter flakes, but there was less reliance on the flint industry and more frequent use of bone, antler, and wood. These materials were better suited for engraving, which the Upper Paleolithic craftsmen worked with a *burin,* or stone flake featuring specialized, chisel-like edges. Also called a *graver,* the burin is diagnostic of Upper Paleolithic cultures in Europe, but archaeologists have also identified it in North American cultural assemblages. Thus, the burin represents another transatlantic connection during the Old Stone Age; this one, Magdalenian.

It is by no means the only indication for a post-Solutrean impact on the Americas. Clovis points found at Lapa do Boquete, in Brazil, yielded a radiocarbon date of 12,070 ±170 Years Before Present. Other American event horizons contemporaneous with Upper Paleolithic times were established at Monte Verde in Chile, Peru's Pikimachay Cave, Taima-Taima in Venezuela, and South Carolina's Topper Site. These are the same locations where older, Solutrean artifacts were found, an observation tending to suggest that Magdalenian seafarers inherited knowledge of an opposite continent from their immediate predecessors, and acted upon that information by voyaging to America.

At what appears to have been the zenith of their cultural development, 40,000 years of the Old Stone Age came crashing down with the abrupt termination of Earth's last glacial era, around 10,900 BCE. In North America, a 2,000-foot-high ice dam blocking the mouth of the Clark Fork River to create Lake Missoula ruptured catastrophically. The resulting deluge discharged 1.3 billion gallons per second, about 1,000 times the Columbia River's current average flow, at speeds approaching thirty-six meters per second, or eighty miles per hour. Water flow was nine cubic miles per hour, more than ten times the combined flow of every river on Earth. For the next thirteen centuries, average coastal temperatures ranged from -20°C in winter to no more than 10°C in summer. Pack-ice and icebergs dominated the waters off Atlantic Spain, while cataclysmic hurricanes and blizzards raged across the Northern Hemisphere from September to May.

In a period known as the Younger Dryas, ice caps reappeared over high ground, the glaciers resumed their inexorable march southward, and sea levels plummeted; forests and grasslands perished, together with the gathered fruits, cereals, and animals on which human existence had depended for thousands of years. Thirty-five different groups of animal species disappeared all at once. In North America alone, more than half of its large mammals vanished. Across Europe, the dangerous cave lions, bears, dire wolves, and wooly rhinos were suddenly gone. But so were the aurochs, bisons, giant ground sloths, mastodons, and mammoths Paleolithic man used as his primary food source.

Dr. David Nogues-Bravo from the Center for Macroecology, Evolution and Climate at the University of Copenhagen, found that "sixty-five per cent of mammal species weighing over one hundred pounds went extinct, together with a lower proportion of small mammals."[6] In total, thirty-five different genera—groups of species—all of different habitat preferences and feeding habits, disappeared. The remains of some of these creatures were discovered around the turn of the twentieth century, but often under peculiar circumstances.

Although their carcasses were often found in groups, mostly intact, and belonged to a variety of ages at the moment of their demise, few exhibited the kind of physical trauma caused by animal predators or human hunters. More perplexing, death overcame many of the specimens so quickly that buttercup flowers they were eating at the time had been preserved in their mouths and stomachs. The animals had been literally quick-frozen to death. Other Siberian discoveries were made in the cul-de-sacs of deep gullies, where bones of ice age megafauna had piled up by the tens of thousands.

Findings from J. Tyler Faith, Ph.D. candidate in a hominid paleobiology doctoral program at the University of Wyoming, and Todd Surovell, associate professor there of anthropology, reveal that mass extinction occurred in a geological instant between 13,800 and 11,400 years ago.[7] Previously, the sudden disappearance of so many species was presumed caused by human predation.

"Until now, global evidence to support the climate change argument has been lacking, a large part of existing evidence was based on local or regional estimates between numbers of extinctions, dates of human arrivals and dates of climate change," explained Dr. Nogues-Bravo. "By dealing with the issue at a global scale, we add a new dimension to the debate by showing that the impact of climate change was not equal across all regions, and we quantify this to reveal each continent's 'footprint of climate change.' Our results show that continents with the highest 'climate footprints' witnessed more extinctions then continents with lower 'climate footprints.' These results are consistent across species with different body masses, reinforcing the view that past climate changes contributed to global extinctions."[8]

The cause of that "climate footprint" was unknown until early 2012, when telltale sediment was brought to light by James Kennett, professor of earth science at the University of California (Santa Barbara) and his sixteen-member team of international investigators. Buried in the floor of Lake Cuitzeo was a thin, dark layer containing unequivocal evidence for a large, cosmic body that struck central Mexico just when the Younger Dryas period opened with such violence. Virtually identical sediment strata dated to the same period have been previously located at numerous locations throughout North America, Greenland, and Western Europe.

According to *Science Daily,* "The data suggest that a comet or asteroid—likely a large, previously fragmented body, greater than several hundred meters in diameter—entered the atmosphere at a relatively shallow angle. The heat at impact burned bio-mass, melted surface rocks, and caused major environmental disruption."[9] The resulting crater became Lake Cuitzeo, measuring twelve and a half miles across, with an average depth of ninety feet.

Professor Kennett told the Proceedings of the National Academy of Sciences, "These results are consistent with earlier reported discoveries throughout North America of abrupt ecosystem change, megafaunal extinction, and human cultural change and population reduction. These changes were large, abrupt, and unprecedented, and had been recorded and identified by earlier investigators as a 'time of crisis.' The timing of the impact event coincided with the most extraordinary biotic and environmental changes over Mexico and Central America during the last approximately twenty thousand years, as recorded by others in several regional lake deposits."[10]

The floor of Lake Cuitzeo is rich in spherules formed when they collided with each other at high velocities during the whirling chaos of an extraterrestrial impact. They are joined by numerous specimens of *lonsdaleite*—an identifiable configuration nanodiamonds assume when they are pressured by large meteorite collisions—and aciniform soot, the acnelike appearance of dust residue resulting from the same cause.

"These materials form only through cosmic impact," Kennett explained, not through volcanic or other natural terrestrial processes.[11] In the entire geologic record, the only other known continent-wide layer with abundant peaks in lonsdaleite, impact spherules, and aciniform soot is in the 65-million-year-old Cretaceous-Paleogene boundary layer that coincided with the extinction of the dinosaurs.

Before the middle of the twelfth millennium BCE, the Younger Dryas began to relinquish its icy grip on southern Asia Minor, dispelling the aridity that had stunted plant growth throughout the Near East. "As temperatures fell," stated archaeologist Brian Haughton, "ice caps moved farther south, snow cover increased, and the once-forested landscape that sustained the large herbivores disappeared. As the landscape was transformed into a sparsely vegetated steppe, big-game species like mammoth bison, red deer and other animals moved south, and . . . indeed early humans had no choice but to follow them."[12]

The relatively few animal herds that survived this period in Europe began to migrate out of the continent, pursued by their Magdalenian hunters into the reviving grasslands of Anatolia beyond the Taurus Mountains and River Euphrates. Even here, animal populations were less profuse than they had been during Pleistocene times, and the human émigrés were compelled to rely primarily on what grains they could gather. In the process, they learned that certain seeds ripened at different times of the year, an observation that inevitably led to the invention of farming and the "Neolithic revolution"; that is, the development of broader, more diversified cooperation in settled villages, necessitating a hierarchy of tasks, sharing of goods, plus social stratification according to specialized tasks, with the innovation of agricultural tools and pottery for storage. While this process seems rather straightforward, even clearly defined, it is shockingly contrasted by the first known building ever made.

Göbekli Tepe is a monumental stone structure standing on the highest point of an elongated mountain ridge in southeastern Turkey. At 11,600 years old, it predates the advent of farming, the domestication of animals, invention of the wheel, pottery, metallurgy, or writing by millennia, and is at least sixty-six centuries older than either Britain's Stonehenge or Egypt's Great Pyramid. As such, the discovery of Göbekli Tepe is not unlike finding a modern skyscraper deliberately buried beneath Tutankhamun's tomb.

Although artifacts at the site were first noticed by archaeologists and dismissed as Byzantine-era by-products in the 1960s, the location's pre-Neolithic provenance finally came to light during a 1994 dig. Excavators revealed a massive, U-shaped monolith surmounted by a pair

*Fig. 7.2. Göbekli Tepe. Photo by Teomancimit, courtesy of Wikipedia.*

of sculpted feline figures facing away from either side of the entrance of a twenty-foot-long corridor. It leads to a series of unworked, dry-stone, concentric walls abutted by stone benches between sets of pillars around the edges.

The ninety-eight-foot-diameter enclosure is floored with a burnt-lime technique popular during the Roman Era as *terrazzo* for its uni-formally smooth surface. At hand are several stone basins that may have been used for fires to illuminate the interior. Built into the walls and interspersed irregularly at arms' length are dozens of eight-foot-tall, T-shaped monoliths—some pressed up against each other—made of limestone and averaging seven tons each. They surround a central pre-cinct, where a pair of larger, sixteen-ton, T-shaped pillars stand thirteen feet high. For their creation, limestone slabs were cut from bedrock pits at the plateau itself, then transported without benefit of wheeled vehi-cles or draft animals some 1,600 feet to the hilltop site. An estimated five hundred men were involved in the process, and they left behind some unfinished pillars.

Although less than 5 percent of Göbekli Tepe's twenty-two acres has been excavated, archaeologists are already speculating that it was a temple for the celebration of religious rituals. They point to the buried location's abundance of deer, gazelle, pig, and geese bones, the remains of sacred feasts at a time when the surrounding countryside was lush and alive with such game. Overcultivation has long since reduced the region to an uninhabitable dust bowl. While the temple's builders and earliest celebrants appear to have been hunter-gatherers, their descen-dants may have become the first farmers. According to genetic analysis, the DNA of wild wheat from which today's wheat is derived is closest in structure to wild strains found just twenty miles from the ringed structure. This recent discovery suggests that modern wheat was first domesticated in its vicinity—not, as still described by history teachers, in Mespotamia's Fertile Crescent.[13]

As such, Göbekli Tepe would seem to have been the focal point for one of humankind's most crucial transitions: from hunting to agriculture. Although unprecedented, it also appears to have been the first of its kind, because Nevali Cori—a similar, less well-worked site about twenty-five miles northwest—was built 3,000 years later.

But the basis for Göbekli Tepe's definition as a "temple" might be signified by the bas-relief imagery crawling over its T-shaped monoliths, which are otherwise made to resemble standing, anthropomorphic figures with long arms and fingers above stylized loincloths. Most are covered with dozens of well-executed reliefs featuring lions, bulls, boars, foxes, gazelles, donkeys, three-headed snakes, herons, ducks, scorpions, vultures, and spiders. Another minority group comprises carved phalloi and abstract pictograms or geometric patterns occasionally met with in later Neolithic cave art, their significance unknown. No representation of deer or other local prey the celebrants hunted are portrayed, implying that the beasts adorning the monoliths belonged to an entirely different class of animals.

Remarkably, virtually all of them are known to have been associated with celestial configurations in the night skies of Classical and Pre-Classical times. There were (and still are):

**Leo:** The Lion

**Taurus:** The Boar, a tight group of thirteen stars forming the image of a charging, long-tusked boar, later more usually associated with the Bull

**Vulpecula cum ansere:** "The little fox with the goose," today a faint constellation, brighter 10,000 years ago in the northern sky, located at the center of the Summer Triangle (which is itself an asterism consisting of the bright stars Deneb, Altair, and Vega, known as Vulture Cadens in Latin)

**Smaragdaus:** The Donkey

**Hydra:** The largest of the eighty-eight constellations and represented in Göbekli Tepe's three-headed snake

**Heron:** A wide constellation of some fifty stars in mid-summer

**Wild Duck:** A cluster of stars in the constellation Scutum

**Scorpius:** A large constellation located in the Southern Hemisphere near the center of the Milky Way between Libra to the west and Sagittarius to the east

**Spider constellation:** A huge mass of hundreds of stars that form a web across the entire sky, in the center of which is perched a large arachnid with two bright red stars for its eyes

**Talitha:** "The third leap [of the gazelle]," is the name of two stars, Talitha Borealis and Talitha Australis, in the Ursa Major constellation.

These celestial connotations seem confirmed by Göbekli Tepe's engraved figure of a vulture balancing a sphere—most likely the Sun or Moon—on its outstretched wing.

While the persistence of these astronomical identifications over the course of some 9,000 years may seem a stretch, several pre-Neolithic, even Old Stone Age examples survived the passage of millennia. A wall painting inside the Upper Paleolithic cave at Lascaux "depicts a stick-man with erect phallus sprawled between a rhinoceros, who appears to be departing the scene, and a bison, entrails spilling prodigiously from its genital area. Near the stricken stick-man is the image of a bird surmounting a stick as a kind of *baton de commandant,* or scepter." This 17,300-year-old artwork "perfectly illustrates the cosmological myth from a Zoroastrian scripture known as the Bundahisn," according to the critically acclaimed scholar specializing in Neolithic studies, Mary Settegast.[14]

Although composed as late as the ninth century CE, the Bundahisn preserves an account of creation and the nature of the universe based on admittedly much older, pre-Persian material. The oldest Iranian version tells of Yima, the earliest king, and a primordial bull, who lived happily together until Evil appeared for the first time, killing them both. From the body of the bull gushed forth marrow and semen to create the cosmos and the animal kingdom. Yima's body transformed into all the metals of the Earth; his seed engendered humanity. Among Upper Paleolithic rock art in Europe and Africa, the rhinoceros embodied the principle of evil. Hence, its depiction at Lascaux, where it appears to have gored the bison (its entrails spilling out) and slain the ithyphallic stick figure, mirrors the Bundahisn creation myth. Yima lost his command of *xvarenah,* or the "kingly glory" (i.e., immortality) in the form of a bird, as similarly depicted in the bird-headed scepter laying beside the stick man illustrated at Lascaux. Only a few anthropomorphic figures are depicted at Göbekli Tepe, including the bas-relief of a decapitated corpse surrounded by vultures. The same scene is repeated on the wall of a shrine room at another Turkish site, the Neolithic condominium of Çatalhüyük, built forty-one centuries later.

Portrayed near the top of at least one of Göbekli Tepe's T-shaped monoliths are three joined figures resembling women's handbags. They are identical to incense pouches commonly depicted in Sumerian cylinder-seals from as early as 3000 BCE, and carried by a pair of Assyrian winged deities engraved on stone stele from the reign of Ashurnasirpal II, as late as 860 BCE. These examples demonstrate the continuity of fundamentally important cultural details over vast stretches of time.

Contributing to the impression of Göbekli Tepe as an astronomical observatory was its abandonment and deliberate burial after 8000 BCE, when it was backfilled under as much as 650 cubic yards of sand brought from outside the vicinity, because no deposits existed in the immediate area.

Geophysical surveys of the site revealed at least 250 more standing stones in sixteen other structures similarly buried at the same hilltop. So far, four—ranging from thirty-three to ninety-eight feet across—have been uncovered. None are perfectly circular, but intentionally oval, resembling Britain's megalithic observatories. Although a pair of tallest stones in the central precinct face southeast, suggesting a purposeful orientation of some kind, whatever specific alignments the others may have incorporated or still maintain have not yet been determined, save one—an orientation with Deneb, constellation *Vulpecula cum ansere* signified by Göbekli Tepe's bas relief image of a fox.

Building, abandoning, burying, and replacing one ringed edifice after another was a pattern followed by many of the site's ancient watch-posts, while covering them under sand was a ritual entombment aimed at revering the sacred character of an astronomy-based religious location. Illinois' pre-Columbian Woodhenge—an arrangement of two dozen celestially aligned poles at the ceremonial city of Cahokia across the Mississippi River from St. Louis—stands above four previous circles. According to Cahokia's official web page:

> The first circle [date unknown], only partially excavated, would have consisted of twenty-four posts [representing the hours in a day, twice the cosmic number of Twelve]; the second circle had thirty-six posts [Western astrologers admit cycles of thirty-six years at the end of which the various planetary influences similarly combine; Chinese astrology's thirty-six "beneficial" stars, and so on]; the

*Fig. 7.3. Woodhenge, at the pre-Columbian city of Cahokia, on the Illinois side of the Mississippi River, across from St. Louis. Photo by the author.*

third circle [1000 CE], the most completely excavated, had forty-eight posts [two days]; the fourth, partially excavated, would have had sixty posts [the sexagesimal base of Sumerian, later Babylonian astronomy]. The last Woodhenge was only twelve [the twelve Labors of Heracles, a solar figure, who traveled through the twelve Houses of the Zodiac; twelve months of the year; twelve Olympian gods; the twelve tribes of Israel; Jerusalem's twelve gates; Christ's twelve disciples, etc.], or possibly thirteen posts [the thirteen-Moon lunar-solar calendar], along the eastern sunrise arc.[15]

So too, the Maya often buried city upon city, piling up level after level, most famously at Guatemala's Copán, with its prominent celestial alignments. "Astronomically aligned temple sites are astro-theological," correctly observes the controversial but insightful cosmologist, D. M. Murdock.[16]

Göbekli Tepe then, is not only the most ancient temple on Earth, but the first celestial observatory. As such, its levels of bas relief sculpture, monumental construction, and applied astronomy are beyond and far above anything associated with hunter-gatherers, and not encountered until the creation of Western European megaliths more than 6,000 years later. Yet, the site has yielded no trace of permanent residence. A profusion of deer and antelope bones by the thousands point to communal feasts, not human habitation. Nothing suggesting domesticity—neither houses nor hearths—has come to light, although some sculpture in the round were discovered.

The oldest known life-size statue of a man was found just nine miles away. Despite its supreme antiquity, the figure is well wrought and dressed in a tailored, double v-neck gown—more sophistication far ahead of its time. To give the head a lifelike appearance, dark-blue stones were set in its eye sockets. Other, free-standing sculpture at Göbekli Tepe depict boars and foxes. These artworks, too, represent the first of their kind. They and all other aspects of the site form an enormous, inexplicable cultural gap unbridged from the close of the Late Paleolithic to before the dawn of agriculture. Either some precedent—perhaps a series of precedents—is missing, or postglacial humanity, for causes we cannot guess, experienced its single most potent surge of innovative genius that additionally included the invention of farming, the basis of civilization. These developments came at a terrible cost, however. Smallpox genes suggest that the disease was once a rodent virus that made a transspecies jump to humans in one of the first agricultural river valleys. Investigator Olga Belinskaya writes how

archaeologist Klaus Schmidt believes Göbekli Tepe is the Temple of Eden, because hunter-gatherers built it at a time of abundant wildlife, when people had time to cultivate art and complex ritual. Then, deforestation and erosion caused ecological collapse, and they had to transition to a harsh farming life, the world's first agriculture. Evidence supports this: People from what today is eastern Turkey were the first to domesticate sheep, cattle and goats (of course, there were no Turks living here at that time). The first farmyard pigs were domesticated sixty miles away, at Cayönü. Rye and oats were first cultivated in the hills of Göbekli.

Writers of the bible must have been describing this corner of Turkish Kurdistan when they spoke of Eden: Eden was west of Assyria; so is Göbekli. Eden was by four rivers, including the Euphrates. Göbekli lies between the Euphrates (or Perath) and the Tigris (possibly the biblical Hiddekel). In biblical lore, the four rivers produced by the river of Eden were the Pison (unidentified), Gihon (unidentified), Hiddekel and Perath, identified as the Euphrates. Beth Eden, the biblical House of Eden, lies fifty miles from Göbekli. The Old Testament talks about "the children of Eden, which were in Thelasar," a town in northern Syria near Göbekli. Lastly, "Eden" comes from the Sumerian word for "plain." Göbekli lies on the plains of Harran.[17]

Göbekli Tepe is not only unprecedented, it is incomparable—there is nothing like it anywhere in Anatolia. But as we broaden our perspective to include the outside world, some startling parallels begin to emerge. The closest, at least geographically, stand in the Western Mediterranean Sea, on the Balearic Island of Minorca, off the south coast of Spain. There, visitors admire the Torre d'en Gaumés, the largest prehistoric village in the Balearics, its U-shaped stone wall enclosing a trio of *talayots*—megalithic towers—and an open-air, T-shaped pillar, its broken crosspiece lying on the ground beside the upright.

Other T-shaped monoliths are scattered across the island, with better-preserved specimens at Torre Trencada and Talatí de Dalt. Like their Anatolian counterparts, the Balearic versions are often ten feet tall, but archaeologists are at a loss to identify their builders or original purposes. The Minorcan pillars are not only removed from Göbekli Tepe by 2,100 miles, but 8,600 years. In terms of both space and time, any sort of relationship between the two seems impossible. Virtually identical T-shaped megaliths are found even farther away, in the Atlantic Ocean, on Tory Island, off the northern tip of Ireland.

A yet more impossible comparison lies on another island—this one on the other side of the world, in the distant Eastern Pacific Ocean. Easter Island, located 2,180 miles from the Chilean shores of South America, is the world's most remotely inhabited place, chiefly famous for its *moai*. These are free-standing, anthropomorphic statues erected before they were brought to the attention of the outside world in the early eighteenth century. The 887 examples average thirteen feet high, weighing fourteen tons, although the tallest moai was over thirty feet tall with a weight of eighty-two tons. While most were carved from tuffa (a compressed volcanic ash), thirteen have been fashioned from basalt, seventeen from red scoria (volcanic, holed rock), and twenty-two from trachyte (igneous, fine-grained rock).

They may represent winners of an annual swimming contest or deified ancestors, although individually the moai are virtually indistinguishable from one another, except for variations in size. The eastern Polynesian word for "sacred" is *moa,* and is a common root signifying "ancestry." Whatever astronomical orientations the statues may have originally possessed vanished when they were overturned, as anarchy overwhelmed the island during the mid-eighteenth century.

Conventional chronologies date their creation to after 1200 CE, although independent investigators, such as World Explorer Club president David Hatcher Childress, cite widespread lichen leeching into the cut stone, suggesting a far deeper antiquity.[18] Because lichen advances incrementally over millennia at a steady rate—save for brief, calibrated surges occasioned by rare and extreme temperature fluctuations—its growth required far longer than the last eight centuries to have migrated by such a prodigeous extent over the surface of the statues.

Childress notes more compelling evidence for their greater age: the island's modern discovery was on Easter Sunday 1722, and for more than 200 years thereafter, the moai were regarded by foreign visitors—and even learned anthropologists—as "stone heads." Not until their proper excavation—initiated by rogue archaeologist Dr. Thor Heyerdahl following World War II—were the monoliths fully exposed to reveal monumental heads connected with legless torsos.

Investigation showed they had not been deliberately interred up to their necks during the native *huri mo'ai,* or "statue toppling," that lasted into the 1830s. As the term signifies, they were "toppled," not inhumed. Instead, many—if not most—of the anthropomorphic monoliths were buried an average of eight feet by natural deposition. The time required for this geological process involved not a few centuries, but many thousands of years, thereby backdating the statues at least several millennia before the first human arrivals at Easter Island—supposedly no earlier than around the turn of the thirteenth century, according to carbon-datable materials collected by mainstream scholars.

While their rendition of statue-erecting, followed by environmental abuse, with subsequent civil upheavals and cannibalism, climaxing in "statue toppling," could be at least fundamentally correct, the *huri mo'ai* is its own story, belongs to a time very long after the figures' creation, and has nothing whatsoever to do with the anthropomorphic monuments—save their desecration by Polynesians. Upon their arrival

800 years ago, the latecomers found these mysterious, neglected colossi on an uninhabited Easter Island that had been abandoned thousands of years before by an entirely different and unrelated people. Such a conclusion results from combined physical evidence of the statues' eight-foot deposition and their venerable lichen patches, which together remove the figures to some period far anterior to visiting Polynesians.

The arms of each moai were carved in bas relief to lay against either side of the body, allowing the hands' long, slender fingers to rest along the crests of the hips, meeting just above a loincloth (known as a *hami*), where they point toward the navel. Their description matches Göbekli Tepe's own limestone monoliths detail for detail, save that the Anatolian versions lack heads. Otherwise, they are without parallel anywhere else in the world, throughout time.

Neither does either set have legs, another unique comparison. The Polynesian moai's fingers intentionally point at the stomach to signify the

*Fig. 7.4. Slow-growing lichen on their exterior surfaces and the figures' burial under eight feet or more of natural deposition suggest that these Easter Island statues are far older than conventional archaeologists believe. Photo from* Ancient American *magazine.*

island's original name, Te-Pito-te-Henua, "the Navel of the World." So too, the site for Anatolia's similarly anthropomorphic monoliths is Göbekli Tepe, Turkish for "navel hill." At sixty-nine feet tall and approximately 270 tons, Te-Pito-te-Henua's largest moai lies unfinished in the crater of Rano Raraku, an extinct volcano, from which the Easter Islanders quarried volcanic rock for their ambitious statue-building program.

*Fig. 7.5. The statues of Easter Island are sculpted in low relief toward the navel, which is similar to the standing monoliths of Göbekli Tepe on the other side of the world in Turkey. Photo from* Ancient American *magazine.*

Similarly unfinished, Göbekli Tepe's largest pillar—twenty-three feet long and fifty tons—is still bound by its matrix to the floor of a quarry 1,600 feet from the concentric temple. The monolith's T-shape is known as a *tau,* after the nineteenth letter in the Greek alphabet. Churchward's statement that "the word *tau* (ta-oo) is one of the few of the Motherland that has been handed down" to survive in various languages around the world appears borne out in the Hawaiian Hora-nui-a-Tau, "the Great Out-Stretched Land of Tau," and Hau-papa-nui-a-Tau, "the Hilly Land of Tau."[19]

In Maori folk tradition, these were the homelands from which the Tangata-Whenua, the original inhabitants of New Zealand, arrived during the ancient past. In the Hawaiians' own oral traditions, Lono was a fair-haired, light-skinned culture-bearer, the most popular figure in their mythology. His personal emblem, known as the *Lonomakua,* or "Father Lono," was a tall, wood pole, at the top of which was a cross-piece, forming the same tau Colonel Churchward insisted symbolized Mu. The portable Lonomakua was carried all over Ohau during the annual Makahiki festival that celebrated Lono's arrival from a sunken kingdom—"the Hilly Land of Tau"—in the ancient past. In these Pacific realm oral traditions, Tau is the Tree of Life, Lemuria's chief symbolic image and another name or title by which the Pacific Motherland was known. Even on the other side of the world, Minorca's great, T-shaped monoliths are referenced in Catalan dialect as *taulas,* or "tables."

These comparisons are either entirely coincidental and, therefore, meaningless, or they indicate a relationship of some kind—however unthinkable—between the Easter Island and Göbekli Tepe of profound antiquity. If the latter, the only conceiveable, if far-fetched, conclusion might explain that missionaries from Göbekli Tepe's "Navel" religious cult, celebrating an apparent rebirth theology, ventured westward to the Balearic Islands and as far afield as the Eastern Pacific. There, the spiritual roots they sank continued to directly influence all subsequent cultural development, as expressed in the ubiquitous tau and similarly carved moai of Te-Pito-te-Henua.

While assigning such wide-flung proselytizing to pre-Neolithic hunter-gatherers is outside consensus anthropology, the influences described may not have arisen first in Anatolia after all, but flowed conversely into Asia Minor from Mu, Churchward's "Mother of Mankind," their real source of origination. Such an alternative would at least explain the otherwise inexplicable aberration presented by Göbekli Tepe's unprecedented appearance between the end of the Old Stone Age and the birth of agriculture. In other words, its anomalously advanced technology was imported by visitors from an outside, higher culture.

Chapter 4 followed some *Homo erectus* survivors of Mount Toba's nearly genocidal eruption 75,000 years ago through Indonesia and out into the Pacific. It may have been here, under conditions very different from those their cousins found in East Africa or, later, in ice age Europe, that their genetic destiny took a separate path in isolation, molded by stimuli less challenging to bare survival, but more conducive to civilized development.

Over the millennia, they followed a somewhat more advanced, parallel evolution with survivor descendants elsewhere, emerging in their Pacific Eden as the first fully modern humans. Remarkably, this conclusion suggested by a great deal of relevant evidence unavailable to Churchward in his time is fundamentally the same version he learned from Hindu monastery records near the Brahmaputra River, nearly 150 years ago.[20]

# 8

# The Mother of Invention

Göbekli Tepe's identification with the Garden of Eden—or, at any rate, *an* "Eden," following the Lemurian original—is underscored in Genesis 3:22–24, when an enraged Yahweh expels Adam and Eve from their earthly paradise: "he placed at the east of the garden of Eden . . . a flaming sword which turned every way, to keep the way of the tree of life." If we understand that the Old Testament is a collection of Semitic and non-Semitic traditions commonly known and retold over numerous generations throughout the Near East many thousands of years before its Hebrew compilers wrote them down around 600 BCE (Jeremiah 30:22), God's "flaming sword" appears to have been a metaphor for a brilliant, even threatening, comet that made close passes near our planet around 8000 BCE.

**Plate 1** (above). Human infants are natural-born swimmers, testimony to the aquatic phases that shaped our evolution.

**Plate 2** (below). Many human infants are born with webbed fingers. Might this be a remnant from our aquatic past?

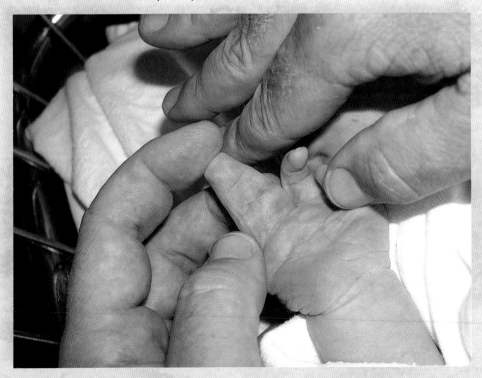

**Plate 3** (above). This photograph shows to good advantage how Britain's Stonehenge was built as a contiguous formation of dolmens.

**Plate 4** (below). Megalithic field at Carnac, Brittany

**Plate 5** (above). An image of the so-called Thunder Ax engraved in the ceiling of Brittany's *Table de Marchand*

**Plate 6** (below). The Stone Age *Table des Marchand*, in western France, is stylistically related to very similar versions found in North America.

**Plate 7.** "America's Stonehenge" in New Hampshire

**Plate 8** (above). Oracle Chamber at America's Stonehenge, Mystery Hill, New Hampshire. Photo by Brian Sullivan.

**Plate 9** (left). Recalling the sacred column of Atlantis described by Plato, an undressed pillar stands alone in its own square, subterranean precinct on the Greek island of Delos.

**Plate 10.** Identically configured to its Aegean counterpart, this lone monolith stands at the pre-Inca ceremonial center of Tiahuanaco. Its name is a corruption of the original Quechua Typi Kala, "Stone-in-the-Center," just as Delos was similarly known as the Omphalos, or "Navel of the World."

**Plate 11.** This modified granite boulder was originally an upright stone installed centuries ago atop an earthen mound appropriately known as the Pyramid of the Sun; it is the largest such structure in Aztalan, a pre-Columbian ceremonial center located in southern Wisconsin between Milwaukee and Madison. Before its 1960 removal by a bulldozer during restoration of the archaeological park, the three-ton, six-foot-tall monolith was precisely oriented to several sunrise positions on the eastern horizon—such as the winter solstice alignment with the peak of another properly named feature, Christmas Hill. Aztalan was an important waystation in the ancient copper trade.

**Plate 12** (above). One of New England's numerous vaulted stone chambers compares favorably with its Neolithic counterparts in Western Europe.

**Plate 13** (left). Petersham stone chamber, Massachusetts. Photo by Scott A. Brown from *Ancient American* magazine.

**Plate 14.** Burnt Hill in Massachusetts is one among dozens of standing-stone sites throughout New England. Photo from *Ancient American* magazine.

Plate 15 (above). This hole in the ground lined with rocks is yet another example of an ancient, enigmatic man-made structure in New England.

Plate 16 (below). Peru's Intihuatanu, or "sun circle," near the shores of Lake Umayo. Photograph by Jay Stuart Wakefield.

**Plate 17.** Etched rock, part of the sun circle near the shores of Lake Umayo, Peru.

**Plate 18** (left). The standing stones of Tokushima, Japan

**Plate 19** (below). Dolmen in Chukrimri, Gochang, Jeolla-bukdo, South Korea

**Plate 20.** Summer solstice sunset near New Jersey's Tripod Rock. Photo by Bruce Scofield.

**Plate 21.** California's Pinnacles National Monument, where strange lights have been seen and where native peoples have gathered for centuries to explore the altered states that the site mysteriously induces.

**Plate 22** (above). Detailed scene on one of the Late Bronze Age Vapheio cups portrays the bull round-up described in Plato's account of Atlantis.

**Plate 23** (below). Ggantija, Malta's Neolithic temple

**Plate 24.** Geologist Virginia Steen-McIntyre doing fieldwork near Mexico City. Photo from *Ancient American* magazine.

The renowned archeoastronomers Victor Clube and William Napier tell how the disintegration of "Kronos" caused large fragments to form streams of cometary debris falling in meteoric bombardments with major consequences for Earth's natural environment.[1] Geologists concur that the Alps suffered their greatest landslide, when nearly three cubic miles of limestone fell 8,858 feet above sea level north of Flims, at Mount Fil de Cassons. The collapsed debris formed a dam on the Vorderrhein River, which backed up into a lake in the Ilanz area. The Rhine was forced to create the Ruinaulta canyon and shaped a huge forestland surrounding Flims.

Similarly catastrophic events brought the last glacial era to a sudden close, just as long-term melting of the Antarctic ice sheets began. Climate change shifted abruptly from the frigid Boreal to temperate Atlantic periods, while sea levels rose to generate catastrophic flooding in many parts of the world. Around the Northern Hemisphere, a series of at least seven massive volcanic events triggered in unison by meteor and asteroid impacts disgorged so much debris into the upper atmosphere that previously warming temperatures fell over the next several centuries, until 7090 BCE. While the precise location of these volcanoes has not been determined, their simultaneous eruptions left a prominent ash print in polar ice cores.

Declining conditions particularly afflicted Asia Minor, where severe aridity dried up the formerly lush ecology. As this period coincides with the abandonment of Göbekli Tepe and simultaneous construction of the famous Tower of Jericho, it appears the caretakers and celebrants at Navel Hill left southern Turkey for better prospects elsewhere. Evidence of their exodus survives in bladed tools made from Anatolian obsidian dating to 8000 BCE found in southwest Iran. Most immigrants from Göbekli Tepe arrived in Palestine near the Jordan River, ten miles north of the Dead Sea. The less afflicted area had been already settled by a culture known as the Natufian for the previous 3,000 years, making Jericho the oldest continuously inhabited city in the world. Situated well below sea level, it is also the lowest permanently inhabited site on

Earth. Protofarmers were attracted to its copious springs and shady palm trees.

The Tower of Jericho was a feat of engineering, built around 8000 BCE. The Anatolian immigrants constructed a massive stone wall over ten feet high, and nearly six feet wide at the base. Behind and connecting it, they raised a conical tower made of undressed stone, internally and externally plastered, twenty-eight feet tall, twenty-nine feet wide at its base, decreasing to twenty-three feet at the top, with walls nearly five feet thick. Inside rose a spiral staircase of twenty-two steps. In an alignment reminiscent of astronomical associations at Göbekli Tepe, computer modeling by archaeologists from Tel Aviv University demonstrated that the shadow cast by Quruntul Peak in the Judean Mountains, about three-quarters of a mile away and over a thousand feet higher, touched the tower each summer solstice before spreading across the rest of Jericho.

The axis created by the tower, spiral staircase, and mountaintop at this moment comprise 290 degrees, the exact azimuth of the setting sun on June 21. An azimuth is the horizontal angular distance from a reference direction to the point where a vertical circle through a celestial body intersects the horizon, usually measured clockwise. Jericho's incorporated alignment and the temple-observatory at Göbekli Tepe are not only the earliest known examples deliberately oriented to the heavens, but they predate what are generally considered the first astronomically positioned megaliths by 2,500 and 3,100 years. Given these millennial gaps, structures such as Stonehenge could not have possibly owed their descent from earlier—however similar—achievements in southern Anatolia and the Jordan Valley. Even so, Jericho's far more ancient tower shares the same summer solstice with its counterpart on the Salisbury Plain. (Please see an image of Stonehenge in plate 3 of the color insert.)

Jericho does not appear to have been threatened by invaders when the stone tower was built, and no burials were made in its immediate vicinity. Accordingly, the structure's presumed military identity seems no longer tenable. More certainly, its construction signaled a transition from mobile hunter-gatherers to sedentary food producers in the Levant. This changeover progressed throughout the next eighteen centuries—with an increasing use of natural resources, selecting certain plants and animals for domestication, storing food, inventing new technologies, along with intensified social cooperation and complexity. Results materialized in demographic growth and the spread of agricultural settlements throughout the Near East.

The nearly two millennia following Comet Kronos and its cataclysmic impact on Earth's climate may have comprised the fabled Golden Age described almost as an archetypical legacy in the mythic traditions of virtually every people. In truth, the next eighteen centuries witnessed a florescence of human ingenuity, unprecedented before or since. World human population stood at 5 million, but its numbers were mostly widely dispersed, with small concentrations in the Near East. Their separateness and lack of density insured against pandemic or social exploitation and unrest. Although trade grew actively, there were no wars, as indicated by the total absence of weapons during this extensive period. Instead, emphasis was focused on developing agriculture and extensive commerce, much of it by sea.

Undertaken was lentil, almond, and obsidian trade with the Aegean island of Melos, some eighty miles across open water, proving that as long ago as 8000 BCE, long-distance sea-travel was clearly in regular use. These voyages included the discovery of Ireland, where the first human arrivals stepped ashore before 7500 BCE. Evidence for maritime expansion piled up in large fish bones, characteristic of deep-sea fishing, at Franchthi Cave, on the Greek Peloponnese. It was here that the earliest known evidence for seed and animal stockpiling took place. As early as 7300 BCE, peas and wild pears, not native to the region, were imported from Asia Minor. Thereafter, domesticated animals and plants, such as emmer and einkorn wheat, were common inside Franchthi Cave. Elsewhere in Greece flourished a food-producing economy of wheat, barley, goats, and sheep for the first time, occasioning the invention of knotless knitting.

On the northern Iraqi foothills of the Zagros Mountains, hogs were domesticated at Jarmo, the oldest agricultural community in the world, while cattle-raising began in Turkey. Apiculture, the science of beekeeping, is first recorded 10,000 years ago on the walls of caves near Valencia, in eastern Spain. The red-painted murals depict workers, swarmed by bees, gathering honey from trees and rock crevices. Agriculture spread throughout the Balkans, cows were domesticated in the Middle East, and two different breeds of non-wolf dogs were bred in Scandinavia. Profusion of these flourishing developments gave rise to the earliest bureaucracy in the form of incised "counting tokens" found in the Fertile Crescent region. An elegant stone mask from Palestine, dated to 6200 BCE and now at the Musée de la bible et Terre Sainte, is the oldest artifact of its kind in the world. Urban civilization was foreshadowed at southern Anatolia's Çatalhüyük, where its 5,000 residents lived in condominum-style structures, and one of its walls was emblazoned with the earliest-known city map of another, similar, as-yet-unidentified metropolis.

Such cultural innovations did not cause the Neolithic Golden Age, but were its results. The success of this era was generated instead by village life substantial enough for interactive social stimuli, but of sufficiently low population density to escape the dehumanization, exploitation, and strife endemic to larger settlements. In other words, a harmonious balance was established not only between humans and their natural surroundings, but between themselves. People naturally need room to become what they are. More populous environments engender struggle for less available resources, promoting competition over cooperation; social focus then shifts from the common good to self-gratification, with the antagonistic division of privileged and under-privileged classes as a natural consequence.

Inevitably, internal dissention boils over into the external strife of war against outside competitors, culminating in an ultimate collapse. This repetitive cycle has typified civilization throughout history. It did not apply, however, to our Neolithic ancestors, who enjoyed cultural progress without self-destructive self-indulgence, within a proper balance of their own numbers. Although they showed no signs of internal disintegration or external stress, their exciting, long-lived Golden Age of peaceful innovation began to come apart in 6200 BCE for other causes not understood. That is, until a fresh archaeological discovery far to the east exposed the culprit.

Sprawling more than seventeen acres atop a rocky promontory overlooking the arid, sparsely populated landscape of southern Armenia, hundreds of weirdly configured stones towering six to nine feet tall have been thrust into the flinty earth. Forming an immense, oval configuration, they average ten tons apiece, but the largest of their number is five times heavier, and all were excavated from basalt quarries several miles away. Curiously, eighty-four of the 223 monoliths feature a smooth, internally angled, cleanly carved, 1.9-inch to 2.7-inch diameter hole drilled with modern-day industrial precision at human eye level (about five feet eight inches from ground level).

A short wall of rocks mixed with compacted soil (known as loam) has been firmly packed around the base of each massive stone, heavily eroded by millennia of wind and rain. This stark and lonely place near the Vorotan River lies not far from the city of Sisian, in Syunik province, 135 miles from the national capital at Yerevan. Known for time out of mind to generations of local residents as Karahunj, the great stone circle is sometimes also called Zorats Karer—the "Stones of Zorats," a neighboring hamlet—although its antiquity escaped the attention of scholars until as recently as the early 1990s.

Only then did they notice the obscure location's obvious physical resemblance to megalithic sites in Western Europe, and soon talk spread of an "Armenian Stonehenge." Word eventually reached Germany, where a team of professional investigators from the University of Munich's Institut für Vorderasiatische Archäologie was dispatched to survey, partially excavate and date Karahunj. After nearly five years collecting relevant data and physical material, the archaeologists published their findings during 2000.

*Fig. 8.1. The stone cirle of Karahunj.*
*Photo by Rita Willaert, courtesy of Wikipedia.*

"In contrast to the opinion that Zorats Karer may be called an 'Armenian Stonehenge,'" their findings indicated that it "was mainly a necropolis from the Middle Bronze Age to the Iron Age," about 1500 BCE to 700 BCE, and may have served "as a place of refuge in times of war," possibly from the Hellenistic period to Rome's Late Imperial Era, circa 300 BCE to 300 CE.[2] As such, the place was interesting, but nothing out of the ordinary. While their assessment was entirely correct, it would prove to be far from complete or comprehensive.

In 1994, shortly before the Germans arrived, lingering conjecture regarding possible celestial alignments at Karahunj prompted other investigators to reconsider the site in terms of archaeoastronomy. Their suspicions were confirmed on dawn of Midsummer Day, when the sun rose perfectly into the holes of four standing stones, signifying the four cardinal directions. Subsequent examination of the monoliths revealed their additional orientations to the solstices, equinoxes, and lunar phases. "The necropolis thesis is certainly true," conceded Vachagan Vahradyan, an Armenian biologist who joined other scientists at Zorats Karer, "but after our initial investigations of the central circle, it is clear the site was aligned to the Sun, most likely aligned to the Moon and— what is really exciting—even some stars or planets."[3]

His pronouncement was met with skepticism, even adamant denial by European and American archaeologists. They argued that the existence of a Neolithic observatory in so extremely remote a location, cut off from the centers of megalithic activity in the British Isles by more than 2,000 miles, was too isolated for credibility.[4] In response, Elma Parsamyan, chief astronomer at Armenia's Biurakan Observatory, made a close study of Karahunj's attributed celestial orientations, and thereafter sent her calculations to Mihran Vardanyan, Ph.D., a specialist in the interpretation of cosmological data at Oxford's Astrophysics Department, in England. Vardanyan was so impressed with Parsamyan's computations, he organized "Stars and Stones 2010, Oxford University Expedition to Karahunj, Armenia." The venture was officially approved and supported by the Oxford University Expedition Council and Royal Geographical Society.

Vardanyan and his colleagues no sooner arrived at Zorats Karer than they realized, "it is clearly pointing to the Sun on the summer solstice day. Karahunj is unique, as it is very well preserved; the stones have never been moved, preserving all the archaeological information."[5] Expedition members made three-dimensional maps based on stellar, lunar, and solar positions indicated by the megaliths, confirming their validity and surprising variety. An important part of their agenda was to either confirm or discredit conclusions made just before the turn of the twenty-first century, when a prominent scholar declared that Karahunj was built about 7,500 years ago, making it not only 2,500 years older than Britain's Stonehenge and Egypt's Great Pyramid, but many centuries older than even the earliest known astronomical observatories.[6]

Had this pronouncement been made by anyone less distinguished than Paris M. Herouni, it would have doubtless excited far less controversy than it did. He was among the most renowned scientists of his time: inventor of the first radio-optical telescope and of the "Herouni Mirror Radio Telescope," the largest and most efficient antenna array of its kind; discoverer of Etta Gemini, a "red giant" star featuring the most powerful flares so far observed; author of 346 published scientific papers, and holder of twenty-one international patents; the recipient of numerous awards for scientific excellence, including the French Foreign Ministry's Bronze Medal, the Gold Medal of Moscow's All-Union Industrial Exhibition, the Catholic Silver Medal of Greater Armenia, and so on. But Professor Herouni's extraordinary scientific credentials were not alone responsible for the excitement generated by his statement concerning Karahunj.

No one had devoted as much time, expertise, or intensity to the site, qualifying him as its chief expert. During five years of meticulously surveying the entire archaeological zone and recording every alleged alignment, he used four independent methods to cross-reference Zorats Karer's megalithic orientations with the paths of the sun, moon, stars and planets, their declination and precession—the apparently backward motion of the vernal equinox, which marks zero degrees Aries, against a backdrop of fixed stars.

A complete cycle takes about 25,800 years. When factored into this vast, cosmic scheme, Karahunj yielded an operational date of around 5500 BCE. Before releasing his findings, he shared them with another world-class authority, the English astronomer who discovered Stonehenge's identity as a celestial observatory. Gerald S. Hawkins (1928–2003) confirmed his Armenian colleague's conclusions, adding, "I admire the precise calculations you have made. I am most impressed with the careful work you have done, and hope that the result will ultimately get recorded in literature."[7]

Herouni continued to research Karahunj, and, before his death in 2008 at seventy-five years of age, he found that some of its stones were oriented to Deneb, the largest star in the constellation of Cygnus. This was an intriguing discovery, because the same alignment may have occurred at Göbekli Tepe, the earliest man-made place of worship yet discovered, older even than Zorats Karer by forty centuries.

Whether this southeastern Turkish site and the Armenian location were directly related somehow—despite their vast separation in time and distance—or coincidentally shared a common astronomical alignment has not been established. The significance of Karahunj's alignment with constellation Cygnus may be found in its mythological identity. Ancient Armenians revered Karapet, the "Swan Lady," a female oracle, also known as the "Swan Bird." "Cygnus" is a Latinized version of the constellation's Greek name for "swan." Given the astrological impetus for astronomy throughout the ancient world, a prognosticating deity's relationship with the stars seems likewise appropriate.

A northern constellation lying on the plane of the Milky Way, Cygnus is one of the most recognizable star clusters of the northern summer and autumn, featuring a prominent asterism known as the Northern Cross, in contrast to the more famous Southern Cross. Deneb, a brilliant white star in the tail of the Swan, was previously known as Arided and Aridif, both archaic Armenian names, suggesting south Caucasian origins for the star's reverence at Karahunj. "Deneb" itself derives from a much later, post-Classic Arabic Al Dhanab al Dajajah, or "Hen's Tail." In the Greek mythic version, Cygnus represented Zeus disguised as a swan while seducing Leda, queen of Sparta. She, as a consequence, gave birth to a baby girl, who grew up to become the notorious Helen of Troy: Sin begets disaster!

Referring to Cygnus sometime during the first century CE, the Roman astrologer Marcus Manilius declared, "From this constellation shall flow a thousand human skills," suggestive of profuse astronomical data perpetually streaming through the celestial observatory at Karahunj.[8]

Megalithic Armenian migration westward during prehistory appears to have left linguistic traces in the revered goddess's name. According to Croatian historian O. Sakač, "the word Karapet fathered the Croatian Zagorje, and the result was the word Krapina, meaning the 'Swan Lady.'"[9] Hrvatsko Zagorje is a region in northern Croatia, locally referred to as Zagorje, a word for "upland," "hinterland," or, literally, "beyond the mountain." Its town of Krapina is the cultural capital of the Kajkavian dialect, the northwestern dialect of the Croatian tongue that paleolinguists find fascinating for its apparent roots in a primeval Indo-European language probably spoken by the New Stone Age megalith-builders—yet another possible point in common with

Karahunj. But these parallels are not the only connection Zorats Karer appears to have made with the outside world.

Its very name echoes as far away as Britain's Salisbury Plain, where "Stonehenge" is a close linguistic variant of Karahunj—in Armenian, *kara* is "stone"; *hunj,* "voice, sound." A proper rendering of Karahunj is: "The Stones That Make Sounds," or "The Speaking Stones." The earliest recorded name for England's Stonehenge was *Stanenges,* literally, "stone gallows," from the formation's resemblance to an old-style gibbet with its twin posts; "-enge" was related to the verb, "to hang."

But this circa 1130 CE version was preceded by Stonehenge's pre-Christian appellation, "the Giant's Dance," as much a reference to its monumental construction as to an immigrant race of giants believed to have governed Britain after a catastrophic deluge engulfed their Atlantic Ocean homeland. Their leader was a brother of Atlas, called Albion—literally, the "White Giant"—who gave his name to Britain. A philiological relationship still resonates between the British *henge* and the Armenian *hunj.*

The country's foremost megalithic structure has only been known as "Stonehenge" since 1932, when Thomas Kendrick—later the Keeper of British Antiquities at the British Museum—so designated it, even though the site is not, properly speaking, a henge. The term refers to an earthwork typically consisting of a roughly circular or oval-shaped bank with an internal ditch surrounding a central, flat area of sixty feet or more in diameter. The three largest stone circles in Britain—Avebury, the Great Circle at Stanton Drew, and the Ring of Brodgar—are each configured into a henge, but not Stonehenge, because its ditch is outside the main earthwork bank. Neither is Karahunj a true henge, not, at least, in a strictly archaeological sense. More important than these linguistic parallels is the fact that the Armenian "monument has the same orientation as Stonehenge . . . the latitude difference between Karahunj and Stonehenge is about +10°; Karahunj and the Great Pyramid is about −10°."[10]

Tantalizing as these facts may be, they cannot explain why the world's earliest known observatory was set up in remote Armenia, of all places, nor identify its builders. The inexplicable appearance of

Karahunj in Syunik province was preceded by and related to a critical phase during Neolithic development about 1,000 years earlier in the Fertile Crescent—a region comprising Iraq, Syria, Lebanon, Jordan, Palestine and Israel, besides the southeastern fringe of Turkey and the western frontier of Iran.

Beginning around 6500 BCE, New Stone Age farmers were using pottery for the first time throughout Mesopotamia. This useful innovation improved agricultural efficiency, with consequent increases in crop yield and regional human population, resulting in village growth and hitherto unprecedented levels of material prosperity, as expressed in the postglacial Golden Age cited earlier.

Not surprisingly, the dominant religious conception that emerged from these flourishing rural communities was the Mother Earth goddess, the great nurturer, from whom natural abundance flowed in such profusion. Overproduction allowed for expansion of trade with other communities along the shores of the Black Sea, beyond to the northern Steppes, regarded by a growing number of anthropologists and paleolinguists as the original homeland of the Indo-European peoples. The region is known as Transcaucasia, from the Russian *zakavkazie* for "the area beyond the Caucasus Mountains"—a broad swath of grasslands ideal for cattle herding, extending into Georgia and Armenia, the Southern Caucasus. This vast expanse was well known and to some degree occupied by Neolithic settlers during their Neolithic Golden Age. It was not to last, however.

Paleoclimatologists point to something they call "The 8.2 Kiloyear Event."[11] Its name derives from a natural catastrophe that occurred 8,200 years ago, when an abrupt decrease in global temperatures ushered in prolonged drought and caused a widespread plant die-off. The natural catastrophe had been centuries in the making. Since the end of the last glacial epoch, gradually warming temperatures finally melted North America's Laurentide ice sheet—releasing many billions of gallons of fresh water into the salty North Atlantic Ocean, and producing tsunami-like flooding that instantaneously drove up worldwide sea levels by twelve feet, drowning all human coastal settlements.

Rising sea levels cut off Australia from New Guinea, and the Mediterranean spilled over a rocky sill at the Bosphorus, flooding 60,000 square miles of land. Some ten cubic miles of water deluged into the Black Sea every day. Northward heat transport ceased, dropping temperatures by as much as eleven degrees Fahrenheit around the planet, and causing a global $CO_2$ decline of 25 parts per million for the next 300 years. Mesopotamia was especially hard hit. The Fertile Crescent could no longer live up to its name, as Neolithic farmers there struggled to survive by inventing irrigation and food storage. Radical climate deterioration was accompanied by geological violence on an epic scale.

At the edge of Norway's continental shelf, a trio of landslides—the largest ever known—fell into the sea, generating a 400-foot-high wall of water that traveled fifty miles across Scotland. This so-called Storegga collapse coincided with cataclysmic eruptions throughout North America's Indian Heaven Volcanic field in Washington State, located midway between Mount St. Helens and Mount Adams. The nineteen-mile-long area of 232 square miles enfolds approximately sixty volcanos, all of which were simultaneously active during the 8.2 Kiloyear Event.

This was no passing phase, but would persist for the next three centuries after its sudden onset around 6200 BCE. This date coincided with the precipitous decline of the New Stone Age in Mesopotamia, followed soon after by its Armenian revival, referred to by archaeologists as the Shulaveri-Shomu. The Central Transcaucasian culture produced the same decorated pottery; circular, mud-brick architecture; long, prismatic, obsidian blades; and anthropomorphic, female figurines diagnostic of Neolithic Mesopotamia. Clearly, the New Stone Age agriculturalists, after balancing on the knife-edge of survival there for 200 years, migrated en masse across the Caucasian Mountains into southern Armenia, where deteriorating conditions were less severe. What the otherwise identical Shulaveri-Shomu Culture did not share with its Near Eastern predecessor, however, was Karahunj. Nothing like it had ever been built before.

Why did the same Neolithic farmers, who never set up any astronomically aligned standing stones, decide to do so after leaving Mesopotamia? In other words, why did they build the world's first megalithic observatory in Armenia? It had been preceeded, of course, by Göbekli Tepe. But that site was built more than 4,000 years before Karahunj was envisioned, rendering any continuity connecting the two structures utterly impossible. Turkey's innovative achievement atop Navel Hill was long buried and forgotten when Zorats Karer was being assembled by Armenian construction engineers, who, oblivious to Göbekli Tepe, independently reinvented applied astronomy.

For 4,500 years, beginning around 10,700 BCE with their first settlement at Tell Qaramel, in Syria, people of the New Stone Age lived off the unchanging bounty of the soil. During the course of that prolonged period, they understandably developed an agricultural religion centered on Mother Earth and her continuous abundance. Then came the 8.2 Kiloyear Event. The habitual cycles of four-and-a-half millennia were abruptly overthrown. Suddenly, without either warning or precedent, Mother Earth, on whom so many generations had based their existence, could no longer be trusted.

Out of this psychospiritual trauma arose a desperate need, in the midst of an ongoing environmental catastrophe, to find something more permanent on which they could depend for natural stability. They found it in the rotation of the heavens, that clockwork cosmos of unerring regularity by which humans could reorder their lives and bond again with the perennial forces of life. Accordingly, the first few generations of Mesopotamian immigrants in Armenia studied the sky, preserving everything they learned, until their accumulated knowledge went into the construction of an astronomically aligned megalithic center. For them, such a place was a temple celebrating their new spiritual concept. It represented a fundamental shift from worshipping Mother Earth to Father Sky. For that major transformation of folkish consciousness, a structure oriented to the heavens was needed. Hence, the original creation of Karahunj.

This interpretation of the evidence is borne out by a comparison of religious artifacts found at Late Neolithic sites in the Near East with others belonging to the successive Shulaveri-Shomu culture responsible for Armenia's ancient standing stones. The former set lacks any reference to the heavens, and is composed almost entirely of anthropomorphic, female figurines self-evidently depicting a Mother Earth fertility goddess, with characteristic Neolithic emphasis on oversized thighs and breasts. Little of such imagery lingered into Shulaveri-Shomu times. Instead, overwhelming attention was lavished on male sky deities, particularly solar figures.

Their chief divinity was Aramazd. The first two letters in his name formed the root for "sun," "light," and "life." His son, Mihr, was another sun god, as was Hayk, the legendary forefather of the Armenian people. Aragil was a mythical stork that personified the sun, and Akahi was a rooster identified with dawn. Among mortals, the most powerful oaths were sworn by the sun, to which the ancient Armenians sacrificed horses.[12] The fifth-century scholar Movses Khorenatsi compiled the earliest known historiographical work about Armenia, a series of volumes rooted in very deep antiquity, when the sun, moon, stars, and planets were worshipped at sacred sites such as Karahunj.[13]

Although these deities were revered throughout the Classical Period, their origins are steeped in a post-Neolithic age. They were celestial replacements for the still vital and honored, but less dependable, now secondary-in-importance Mother Earth. From those first standing stones erected in the southern Caucasus, their megalithic technology spread westward to Europe and North Africa. The hitherto earliest known celestial observatories were simultaneously established at two locations in Germany and Egypt, separated from each other by 2,300 miles.

That the Goseck Circle in the Burgenlandkreis district of Saxony-Anhalt and the standing stones of Nabta Playa, in the Nubian Desert, 500 miles south of Cairo, were built at the same time—circa 4900 BCE—suggests both locations were independently influenced by a common influence arriving from outside their respective cultural orbits. The six centuries separating them from Karahunj further implies that other, similarly oriented, yet older sites remain to be discovered radiating outward from the Armenian birthplace of megalithic astronomy.

While Zorats Karer may be the first of its kind, it shares the region with dozens of other standing stones thereafter erected in mountains near the sources of rivers or lakes, which they appear to mark or delineate in some way. The ten- to twenty-foot-tall monoliths are cigar-shaped, and often sculpted in the shape of a fish. They are referred to as Vishapakar, or "dragon stones," the same title by which many megalithic sites from Western Europe to China, Korea, and Japan are still known, suggesting the outward migration of megalith-building from its central birthplace in Syunik province.

The profusion of radiating Vishapakar further implies a cultural ripple effect that reverberated across Armenia and far beyond. Interestingly, early-twentieth-century archaeological consensus held that the Megalithic Age began in the Middle East and spread to Europe, a view abandoned after World War Two, but opened for reconsideration now by the discovery—not far outside the Middle East—of Karahunj and its local scions. But another, more distant offspring has more to say about the dynamic diffusion of Neolithic influence.

# 9

# Older than Sphinx or Pyramid

*Astronomy compels the soul to look upwards and leads us
from this world to another.*

PLATO, *THE REPUBLIC*

Beginning in 1973, a Texas Professor of Anthropology from Southern
Methodist University in Dallas was leading his team of fellow American
scholars through the Nubian Desert. Trudging across one of the driest,
least inhabitable regions on Earth, Fred Wendorf and company were
aided solely by one handheld compass in their attempt to find a remote,
unmarked archaeological site unconnected by any roads. As he ordered
a halt to ascertain their bearings and his colleagues rested for a much-
needed water break, they noticed that the sands around them were lit-
tered with dozens, possibly hundreds, of potsherds going back centuries
before the rise of Egyptian civilization.

All that was known about this excessively obscure and inhospitable spot was its name—Nabta Playa—located some 500 miles south
of Cairo; about sixty miles west of Abu Simbel, most southerly of the

pharaohs' monumental, rock-cut temples. Physical evidence here of a human population center was not only surprising, but seemingly impossible, given such severe environmental conditions.

Over the next twenty-five years, Wendorf and fellow investigators often returned to Nabta Playa for answers. They learned that it was not always a hostile desert, but had once been a large water basin receiving as much as twenty inches of annual rainfall. A resulting lake was the centerpiece of lush savannah inhabited by extinct buffalo and large giraffes, together with varieties of antelope and gazelle, until the onset of hotter temperatures beginning around 6,000 years ago dried up the water and expunged Nubia's ephemeral paradise.

Before that climate change, Nabta Playa had obviously attracted human settlers, perhaps as early as the tenth millenium BCE. Wendorf found that they consumed and stored wild sorghum. Traces of this grass raised for grain and used as fodder plants, either cultivated or as part of pasture, led him to presume that the inhabitants were early pastoralists practicing animal domestication. They were also artistically inclined, as demonstrated by surviving ceramics painted with complex patterns.

Into the seventh millenium BCE, these successful attempts at organizing society swelled the local population and further stimulated human ingenuity. Deep aquifers were excavated; huts—many with large hearths—were organized into straight rows, resulting in village streets; and diet was expanded to include fruits, legumes, millets, and tubers. But Nabta Playa was only occupied during summer months, when the local lake filled with water for grazing cattle, some of which were sacrificed and entombed in stone-roofed chambers, foreshadowing by millennia Pharaonic Egypt's cult of the cow-goddess, Hathor. She was the divine personification of love, beauty, music, motherhood, and joy—commonly depicted in Dynastic temple art as a woman wearing a headdress of cow horns with the sun in between them. In what may have been a dim reference to her origins at Nabta Playa, Hathor's title was "Mistress of the West."[1] By 5500 BCE, the site had grown into a ceremonial center attracting celebrants from around the region.

Precisely who these people were has not been determined, although sub-Saharan roots are speculated by some researchers, more by baseless inference than physical proof. Instead, "the repetitive orientation of megaliths, stele, human burials and cattle burials, reveals a very early symbolic connection to the north"; that is, the Upper Nile Valley.[2] As Nabta Playa flourished in human numbers and cultural wealth, its sometime residents erected a monumental structure that took Professor Wendorf and his accompanying investigators by surprise.

Among the scattered debris of a vanished, New Stone Age settlement were unusually configured outcroppings and slabs more than half-concealed by the desert sands. When these peculiar rocks were dug out and thoroughly exposed, the archaeologists were astounded to behold a cromlech not unlike megalithic structures erected in Western Europe during Neolithic times. Nabta Playa "consists of an outer rim of sandstone slabs with four sets of lager stones that form two line-of-sight 'windows' in the calendar circle," as described by Thomas G. Brophy, Ph.D., a former NASA astrophysicist.

"Inside the circle are six larger stones. The largest of the slabs are almost three feet long, and the smallest are slightly less than a foot. The circle is ten to eleven feet across."[3] Outside the circle lies "Megalith X-1," more than twelve feet long, before it was deliberately toppled and broken

*Fig. 9.1. The standing stones of Nabta Playa. Photo by Raymbetz.*

apart unknown centuries ago. Nearby is another fallen stone over seven feet long. Both were originally planted upright at the top of a knoll. This pair and the oval circle belong to an estimated thirty similar complexes throughout the vicinity. None have been fully excavated, and only twenty-five stones in the small cromlech have been closely studied. Its characterization by Brophy as a "calendar circle" was confirmed by Professor Wendorf, who demonstrated that it marked sunrise of the summer solstice, an event that coincided with archaeological traces for the annual surge of human activity at Nabta Playa.

According to science writer Mark H. Gaffney, the stones of Nabta Playa were placed

in straight lines that radiate out from a central point. The arrangement employed a simple, star-coordinate system that assigned two stones per star. One aligned with the star itself and marked its vernal equinox heliacal (i.e., rising together with the Sun on the first day of spring) position on the horizon. The other aligned with a reference star, in this case, Vega, thus fixing the first star's rising at a specific date in history. In archaeo-astronomy, single, megalithic alignments with stars are considered dubious, because at any given time, several stars will rise at or within a few degrees of the point on the horizon denoted by a lone marker. Over long periods of time, many different stars will rise over this position. The creators of Nabta Playa eliminated uncertainty with the Vega alignment and the specificity of vernal equinox heliacal rising, which occurs only once every twenty-six thousand years for a given star. This fixed the star's rising date. Vega was a logical choice, because it is the fifth brightest star in the heavens, and dominated the northern sky in this early period.[4]

Brophy took the evidence further to show how another set of stones "would have applied to Orion's belt," explains Boston geologist Robert M. Schoch, Ph.D., "as it appeared on the meridian [an imaginary line in the sky running from the north to the south through the zenith] each night at around the time of the summer solstice [when the Sun rises from the eastern horizon farthest north and is highest in the sky at noon in northern latitudes] during the period of 6400 B.C. to 4900 B.C."[5] Wendorf and most archaeologists likewise date the Nabta Playa circle to after the beginning of the fifth millennium BCE. This period illuminates the Nubian Desert complex within the context of its times. Dr. Schoch's own research has capably shown that the low date—and most likely period—for construction of the core-body in the Great Sphinx is circa 5000 BCE. Far to the north, another "calendar circle" was built at the same time Nabta Playa was erected, 2,300 miles away.

The Goseck Circle is Europe's earliest-known astronomical observatory, located in Sachsen-Anhalt's Burgenlandkreis district, in central-northeastern Germany, south of Berlin, outside the small town of Goseck. It was discovered during a 1991 aerial photographic survey that revealed circular ridges under a wheat field. But they were not excavated for another eleven years, when University of Halle-Wittenberg archaeologists Francois Bertemes and Peter Biehl arrived at the site. They found that it comprised four raised, concentric circles 246 feet across, together with a mound, a ditch, and two wooden palisades interspersed with three gates facing southeast, southwest, and north. The rings and gates leading into the inner circles become narrower as someone entering the complex progresses to its center, indicating perhaps that only a few, privileged persons were allowed access to the innermost ring, the sacred midpoint.

When Bertemes and Biehl combined possible celestial orientations with GPS coordinates, the two southern openings marked the sunrise and sunset of the winter and summer solstice.* At the winter solstice, observers at the center would have seen the sun rise and set through the southeast and southwest gates. Wolfhard Schlosser,

---

*The Global Positioning System (GPS) is a space-based global navigation satellite system. It provides location and time information in all weather, anywhere on or near Earth where there is an unobstructed line of sight to four or more GPS satellites.

Professor of Astronomy at Bochum's Ruhr University, found that the Goseck Circle combined "an easily judged lunar calendar with the more demanding measurements of a solar calendar," plus several alignments to certain stars, although he did not specify which ones. "The formation of the site," Schlosser added, "its orientation and the marking of the winter and summer solstice show similarities to the world-famous Nebra Disc, though the object was created twenty-four hundred years later."[6]

The Nebra Disc was discovered just twelve miles from Goseck, in the wooded region of Nebra, and is considered the oldest-known image of the cosmos. The thirteen-inch, bronze plate with blue-green patina is inlaid with gold leaf symbols clearly representing the sun, crescent moon, and stars—including a cluster of seven dots signifying the constellation of the Pleiades as it appeared 3,600 years ago. Celestial data provided by the Nebra Disc, Schlosser believes, derived from previous astronomical observations possibly made at Goseck.[7] If so, relationship between the device and the site indicates Middle Europe's profoundly rich scientific-cultural heritage. Indeed, subsequent aerial surveys have identified more than 250 ring-ditches across Germany, Austria, and Croatia; barely 10 percent of them have been investigated so far by archaeologists, who previously assumed the enclosures were no more than Neolithic forts, though the lack of any building foundations inside was puzzling.

Western Germany's Goloring, near Koblenz, is similar to—if later than—the Goseck Circle, but dates to the same period as the Nebra Disc. Potsherds at Goseck indicate that the observatory was built around 4900 BCE, because they are adorned with linear designs compared to standard chronologies of pottery styles. The period they suggest was supported by carbon dating of two arrowheads, the remains of what may have been ritual fires, plus human and animal bones found within the circular compounds. Their constructions are attributed to the Middle Danubian Culture, when its representatives moved down the Vistula and Elbe Rivers into the Sachsen-Anhalt area. Unlike their regional predecessors, the Middle Danubians cremated their dead, a diagnostic Aryan practice underscored by origins in Transcaucasia.[8] Here, the first celestial observatory was built at Armenia's Karahunj stone circle, as described in the previous chapter.

It is conceivable then, that pioneering Caucasian astronomers migrated into central-northeastern Germany, where they are referred to by scholars as Middle Danubian culture-bearers. Their Goseck Circle, with its reconstructed wooden palisade, was opened to the public—fittingly enough—on December 21, 2005, the winter solstice. While Germany's Goseck Circle, Nubia's Nabta Playa, and Egypt's Great Sphinx are structurally very different from one another and separated by considerable distances, they were all built at the same time and shared a common celestial alignment. At 241 feet long, twenty feet wide, and sixty-seven feet high, the Great Sphinx is still the largest monolithic statue on Earth.

Mainstream Egyptologists repeated throughout the twentieth century that it was constructed after 2558 BCE by a Pharaoh Khafre, also known as Chephren—speculation based entirely on dubious circumstantial inference, minus a single scrap of contemporaneous documentation. Outside scholarship directed from the "hard sciences" absolutely debunked this flimsy interpretation with geological facts—most importantly among them, evidence of rain damage the monument suffered as late as 7,000 years ago, proving it existed at that time.

Andrew Collins, a British authority on ancient Egypt, observes, "It is clear that at the commencement of the Pyramid Age [officially, 2686 BCE to 2458 BCE], the monuments remaining on the Giza Plateau were in advanced stages of decay. Yet, in this same, great epoch, the architects and engineers of the 4th Dynasty pharaohs, such as Khufu, Khafre and Menkaure, would appear to have repaired, redesigned and resanctified structures such as the Valley Temple and the Great Sphinx, which were then incorporated into the gradually emerging pyramid field."[9]

In other words, Khafre "repaired" and "redesigned" the Great Sphinx, which he did not build, because it was already decrepit with antiquity by the time he came to the throne. As such, either he or some other Fourth Dynasty king recarved the original head in his own image.* It has a markedly different texture from the body, and shows far less severe erosion, thereby establishing its later addition. In the Old Temple laying at the feet of the Sphinx stand twenty-four columns— one for each hour of the day and night—once accompanied by twelve statues representing the daylight hours. These, too, were all later, but appropriate, additions to the Great Sphinx's original construction around 5000 BCE.

According to author Graham Hancock, "computer simulations show that in 10,500 B.C., the constellation of Leo housed the Sun on the spring equinox—i.e., an hour before dawn in that epoch, Leo would have reclined due east along the horizon in the place where the Sun would soon rise. This means that the lion-bodied Sphinx, with its due-east orientation, would have gazed directly on that morning at the one constellation in the sky that might reasonably be regarded as its own celestial counterpart."[10]

Be that as it may, the ancient Egyptians did not associate the constellation Leo with a lion until Late New Kingdom times, after 1200 BCE. Robert Temple, a fellow of Britain's Royal Astronomical Society, argues persuasively that the Great Sphinx was incipiently conceived not

---

*Khafre's realistic portrait statue at Cairo's Egyptian Museum bears no facial resemblance to the countenance of the Great Sphinx. His restoration of the monument, which had already deteriorated by 2500 BCE, semed to justify reconfiguring an earlier version of the face into the 4th Dynasty pharaoh's own visage. Testing by an associate professor of natural science at Boston University in 1991 demonstrated that the Great Sphinx preceeded Khafre by more than three thousand years. Erosion on its surface, argued Robert M. Schoch, Ph.D., in his book *Pyramid Quest: Secrets of the Great Pyramid and the Dawn of Civilization*, was due less to the effects of wind-blown sand, than rain, which was scarce throughout Old Kingdom times, but heavy in previous millennia. Although archaeologists mostly rejected his findings, their peer review by fellow geologists universally supported them. Schoch's back-dating is significant, because it shows that the Great Sphinx was built by an unknown, pre-Dynastic people in possession of an extraordinarily high culture at a period defined by mainstream science as too primitive for the construction of such monumental projects.

as a lion, but a jackal—an animal associated with Anubis, "the Lord of Rostau," as Dynastic Egyptians referred to their god, who conveyed the souls of the dead to the Afterlife. Rostau was their name for the Giza Plateau, where the monument is located. "'Anubis on his hill,' therefore, became, I believe, the standard way of referring to the Great Sphinx of Giza," Temple concludes.[11]

While Hancock's computer simulations might indeed show that the Great Sphinx aligned with the constellation Leo more than 12,000 years ago, that advanced period would have been no less meaningless to Dynastic Egyptians than the Sphinx's coincidental orientation to any other cherry-picked epoch tens of thousands or millions of years before. Had the Sphinx been engineered to mark a 10,500 BCE date, as Hancock suggests, it is far too much to expect of the Egyptians that such a commemorated period could have still meant anything to them by the time their civilization got going, which was 7,400 years later. There is, of course, no cultural continuity between Dynastic Egyptians and any people in the eleventh millennium BCE. However, this is not to deny the Great Sphinx's deliberate orientation to the rising sun, which it faces directly on the morning of each vernal equinox, associated everywhere with rebirth, just as Anubis personified a new life beyond death.

Its initial association with Anubis appears to have culturally morphed into Leo after the onset of the Old Kingdom, because the Great Sphinx stared directly at the sun as it "rose where the star Regulus, at the heart of the lion of the Constellation Leo, was on the horizon," on the summer solstice.[12] Here is the same solar fix found at such otherwise diverse, contemporaneous sites as the Goseck Circle and Nabta Playa. Professor Brophy believes that three other stones at the center of the latter represent Orion's head and shoulders, as they would have been viewed 18,500 years ago.*[13] He found that three more rocks south of the

---

*"According to Brophy's analysis, three of the stones inside the Nabta circle represent Orion's belt, the same portion of the same constellation that Robert Bauval has suggested the three major pyramids on the Giza Plateau represent."

site precisely define the actual distances of the stars in that constellation from our solar system, while documenting the speeds at which they are moving away from the Earth. These and smaller, nearby stones are supposed to show that their arrangers "had information about planetary systems or companion stars associated with the six stars in question—information that we do not have today!"[14]

Concerning another Nabta Playa stone, Brophy wonders if it encodes "information about the origin of the universe, the age of the solar system or universe, the structure of the galaxy and universe, and/or the fundamental constants of nature?"[15] If so, then no greater contrast can exist than that between such ultrasophisticated data and the crude enclosure it was allegedly meant to record. That seasonal, pastoralist residents herding their cattle through the Nubian Desert 7,000 years ago could have somehow used, much less understood, such information is a more outrageous suggestion than the alleged existence of that data.

Like Hancock's claim that the Egyptians used the Great Sphinx to memorialize something seventy-four centuries before their time, such information would have been utterly useless to its recipients. While Dr. Brophy's plotted alignment of Nabta Playa stones with certain stars is undoubtedly correct, these same stones can be just as coincidentally oriented to any other number of different stars. Archaeoastronomers, for all their intellectual brilliance, are only human, no less liable to get carried away with their work than others in pursuit of their own passions. In any case, his conclusions may have escaped a final judgment for all time.

"The Nabta site deserves further investigation and impartial study," urges Dr. Schoch, "as well as careful preservation for future generations."[16] But Gaffney's 2006 observation that "the site's remoteness protected it from most human disturbance" no longer applies.[17] "It seems that the site has been ransacked by vandals," according to reporter Scott Creighton. "Many of the ancient standing stones have been knocked down, whilst others have actually been stolen."[18]

Today, all that remain of Nabta Playa's original configuration survives in charts and photographs. "Astrophysicist Thomas G. Brophy reported that the vandalism was clear when reviewing his photos from 2007 to those taken in 2008."[19] In other words, an early human achievement that stood for seven millennia could not survive a few years of exposure in the early twenty-first century. That fact says perhaps far more about the difference between our ancestors and our own time than the most bitter commentary.

The 8.2 Kiloyear Event that shut down a Neolithic Golden Age and opened the first celestial observatory devastated fertile territories and forced their evacuation. People were not only on the move in search of less afflicted living spaces, but, having been let down by Mother Nature, they shifted their spiritual focus from the venerable Earth goddess to sky gods. These demographic and metaphysical changes were reflected in new kinds of permanent structures known as megaliths, sometimes deliberately and accurately oriented to specific coordinates in the heavens, despite often weighing many tons.

Several different categories of megaliths raised over the course of forty-three centuries testify to humankind's longest-lived, most enduring tradition of ceremonial construction, numerous examples of which continue to survive—not as ruins, but as still-operative, astronomical markers. By way of comparison, how many buildings made today will be functioning as they were originally intended, 5,000 and 7,000 years from now?

# 10

# Stone Age Astronomers in America

*Archaeologists are slowly beginning to realize that to understand European prehistory, American prehistory must also be considered.*

R. CEDRIC LEONARD, *THE QUEST FOR ATLANTIS*

The best-known megalithic type is the stone circle—begun at Karahunj and most famously perfected 2,700 miles away and forty centuries later at Britain's Stonehenge. A simpler form is the *menhir,* from the French Middle Breton for "long stone," a single, upright monolith standing alone or in groups of similar examples. Although size varies considerably, from a few feet to nearly twenty meters tall, configuration is generally uneven and squared—sometimes cigar-shaped—tapering toward the top.

About 50,000 menhirs still exist in Ireland, Great Britain, and Brittany, while another 1,200 are found across northwestern France alone. Of Northern Europe's original 50,000 standing stones, only 10,000 survived Christian attempts to eradicate them all. Menhirs were commonly engraved with megalithic art, often in such a way as to provide them with human features not unlike Göbekli Tepe's anthropomorphic pillars, suggesting an awesome continuity preceding the advent of Western European megalith-building by fifty centuries.

A yet more common category of megalithic construction is the *dolmen*—Breton for "stone table," a chamber consisting of upright stones with one or more large, flat capstones forming a roof. The dolmen is referred to by archaeologists, not with invariable accuracy, as a "portal tomb." Not all contain human remains, and those which do may—in many cases—have been intrusive burials made long after the builders' original intentions were forgotten. Less often encountered are passage-graves consisting of a square, circular, or cruciform chamber with a slabbed or corbelled roof, and accessed by a long, straight passageway. Structures were themselves either mostly or entirely covered with a circular mound of earth, occasionally surrounded by an external stone curb.

Although the Megalithic Age spread from Armenia to Egypt and Germany, its Western European birth occurred along the continental shores of the Atlantic Ocean. Contemporaneous with Nabta Playa and the Goseck Circle, the megaliths' early profusion and concentration along continental coastlines from Iberian to Scandinavian coasts correctly implies their identification with maritime peoples on the move.

The early fifth millennium BCE dispersal of human populations via long-distance sailing routes is established by the premiere settlement of Malta—some eighty miles across open water from Sicily—during the Għar Dalam phase (circa 4850 BCE) when the island's first structures, the Skorba temples, were built. In fact, the Atlantic Neolithic period began with the earliest megalithic construction in Portugal, at the municipality of Évora, just south of the important Tagus River, eighty-seven miles from Lisbon. There, the Almendres Cromlech, among the largest group of menhirs in the Iberian Peninsula, and one of the biggest in Europe, may still be visited.*

That the megalith-builders were sailors appears in evidence on the Kermaillard menhir, also known as La Motte De Beurre, located near the end of a peninsula on the south side of the Gulf of Morbihan, a natural harbor on the coast of the Département of Morbihan, in the south of Brittany. The fifteen-foot-long monolith was originally found lying on its side. When set upright after the turn of the twenty-first century, observers were surprised at what was revealed. On the whole width of the lower part of an almost perfectly flat side—on which the menhir fell centuries ago—engraved from left to right, were the images of a small-handled ax, a square cartouche, and a ship. Conventional archaeologists believe it does not represent what it appears to depict, but rather signifies a crescent moon. "Have you ever seen an upside down moon?" asks Jay Stuart Wakefield, a Washington State zoologist and lifelong sailor. "Do you think it was carved when the menhir was lying on its side? Don't you suppose this menhir was upright quite a long time (megalithic times)? Have you ever seen a moon that looks like that?"[1]

After a careful, twenty-year-long study of Western European megalithic sites, Peter Davidson identified many standing stones as navigational markers originally designed for guiding ships into safe anchorages. They "could be used to establish a dead-reckoning for navigation from one sandy beach to another," concluded the retired British engineer in December 2010. His particular search included megalithic alignments without any obvious or plausible solar or lunar correlations, finding "in many instances they could be used to indicate key landfalls from a local departure-point." These standing stones "seem to show a picture of routine marine transport over the Atlantic seaboard from Carnac (Brittany), in the south to Callanish (in the Outer Hebrides),

---

*"Cromlech" (from the Brythonic, or Breton/Welsh crom for "bent" and llech, "flag-stone") is a word used to describe ancient stone circles and dolmens, although the term is no longer current among most modern archaeologists.

in the north, with a high level of statistical support."[2] (Please see plate 4 of the color insert.)

The greatest such example, known as the Grand Menhir Brisé, or "The Broken Menhir of Er Grah," towered over Locmariaquer, Brittany, where it was erected between 4800 and 4700 BCE. At 355 tons, it was not only the largest single block to have been erected by Neolithic man, but the heaviest object humans ever moved without powered machinery— a record that stood for the next 4,000 years, until a 517-ton stone was installed in the lower level of Jerusalem's Western Wall. Even today, the French monolith is surpassed only by this "Western Stone" and St. Petersburg's "Thunder Stone," transported at the command of Catherine the Great, in 1770. Just forty-eight years earlier, a severe earthquake—Brittany is the most seismically active area in France— toppled the 67.6-foot-high Grand Menhir Brisé, which broke into four sections. Until then, it was visible as far away as twelve miles out to sea.

The monolith is no crude structure, but has been worked over its entire surface. Its center section (now a middle fragment) is skillfully engraved with the likeness of an axe. (Please see plate 5 of the color insert.) Although the severely weathered image is very difficult to

*Fig. 10.1. The greatest megalith, Brittany's Er Grah, lies fallen after a severe earthquake that shook western France. Photo by S. Möller.*

discern, it is clearly duplicated on the ceiling of the Table des Marchand, a magnificent nearby dolmen recently reassembled into its original setting as part of a large cairn. (Please see plate 6 of the color insert.) The axe was a sacred symbol probably associated with a Neolithic storm god. Since time out of mind, local Bretons still call these figures "thunder axes." Accordingly, the Grand Menhir Brisé may have been additionally erected to attract lightning, thereby calling down the storm god— whose own emblem adorned the stone—as part of some ritual activity.

Multiple purposes were typically incorporated in monumental undertakings, as additionally proved by the pioneering Scottish archaeoastronomer, Alexander Thom (1894–1985), who demonstrated that Brittany's great stone calculated an 18.61-year lunar cycle.[3] Based on its orientation, he accurately predicted the discovery of other ancient celestial markers, confirming his hypothesis. The cycle Thom discovered at Locmariaquer is a major lunar standstill, when the Moon appears to move in only two weeks from high in the sky to low on the horizon. For reasons not entirely understood, this period held special significance for the megalith-builders, who often oriented their structures to the 18.61-year cycle, known as the "Metonic," after Meton of Athens, the Greek mathematician, astronomer, and engineer, who rediscovered it in 432 BCE. The foundations of his observatory are still visible just behind the podium of the Pnyx, the ancient parliament building.

How a much earlier, anciently preindustrial people could have moved a 355-ton-stone more than six miles from a rocky outcrop north of Auray—a commune in Brittany's Morbihan department—and then perfectly erected its nearly seventy-foot-length with astronomical precision is physical evidence for a society far more sophisticated and advanced in the principles of applied mechanics and social coordination than anything we can imagine. Any race capable of such a stupendous feat was unquestionably able to achieve equally great, or perhaps even greater, things in other fields of human endeavor.

Also, many standing stones are far more significant than their stark simplicity infers. They often simultaneously embody various functions, some of them less obvious than others, such as the 18.6-year lunar cycle mentioned above. No one has done more in recent years to bring out these deeper, multiple subtleties than Jay Stuart Wakefield, and Reinoud De Jonge. Since the end of the last century, their painstaking measurements of numerous megalithic sites in Northern and Western Europe have confirmed that many of them were deliberately built, at least in part, to memorialize sailing instructions for long-distance voyages. Wakefield has melded scientific discipline with personal maritime experience, while De Jonge is a theoretical physical chemist in Holland. Together, they have deciphered convincing evidence for the megalith-builders as seafarers, who ventured outside the hypothetical limitations imposed on our ancestors' abilities by conventional archaeologists.

Wakefield and De Jonge observed that the number, placement, and angles of certain standing stones correspond to the position of landfalls far beyond the continental shores of Western and Northern Europe. This data was encoded in the stones themselves, which served as mnemonic devices for helmsmen during preliterate times. Before the advent of the written word, Neolithic navigators would have acquainted themselves with sailing directions to their overseas' destinations, as graphically spelled out in specific patterns arranged by the monoliths. Ship's company—or, at least, captain and officers—perhaps participated in dramatic recreations of notable voyages among the standing stones, to aid in memorizing their instructions; although, naturally, no evidence for such presumed ritual activity could have survived the passage of millennia.

Among the best-known locations that exemplify the megalithic sites as mnemonic maps occurs on the Brittany coast at the Gulf of Morbihan, not far from the toppled Grand Menhir Brisé. There, in the town of Carnac, is the largest collection of its kind on Earth. More than 3,000 standing stones, all of them hewn from local rock and dating back 6,500 years ago, are arranged in three major sets. The Kermario, "House of the Dead" group consists of 1,029 monoliths in ten columns, about 4,300 feet in length, forming "an enormous arrow pointing to the southwest, toward the Ocean."[4] Beginning with this suggestive orientation, Kermario appears to reference the Azores, with emphasis on the island of Corvo. More than 1,000 miles west from Brittany, the Azores were not officially discovered until the early fifteenth century, as was the island of Madeira (another 600 miles distant), also indicated at Carnac.

Contrary to mainstream archaeologists, who believe neither archipelago was settled by humans before then, De Jonge and Wakefield found that seven rows

> all point 33° WSW, corresponding to the other island of the West Azores, Corvo, 7° above Madeira (33° N), at 33° + 7 = 40° N. The seven rows confirm Corvo from Kermario at 47 – 7 = 40° N. The seven rows all make an angle of 33°, corresponding to the initial sailing direction from Corvo to Cape Race, Newfoundland, 33° WNW. . . . The latitude of the monument of Kermario at 47° N confirms this. . . . The seven main rows also provide the terminal sailing direction in the neighborhood of southern Cape Hatteras, 25° – 7 = 18° WNW. . . . The angle of 35° also encodes the direct sailing distance from southern Cape Hatteras to the West Azores. . . . Together with the seven main alignments, it forms 28° + 7 = 35 units, confirming southern Cape Hatteras and the direct sailing distance to the Azores.[5]

Nor was the Kermario grouping alone in citing the Azores as stepping-stones to North America, as demonstrated by the Carnac's Ménec alignments. They are made up of twelve converging rows of 1,153 menhirs extending 3,822 feet by 330 feet. The largest specimens, about thirteen feet high, are at the wider, western end. Monoliths thereafter stand progressively shorter, down to just two feet tall, along the length of the alignment, before rising in height again toward the extreme eastern end.

De Jonge and Wakefield observed:

The twelve rows symbolize the twelve islands on the crossing of the Ocean from northwest Africa, via the Azores, to Newfoundland. . . . The east and west circles of Ménec represent the Old and New Worlds. . . .The important western rows represent the long crossing from the West Azores to Newfoundland . . . the start of Row XI high in the east circle represents the east coast of America at a high latitude. Menhir C has been placed at the very start of this row. The east-west line from big Menhir A (Ménec at 47°) runs to the start of Row XI, now representing Cape Race, Newfoundland, at the same latitude as the Ménec at 47° N.[6]

At Kerlescan, on the northwest edge of Carnac, thirteen rows of 352 menhirs, plus a U-shaped stone circle of forty-six monoliths, provide additional transatlantic instructions. Beginning at Cabo Fisterra, Cape Finisterre, or "Land's End"—a rockbound peninsula on the Galician coast, Spain's westernmost point—the site indicates the Azore Islands progressively, from San Miguel to Santa Maria, Terciera, San Jorge, Pico, Fayal, Graciosa, Flores, and Corvo. From these, the

> west side of the U has eleven stones corresponding with Cape Hatteras, 11° below Cape Race and Kerlescan at 47 − 11 = 36° N. Rows III and VII contain 11 + 25 = 36 menhirs, confirming this latitude. This is also the latitude of the Strait of Gibraltar, at 36° N, at the other side of the Ocean. The west side of the U has eight stones above the axis, corresponding to Delaware Bay, 8° below Cape Race, at 47 − 8 = 39° N. The most important row, Row V of 39 stones, confirms this latitude of 39° N. Rows IV and VIII contain 19 + 22 = 41 menhirs, corresponding to Nantucket at 41° N. Rows I and VIII have 20 + 22 = 42 stones, encoding Cape Cod at 42° N.[7]

The same sailing directions were essentially repeated by Brittany's Rows of Leure, on the Crozon Peninsula, as revealed by a precisely surveyed ground plan of the demolished site. So too, the Stone Rows of

Lagatjar, just south of Brest, comprise three rows of monoliths representing degrees of latitude and "built to celebrate a new shortcut route for crossing of the Labrador Sea, a new sailing route to America."[8]

If we are to accept that transoceanic coordinates are actually embedded in the megaliths, then they should find at least some corresponding evidence on the opposite shores of the Atlantic. The first such connection appears in New Hampshire, where an arrangement of menhirs lies within the town of Salem. Bruce Scofield, Ph.D., a faculty member at the University of Massachusetts and author of several popular books about Mesoamerican calendrics, describes the site as "a group of chambers, underground passages, alignments and inscriptions. . . . There are over one hundred fifty acres of land containing stone walls, sculpted stones, standing stones, and a quarry from which the slabs were excavated . . . alignments that mark the Sun's position against the background of hills on February 1st, May 1st, and November 1st [are] days of great importance to the Celtic calendar."[9] (Please see plates 7 and 8 of the color insert.)

To be sure, correspondences with Western European counterparts are apparent. At forty-five and seventy tons, the two largest stones erected at the New Hampshire location were far beyond the experience of any aboriginal, colonial, or early industrial Americans, but commonly moved by the megalith-builders of Western Europe. So too were these more recent peoples unlikely to have bothered about precisely orienting Salem's menhirs to various and arcane astronomical phenomena.

According to *Ancient American* writer James Vieira, "Stone markers throughout the site provide over two hundred alignments with the Sun, Moon and forty-five different stars, which have been verified by independent researchers. One alignment wall allows a person to observe the southernmost standstill of the Moon on its 18.61-year Metonic cycle. A period of 18.61 is required to carry the Moon to all of its possible positions in respect to the Sun. The event is marked at Mystery Hill as the Moon passes above the winter solstice, and then aligns with the terminal of the wall."[10]

This, of course, is the same Metonic cycle marked by the Grand Menhir Brisé, that dominated the Atlantic coast of Brittany, from 6,800 years ago. Had the New Hampshire site existed anywhere in Western Europe, mainstream archaeologists would have unhesitatingly catalogued it among the hundreds of similar groupings featured throughout the ancient Old World. "Its construction is quite reminiscent of the Neolithic village of Skara Brae in the Orkney Islands of Scotland," according to the well-traveled archaeologist, Dr. David Zink.[11] "Megaliths densely populate the northern Orkney Islands," writes Dr. Maelee Thomson Foster, a professional photographer of standing stones for the American Institute of Architects, "where an impressive group is organized as a linear system, connecting the chambered tomb of Maes Howe in the east, with the Atlantic Ocean and the well-preserved neolithic village of Skara Brae in the northwest . . . the six-mile ceremonial path terminates in the mid-summer sunset reflected in the sea."[12]

Only because "Mystery Hill," as the location was known until the late twentieth century, occurs in North America did orthodox scholars dismiss it as an eighteenth- to nineteenth-century quarry and/or agricultural storage area; so great was their bias against even the remotest possibilities for outside contacts during pre-Columbian times. For them, "BC" meant "Before Columbus," an irrevocable line drawn in the sand, which no salaried scholar dared cross on pain of expulsion from the scientific community for academic heresy.

In their attempt to demystify Mystery Hill during the early 1990s, they conducted radiocarbon testing of several charcoal pits at the site, which yielded dates from 2,000 to 500 years ago. These time parameters corresponded, as expected, to indigenous occupation from the Late Archaic to Early Woodland time periods, when the area was populated by ancestors of present-day Native Americans. But in 1995, excavation of a wall east of the North Stone generated a C-14 date of 6,530 +/- 40 Years Before Present. This period, circa 4580 BCE, precisely matches the early florescence of megalith-building in Western Europe.

Subsequent radiocarbon analysis of material from a fire pit at the North Stone itself yielded a time frame of 3,470 +/- 30 Years Before Present—around 1350 BCE—toward the close of the Megalithic Age. More recent carbon-14 surveys at Mystery Hill dated it "to at least 2000 B.C. by scientists at Geochron Labs of Cambridge, Massachusetts," reports Viera, "after dating thirteen, different test pits."[13]

Following revelations such as these, the location's name was changed to "America's Stonehenge," as an attempt to move away from its ill-deserved reputation as a roadside oddity, and into more serious reconsideration as an authentically pre-Columbian legacy. "It has been described by Dr. Edward J. Kealy, professor of History at Holy Cross College (Notre Dame, Indiana)," according to Viera, "as 'potentially the most important stone complex in the Northern Hemisphere.'"[14]

Wakefield and De Jonge concur. They found that Rows I, II, and XIII at Kerlescan, in Carnac, "have 8 + 20 + 15 = 43 menhirs, corresponding to 'America's Stonehenge' and the south cape of Nova Scotia

*Fig. 10.2. "America's Stonehenge." Photograph by Brian Sullivan.*

at 43° N. This nautical center for crossing the Ocean is the most important megalithic monument of North America."[15] Ancient Old World reference to the New Hampshire site reemerges at another Brittany location, the Rows of Leure: "Including the central menhir, the SW/NE row possesses 5 + 1 = 6 menhirs, corresponding to Cape Cod at 48 − 6 = 42° N. The western menhir, SW1, represents Cape Cod, literally. The central menhir, NE2, is 'America's Stonehenge,' and the south point of Nova Scotia, at 42 + 1 = 43° N. 'America's Stonehenge' . . . was definitely a 'crossing point' for east and west voyages."[16] If this site was the only one of its kind, even devout cultural diffusionists might be inclined to conclude that the impact of overseas arrivals from Neolithic Europe was a limited, uninfluential affair, confined to the low, pine-covered hill near New Hampshire's Merrimack River.

As Scofield writes:

> Few people are aware that throughout New England there exists a large number of mysterious sites that consist of several stone chambers and peculiarly arranged boulders, or standing stones. [Please see plates 12–15 of the color insert.] Many are on hills with access to a river; some lie in valleys with views to significant features of the horizon. Most have large boulders or standing stones that align with important sunrise or sunset dates, such as the solstices or the equinoxes. The chambers, made of rock walls with huge, flat rocks for a roof, usually face the direction of the winter solstice. Some inscriptions have been interpreted to reinforce the calendrical use of the site.[17]

Without exception, these structures are dismissed by orthodox archaeologists as Colonial Era root cellars, or, at most, ceremonial formations raised by local Native American tribes no earlier than the late sixteenth century. "But colonial farmers were not known to have worked with massive slabs of rock," Scofield continues, "and there is no mention of colonists constructing stone chambers in the old family histories. The Indians that lived in New England at the dawn of the Colonial Period were not known to have worked with stone. . . . It has been noted that the quarrying method employed was an ancient one, utilizing heat and wedging, not one that a colonial farmer with oxen and iron tools would use."[18]

# 11

# Red Paint People

*One sometimes feels that experts have a genius for
swallowing fakes and refusing the authentic.*

JACQUETTA HAWKES, *MAN BEFORE HISTORY*

Encoded sailing directions to Nova Scotia and Newfoundland among
the megaliths of Atlantic coastal France are powerfully underscored by
the presence of the "Red Paint People," who arrived along the shores
of Canada and New England just when Western European megalith-
builders were taking to their boats. Both folk, although allegedly isolated from each other by an ocean and utterly independent from one
another, had many fundamentally significant traits in common: among
them, the use of red ochre—a hematite, or iron pigment—in their
funeral customs.

During the late nineteenth century, bloody liquid began seeping
from the soil not far from Bangor, near the mouth of the Penobscot
River, on the coast of Maine. Investigators determined that the strange
pool appeared after heavy rain mixed with a recently exposed deposit of
red ochre. Probing into the congealed mass, they were surprised to find
many pre-Columbian stone tools distinctly superior in craftsmanship to
comparable tribal Indian examples. Uniquely sophisticated gouges told

of an extensive woodworking industry encountered only on the other side of the continent, among the northwest Haida people of Pacific coastal British Columbia. The Maine location also yielded a profusion of singular arrowheads and other blades artistically manufactured from a sugary-white, translucent chert—a fine-grained, silica-rich, microcrystalline rock never encountered before, its origins unknown.

During 1882, these red ochre finds attracted the attention of Harvard Peabody Museum directors, who dispatched Charles C. Willowby to examine the site in what proved to be the first scientific excavation in the history of archaeology in the United States. He concluded that untypical discoveries made at the Penobscot River could only have belonged to a group he christened the "Red Paint People," a hitherto unknown folk different from all other Native Americans. Willowby's ground-breaking research was followed up by Warren King Moorehead, then widely revered as the "Dean of American Archaeology" for his numerous seminal contributions to that nascent science.

Among them was his pioneering employment of photography—both still and motion pictures, often color-tinted by hand, frame by individual frame, for the most accurate reproduction possible—which he used to document his excavations. Moorehead was astounded by the sophistication of the Red Paints' tools and their exclusive devotion to ochre; earmarks, he declared, of an advanced maritime culture with roots in ancient Western Europe. Based on these informed assumptions, he predicted that the source for their enigmatic chert would be found somewhere in the far north, perhaps as far away as the subarctic, because its prehistoric users must have spread over thousands of miles, up and down the Atlantic seaboard from Canada to New England.[1]

Moorehead's bold statements absolutely enraged most of his professional colleagues, because prevailing academic doctrine had only very recently affirmed zero-tolerance for any consideration of overseas' visitors in the Americas before Christopher Columbus. Equally adamantine was their conviction that no vessels—save for small, wood dugouts or birch-bark canoes—ever plied more than rivers and lakes throughout the whole prehistory of all the Americas. Moorehead refused to recant, however, and the Lilliputian forces of consensus reality quite literally dismantled his career.

Previously, they had lauded him as a leading professor in his field at Ohio State University; the first excavator of Ohio's Hopewell mounds; the savior from developers of Fort Ancient, an immense stone installation at least 2,000 years old, and Cahokia, Illinois' immense Monks Mound, lager at its base than Egypt's Great Pyramid; the first surveyor of Arizona's Chaco Canyon and Mesa Verde; author of the first encyclopedia of Ohio's earthworks, documenting them before they were eradicated by the farmer's plow; science hero of the 1893 World's Columbian Exposition, in Chicago; and head of Massachusetts' prestigious Robert S. Peabody Museum of Archaeology in Andover. All that meant nothing to majority officials, as the professional life of Moorehead the Heretic was permanently brought to an end.

So was any serious discussion of the Red Paint People, branded as no less legendarily ludicrous than Atlanteans or leprechauns. Moorehead died in 1939, and some twenty years later his prediction that the source of Maine's unique chert would be discovered in the far north came to pass. Geologists found the crystals' place of origin 1,500 nautical miles away, around the shores of Ramah Bay, in Labrador. Henceforward known as "Ramah chert," it appears at every Red Paint site uncovered—again, as Moorehead envisioned—from New England to Canada's subarctic shores. Starting in the 1960s, archaeologists could no longer ignore these emerging locations, and grouped them under an ambiguous "Maritime Archaic Culture." That ambiguity began to shortly thereafter unravel with a series of discoveries that continuously distanced the Red Paint People from inland Native Americans.

From Newfoundland's Port au Choix were retrieved barbed and toggled harpoons, leisters—spearlike implements with three or more prongs for stabbing fish—swordfish bones, stone plummets for large nets, and the polished effigies of whales. This site's more than 100 graves yielded yet more elaborate objects, including beautifully crafted daggers of ivory, antler and bone; shell-beaded clothing; and a burial suit made from more than 200 skins of the now-extinct great auk. Not only were such items never encountered elsewhere throughout pre-Columbian North America, they clearly belonged to sailors who ventured far from shore for deep sea fishing—unlike the Indians.

*Fig. 11.1. Finely crafted implements for deep-sea fishing and hunting from a Red Paint People tool kit. Photo from* Ancient American *magazine.*

The first discovery of a Red Paint settlement was made at Nulliak Cove on the coast of Labrador, where twenty-six multiroom stone foundations spread over 300 feet. Nearby, several upright sharp-pointed monoliths appeared to have been standing since the beginning of time. Eskimo refer to these standing stones as *anook-shits,* or "travel markers," capable of being observed from some distance out at sea for purposes of triangulating relative positions in navigating the coastline—an identical function performed by megaliths near the shores of Brittany, such as Locmariaquer's Grand Menhir Brisé.

In 1876, years before modern rediscovery of the Red Paint People, Randall Mitchell, a clerk at Igloolik and later a manager at Arctic Bay for the Hudson Bay Company, was told by local Eskimos that their ancestors were not responsible for the anook-shits, which were raised in the distant past by fair-haired giants, the Toonikdoak, from across the sea. Some of the standing stones at Nulliak Cove have squared notches cut into them to frame solar alignments, likewise incorporated in many Neolithic sites throughout Western Europe.

"At Borango Fjord and Varanger Fjord, in Norway," writes American anthropologist Dr. Gunnar Thompson, "archaeologists uncovered remains of a sixth-millennium B.C. culture [the Maglemosian] having red ochre burials, polished slate tools, polished stone gouges, elbow-handled choppers, soapstone plummets, bird effigy combs, barbed harpoons, and inscribed bones. The similarity of these artifacts to New England specimens, particularly the use of red ochre, establishes that America's Red Paint People and Scandinavia's Ancient Maritime Hunters had a common heritage."[2]

Littoral graves there characteristically feature red ochre, such as the Maglemose site's nineteen burials near Vedbæk, on the Øresund coast of Danish Zealand, facing Sweden, and dated to more than 7,000 Years Before Present. Found among them was a leister identical to its transatlantic counterpart from Port au Choix. The Labrador settlement at Nulliak Cove also features a small monolith—about two feet tall—deliberately placed at the village center, and unlike anything found anywhere else in the world, save among the Laplanders of Finnmark in the extreme northeast of Norway, where shamans still use precisely the same kind of rudely shaped stones as altars.

A prominent Norwegian anthropologist of the mid-twentieth century, Gutorm G. Jessing, observed, "Nowhere on the globe are there to be found remains as closely related as those of Norway and the coast of Maine."[3]

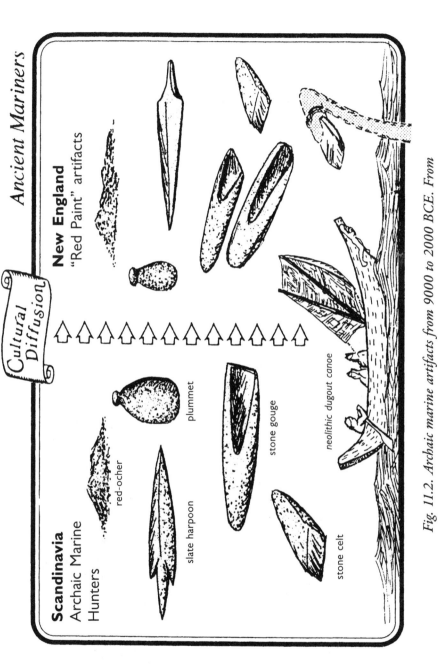

*Fig. 11.2. Archaic marine artifacts from 9000 to 2000 BCE. From American Discovery, by Gunnar Thompson, Ph.D.*

Virtually identical bone combs and carvings produced by North America's Maritime Archaic and Western Europe's Neolithic societies self-evidently resulted from a shared cultural impetus. A carving from Maine appears to depict a lunar representation of some kind. Inside its vertical rectangle are two diagonals bisected below midpoint by a horizontal line. At top left, where the upper diagonal rises into the corner, appears a circle representing the Moon, as suggested by thirteen smaller circles running along the rectangle's left side from top to bottom: thirteen phases of the Moon make up one lunar month of twenty-eight days.

Lunar calendars were particularly associated with seamanship in the ancient Old World. Perhaps Nulliak Cove's most obvious connection to Stone Age Europe is a burial mound with a rectangular entrance formed by a pair of monoliths crossed at the top by a horizontal lintel. It is virtually a mirror image of Brittany's Merchant's Table, the Table des Marchand, at Locmariaquer.

That the Red Paint People built stone burial mounds no different than those raised along the shores of Western Europe, but not by inland Native Americans, indicates a fundamental overseas' connection. "Massing evidence argues they were one folk," wrote George Read Murray in the premiere issue of *Ancient American* magazine. "The cultures shared a spectrum of traits, including long-occupied settlements along the Atlantic from which they sailed to fish the deep ocean. Another signature of their sameness are three-story middens, trash-heaps treasured by archaeologists. The middens' fills are mostly bones of deep-sea game: whales, porpoises, sharks and seals. The middens' mass tells much. They show Red Paint and Red Ochre folks were skilled sailors, fishers, boat-builders and sail-weavers. The heaps suggest the folk cultivated at least sail fiber, likely hemp, and harvested lumber for boat-hulls."[4]

The credibility of these comparisons is confirmed by their shared chronology. The oldest known physical evidence for the Maritime Archaic is likewise the most northerly site of its kind: a burial cairn—

a man-made pile of stones from the Irish Gaelic *carn*—at Labrador's L'Anse Amour, dated to circa 5500 BCE. It compares with a contemporaneous burial mound of discarded mollusk shells on Téviec, an island near the Quiberon Peninsula in Brittany. L'Anse Amour, the "Cove of Love," is a corruption of its earlier name, L'Anse aux Morts, the "Cove of Death," so called because that part of the world is a wicked place opposed to almost all forms of life. Freezing temperatures made worse by high winds and rough weather do not make for a desirable landfall. What then, could have enticed Neolithic seafarers from far-off, relatively comfortable Western Europe to these long stretches of barren, rocky coastline whipped by perilous waves?

However, Labrador and Newfoundland were not always subjected to the subarctic conditions that prevail there today. Wakefield explains, "Paleoclimate records, drawn from deep Greenland ice cores, now reveal that at the time of the discovery of America by the Megalithic Culture, the Northern Hemisphere was experiencing unusually warm conditions."[5]

The time frame embracing both the Western European megalith-builders and North America's Red Paint People is referred to by paleo-climatologists as the Holocene Climatic Optimum, when temperatures reached several degrees Celsius higher than today, and the Earth's mean sea level was fifteen to eighteen feet above present levels. This period is also called the Older Peron transgression, or Holocene Wet Phase, referred to by archaeologists as the Neolithic Subpluvial—a time of unusually warm temperatures, abundant rainfall, lush growth, and mild climate. Barry Fell (1917–1994), a Harvard professor of invertebrate zoology, but more famous for his books about overseas' visitors to America in pre-Columbian times, pointed out that during the sixth millennium BCE, "The North Atlantic was as warm in the winter as it now is in the summer."[6]

As a consequence, Canada's eastern shores were entirely different and far more hospitable than they now appear. They were fertile areas 7,000 years ago, rich in marine life and agricultural possibilities

Heck (1857)

1. Celtic Stone Circle
France

2. Stone Chamber
France

3. Memorial Chamber
Newgrange, Ireland 3000 BC

4. Dolmen
Ancora, Portugal

5. Cromlech
France

Kronau (1892)

Kronau (1892)

1. Stone Circles
Peru

2. Stone Chamber
Acora, Peru

3. Ceremonial Chamber
Dunleth, Ill.

4. Dolmen
Northern Salem, NY

5. Cromlech Altar
Westport, Ma.

*Fig. 11.3. Old World Cultural Diffusion to America, by Gunnar Thompson, Ph.D. From* American Discovery *magazine.*

the Red Paint People found worth pursuing. "For archaic mariners," Murray argues, "the North Atlantic supported an arc of hop-stones two or three days apart. Sailing easterly, they touched Labrador, Baffin Island and Greenland; from Europe, either Norway or Scotland, were the Faeroes Isles. Iceland, at mid-point, had likely been a midsummer gathering point for sea-beasts and their fishers, alike."[7] This direct passage would have been even more accessible during the rise of milder temperatures seven and eight millennia ago.

Most sites associated with North America's Red Paint People are parallel in time with the European megalith-builders, although the former lingered on much longer, gradually diminishing in skills and numbers. Their mostly mixed descendants may have endured as the Beothuk, native Newfoundlanders, surviving into the early nineteenth century. Although at the time of the first modern European contacts—300 years earlier—they consisted of no more than 500 or 700 individuals, they still built stone cairns over shallow grave pits very reminiscent of Maritime Archaic settlements in Labrador. Covey tells tells how "Emerson Greenman of the University of Michigan found canoe, kayak and dugout types painted in red or black in Pleistocene Spanish caves, La Pasiege, Castillo and La Pileta, which included the mid-ship gunwale peak characterizing Beothuk watercraft of Newfoundland."[8]

More tellingly, the Beothuk made ceremonial use of red ochre, with which they painted their bodies, houses, canoes, weapons, household appliances and musical instruments. "It was the practice to cover the bones of the dead with red ochre in ancient times," explains travel authors Elizabeth Pepper and John Wilcock, "a symbolic reinvestiture of the bones with life."[9] Such adornment was not commonplace, but so sacred that it only took place during an annual multiday celebration of the vernal equinox, a throwback, perhaps, to the solar-oriented standing stones at Nulliak Cove. As additional indication of its importance, red ochre designated Beothuk identity: the pigment was applied to a newborn, signifying the child's tribal initiation. Forbidding a fellow tribesman from wearing red ochre was a form of punishment denoting estrangement from his people.

Whether or not these practices were carried down faithfully, partially, or in any way from Maritime Archaic times is impossible to determine. Even so, persistent ritual employment implies at least a cultural memory of the deeply ancient Red Paint People. Highlighting these parallels was the surprise expressed by modern outside observers struck by the non-Indian physical traits displayed by some Beothuk. Individual instances of fair, wavy hair, rosy complexion, and light-colored eyes, while untypical, were nonetheless persistent over the generations. These anomalous characteristics may have been inherited from the Red Paints. Based on DNA analysis conducted in 2007, archaeologists concluded that the Beothuk were solely of indigenous ancestry. Their examination, however, had been limited to material from the teeth of just two Beothuk individuals who died during the 1820s. A single pair of representatives could not determine the racial identity of an entire tribe, even one as small as the Beothuk.[10]

Had DNA testing made use of Demasduit's genetic material, it might have produced different results. Known to her British benefactors as Mary March—after the month in which she was abducted from her tribe—her 1819 portrait realistically portrays a young woman with distinctly Caucasian facial features. Related analysis in 2010 by a team of European scientists revealed a previously unknown mitochondrial DNA sequence in Iceland, where genetic traces of a Native American woman from prehistoric Labrador were found. Their discovery suggested she had been taken to Iceland either by returning Norse Vikings or much earlier Neolithic sailors, who used Iceland as a stepping-stone to and from the subarctic coast of eastern North America.

Linguistics joined genetics on behalf of Red Paint possibilities, when researchers determined that the Beothuk language was an "isolate," utterly unrelated to Algonkian spoken throughout the region, and to any other known language.

*Fig. 11.4. Early-nineteenth-century portrait of Demasduit, a full-blood Beothuk Native American, last living descendant of New England's Red Paint People. Image from* Ancient American *magazine.*

Whatever secrets this remnant tribe may have preserved about the Maritime Archaic Period were lost with the death in 1829 of the last known living Beothuk. Even before their extinction, speculation ran high that Beothuk ancestors may have been responsible for erecting the strange dolmens that were still encountered in parts of New England and the Canadian Atlantic coastal region. In France alone, more than 4,000 such structures were built during Neolithic times.

Dolmens are usually aligned with specific positions on land or in the heavens. Examples in Wales are sighted on Ursa Major, the Great Bear Constellation. While displayed to a far greater degree at the Grand Menhir Brisé, the ability of their preindustrial creators to raise single stones of prodigious weight and set them with delicate precision upon a set of much smaller supports testifies to an engineering skill modern construction specialists cannot satisfactorily explain. The largest capstone in Europe (100 tons) tops La Bajouliere, a dolmen at St Remy la Varenne, in western France.

"How did these men, without the assistance of proper tools," wondered the renowned New England folklorist and author, Robert Ellis Cahill, "lift and balance boulders weighing from thirty to ninety tons squarely on top of three, little boulders?"[11] He did not, however, have La Bajouliere in mind when he expressed his astonishment. Cahill was instead referring to our country's largest dolmen, featuring a ninety-ton capstone supported on five erect peg-stones planted about four feet into the ground beside a stream in a valley at North Salem, New York. Located near the post office along the main road leading through the small town, the stone anomaly was off-handedly dismissed by mainstream scholars as "a glacial erratic," their term of archaeological insignificance for all megaliths outside the Old World. Orthodox archaeologists insist that such structures do not exist beyond Europe, so they cannot be found here, and those mistaken for "dolmens" must have been accidentally deposited as "perched boulders" by glaciers. In other words, "Nature here duplicated what human wit and sweat did there."[12]

*Fig. 11.5. North Salem Dolmen—New York. Photo from* Ancient American *magazine.*

"If all American dolmens are only glacial boulders," pointed out Fred C. Rydholm, a resident authority on Michigan history and prehistory, "they should be rather unequally distributed over areas once covered by glaciers. This is certainly not the case, however. Doubtless, a glacier could, as a rare event, produce a dolmen-like formation, and a small percentage of American dolmens may have formed that way. But their actual locations tell quite a different story. . . . Over most of the vast territories formerly covered by glaciers there are virtually no dolmen-like structures." Rydholm also observed that North American dolmens "stand on three or four supporting stones, as European dolmens do."[13]

"That this boulder could be solely the result of glacial forces," James W. Mavor Jr., a leading physicist at Woods Hole Oceanographic Institution (Massachusetts), wrote of the North Salem structure, "is a notion with extremely low probability. . . . Pedestaled boulders supported by quarried pedestals, clearly erected by man, have been identified in New England."[14]

What appears to be a pictographic image on its surface suggests at least some human modification of the structure during the past. In "The Mysterious Megaliths of New England," science reporter Paul Tudor Angel wrote of America's dolmens, "serious scientists and archaeologists have denied their study because of their monumental implications: It would force them to throw away their pre-conceived notions about the achievements of ancient man into the historical garbage can."[15]

Although North Salem's dolmen may be the largest such example in our country, it is by no means the only such specimen. Phaeton Rock, in Lynn, Massachusetts, was summarily brushed off during the mid-nineteenth century by Joseph Henry, the Smithsonian Institution's earliest director, as having been carried "from Canada and lodged in its present elevated position during what is called the drift period, and was probably transported through the agency of ice."[16] More than 100 years later, after having determined that its three supporting stones were set at a 75-60-45-degree triangle, James P. Whittall III was skeptical: "This dolmen seems to have been erected with mathematical precision." He found it "extremely difficult to consider this monument a glacial erratic."[17]

Founder and first director of the Early Sites Research Society (Massachusetts) in 1973, Whittall was no armchair archaeologist. He is renowned, among other related accomplishments, for his discovery and excavation of a "Red Paint burial in a mound which produced a skeleton (dated to 7500 BP) and one of the earliest fluted points in the East."[18] He went on to investigate another dolmen—referred to by local Coaxets of the Wampanoag tribe as *Hassaneghk,* or "stone house with stone roof"— in Westport, Massachusetts, on the coast of Buzzard's Bay, about 1,500 feet from the sea. "All references to this structure by owners of the property (three families) down to the present day," he noted, "state that the dolmen was an Indian relic, used as a threshing table for corn. It is an established fact that the Indians of this area did not do heavy stone work, much less move a four-ton slab of granite onto leg piers for corn thresh-ing!" Its large capstone stood about two feet off the ground on three much smaller supports, prompting the well-traveled Whittall to observe, "I have seen a matching structure in the Orkney Islands."[19]

He visited another dolmen at Martha's Vineyard, an island located south of Cape Cod in Massachusetts, previously known in Wam-panoag as Noepe, "the land amid the streams." There, atop a small knoll referred to as Quista, he found four large boulders arranged in a rough circle with an opening on the down-hill side. These stones are about two feet in height, and form a remarkably tight wall. The two on either side of the opening were evidently selected for their smooth surface and give the doorway a symmetrical appearance. On top of these stones rests a huge, quarried capstone, roughly circu-lar in shape, and weighing about two tons. A few quoins are placed beneath it, to chink up various openings. The chamber thus formed is about 2.5 feet in height, and slightly more than three feet wide, by about six feet long. The opening faces the southwest . . . if we com-pare this structure to those in Western Europe, we find that we have a chamber that parallels very closely the portal graves or dolmens of the megalithic period.[20]

That the Red Paint People of North America's eastern seaboard and northern Europe's Red Ochre People were the same postglacial seafar-ers who erected standing stones on both continents seems self-evident. More surprising were the megaliths trailing behind their expansion westward across the Upper Great Lakes Region and beyond into the Rocky Mountains.

# 12

# Sacred Hoops

*History, to be above evasion, must stand on documents,*
*not on opinion.*

JOHN DALBERG-ACTON (1834–1902),
BRITISH HISTORIAN

To be sure, at least some "glacial erratics" have been mistaken for mega-liths, but many of New England's stone structures are too self-evidently artificial for natural formations. A case in point is New Jersey's Tripod Rock located in Morris County's Pyramid Mountain Natural Historical Area. Sitting near the edge of a long ridge, the nineteen-foot-long, ten-foot-wide, 7.5-foot-tall stone of granitelike Precambrian gneiss weighs forty tons more than Europe's heaviest megalithic table, La Bajouliere, in western France. Tripod Rock balances on a trio of much smaller boulders, each about three feet in diameter, raising it above the long ridge on which it sits near the edge by about 1.5 feet at the lowest level. Points where they touch the underside of the rock form an approximate 3-4-5 triangle.

The number three is repeated northwest of Tripod Rock, about forty feet away, where another triangle is laid out by three boulders—the two largest partially resting, dolmenlike, on smaller rocks. A line of sight midway between them aimed from a bedrock outcrop near Tripod Rock at a third stone serving as the apex—approximately ten feet away to the northeast—points directly to the next ridge on the horizon in the west. There, the sun went down each summer solstice on its precise setting-point over a large boulder on the far ridge. This annual event occurred for unknown thousands of cycles until the early 1980s, when the stone marker was removed during construction of a private home.

Despite this damage to the original precise alignment, "the effect is still quite striking and worth viewing," according to Bruce Scofield, who tells how

> small crowds gather each June 21st to watch the summer solstice sunset from between the two markers. . . . From the position of the observer, the summer solstice occurs approximately fifteen to twenty minutes before the true horizon sunset at that time of year. During the period around the summer solstice, a few days before and after June 21st, the sun is observed to set over the next ridge to the west, Stony Brook Mountain, at approximately 8:20 p.m., Eastern Daylight Time. . . . The original survey suggested a possible winter solstice alignment, but this was not confirmed visually.[1]

These solar orientations and repetition of the number three are alluded to by a triangular crest running along the length of the top of Tripod Rock from front to rear, suggesting a celestial alignment. Whatever heavenly target it may be sighting still eludes archaeoastronomers, although the crest was either deliberately sculpted, or the 140-ton boulder was specifically chosen for this natural—if unusual—feature. In either case, the structure's man-made character as an astronomical marker is clear. The great stone itself, however, implies at least some dressing or modification, given its untypically barrel-like configuration. Two more smaller dolmens measuring about three to ten feet in diameter stand northeast of Tripod Rock, although their celestial orientation, if any, has not thus far been determined. But the entire site's

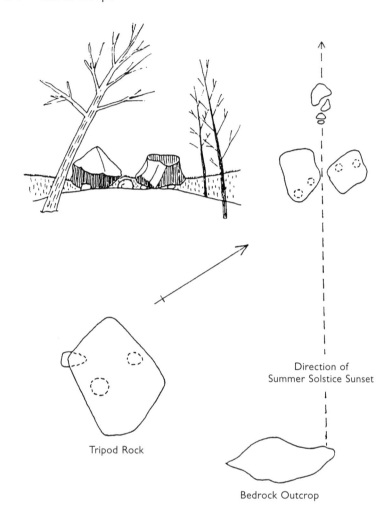

Tripod Rock

Direction of
Summer Solstice Sunset

Bedrock Outcrop

*Fig. 12.1. The placement of New Jersey's Tripod Rock*

astronomical character appears on the outcropping of bedrock where
Tripod Rock sits at the center of a rough oval formed by boulders, each
averaging ten feet across.

So too, Western Europe's megalithic "circles" are more ovals, as
they mimic the ellipsoidal rotation of celestial targets. "The very name,
'stone circles,' is misleading," writes Dr. Maelee Thomson Foster, "as
none are true, geometric circles. . . . Much of the variance between stone
circles is the result of orientation to different cosmic events. Statistical

and astronomical studies, such as those reported in Alexander Thom's *Megalithic Sites in Britain,* indicate that slight asymmetries in the shape result from remarkably accurate observations of cosmic movements that are subsequently recorded within the design of the circle itself."[2]

Ancient Old World parallels continue. Merlin is described by the twelfth-century cleric Geoffrey of Monmouth in his chronicle *Historia Regum Britanniae* ("History of the Kings of Britain") as having floated Stonehenge—likewise aligned with summer solstice sunsets—through the air from its original location atop Ireland's Mount Killaraus to its current resting place on the Salisbury Plain, in England.[3] New Jersey's Delaware Indians, also known as the Abnaki, or Wabanaki—"People of the Dawn," or "Easterners"—were a resident Algonquian tribe whose elders similarly claimed that a sorcerer very long ago employed native "medicine" to levitate Tripod Rock into position.

Not far away, near a brook, is an ancient rock shelter with a typically large overhang. Extensive excavations of Bear Rock, as it is known, during the late nineteenth century recovered numerous artifacts, some still owned by local museums. Among these prehistoric materials were stone tools, perhaps the very implements used to shape Tripod Rock. Despite an abundance of demonstrable celestial alignments, it generates little interest among mainstream scientists, who are sure its astronomical orientations are nothing more than a fortuitous work of Nature. Mary Jasch, a travel writer for *Skylands Visitor,* had her doubts: "Some people may wonder about the odds of three tripods in one location. Is it a monument to the power of sheer chance and geological forces? Or did someone build the tripods?"[4]

They share so many details in common with their overseas' counterparts, even the most conventional archaeologist would unhesitatingly embrace North American structures like Tripod Rock as authentic dolmens if they appeared anywhere in Western Europe. New Jersey's Tripod Rock and its associated formations are not only physically indistinguishable from Western European versions, both feature astronomical alignments—sometimes to the same celestial event. Barry Fell found "it difficult to distinguish the North American examples from the European ones, and believe that both sets were produced by ancient builders, who shared a common culture."[5]

With supportive evidence taken into account, "the relationship of the American examples to those of northern Europe becomes undeniable." According to Paul Angel, there "are in fact over two hundred examples of dolmens in New England alone."[6] Western European impact on ancient North America was not confined to the Atlantic coastal regions, however. That the megalith-builders penetrated deep into its interior is confirmed by their identifiable monuments found mostly in New England, where their transatlantic arrival would be expected, and the Upper Middle West, particularly around the Great Lakes region. It was here that a prehistoric mining enterprise of epic proportions removed in excess of 500 million pounds of the world's highest grade copper, beginning around the turn of the fourth millennium BCE.

"This estimate could miss the mark by a considerable amount in either direction," stated James P. Scherz, Professor Emeritus, University of Wisconsin (Madison), who applied his surveying and civil engineering skills to archaeoastronomy.

> But even if these estimates were in error by 50 percent or more, the conclusions are essentially the same—watercraft, and not the backs of natives must have been used to move the ancient copper nuggets. When we translate this weight of copper into tons, the magnitude of this prehistoric enterprise becomes more comprehensible. For example, if a railroad car of the type used in the 1800s carried about fifty tons of copper, then the number of railroad cars required to haul the prehistoric excavations would have been a quarter-of-a-million tons, for fifty tons per car, equalling five thousand railroad cars filled with copper nuggets. Unlike trainloads of modern ore, which may contain 2 percent or 4 percent metal, these five thousand railroad cars carried essentially pure copper.
>
> If there were one hundred railroad cars per trainload, they would

equal fifty trainloads of copper nuggets. Given the average length of a railroad car at twenty-five feet, each train is twenty-five-by-one-hundred feet, equaling twenty-five hundred feet, about one-half mile long. If all fifty trains were parked on a track, end-to-end, their combined length would be twenty-five miles of railroad cars, with each car carrying about fifty tons of nuggets. If the Michigan copper was removed over a two thousand-year period (roughly 3000 BC to 1000 BC), then in each year, on the average, there had to have been the equivalent of two railroad cars freighting one hundred tons worth of copper each summer. It is hard to imagine this amount of copper being carried on the backs of Indians over trails or even over portages each summer for two millennia.[7]

The engineering skills and man-power organization that went into Michigan's prehistoric mining operations were matched only by the hundreds of multiton megaliths then being erected with astronomical precision on a comparable global scale. Eighteen centuries after they began, the digs came to an abrupt halt. This time frame exactly coincides with the final phases of megalith-building, signifying the arrival of Western Europeans at Michigan's Upper Peninsula, where mining was primarily focused. Archaeologists have been unable to account for the 223,215 or more tons of copper excavated from 5,000 pit mines—some of them sunk sixty feet down through solid rock—by an organized labor force that numbered tens of thousands of workers.

Clearly, such a prodigious task was undertaken for the manufacture of bronze, which requires high-grade copper—not abundantly available in the Old World—combined with zinc and tin. The Upper Peninsula deposits—the highest grade on Earth—disappeared into the Bronze Age furnaces of Europe and the Near East for the mass production of tools and weapons far superior to any previous kinds. Copper was the nuclear fission of its day—the most valuable resource for peoples transitioning from Stone Age tribal society to Bronze Age high civilization, and worth their maximum efforts to obtain it in quantity.

Confronted by the vast stretches and formidable natural obstacles of the North American continent, they required a network of reliable timepieces that were also prominent markers acting as guideposts along optimum travel routes to the mining region and other important locations associated with it. "Trackways and sea-routes provided a linkage of sites," says Dr. Foster, "the megalith itself serving as beacon and territorial symbol."[8] The design of these permanent seasonal calendars and directional indicators was already at hand in the dolmens previously set up by megalith-builders across Western Europe.

A northern Minnesota look-alike standing in the Superior National Forest is the Sawbill Dolmen. Known earlier as the Lujenda Stone, it indicates a water passage from Lake Lujenda, where it crosses over the divide from the St. Lawrence River system into the Hudson Bay drainage, placing travelers squarely amid the copper mining region. Outdoor reporter Bryan Hansel wondered if this and other similar stones, popularly referred to by local residents as "Norse altars," were set up by "5th century Vikings." But the Northmen were not known for erecting dolmens, nor did the so-called Viking Age commence until 300 years later. He nonetheless voices area speculation incorrectly associating Midwestern megaliths with visitors from medieval Scandinavia.[9] The Lujenda Stone or Sawbill Dolmen is not alone in the Upper Great Lakes Region, however.

*Fig. 12.2. Northern Minnesota's Lujenda Stone, or Sawbill Dolmen. Photo from* Ancient American *magazine.*

A specimen of particular importance to the ancient miners still stands in the mountains of Michigan's Upper Peninsula, overlooking Lake Superior. Northwest of Marquette, Huron Mountain is "used today as a recognizable landmark for summer sailors of the Great Lakes," observes Professor Scherz, "just as it may have served prehistoric mariners freighting copper cargoes."[10]

Huron Mountain's dolmen comprises a granite boulder some three feet high, four feet long, and three feet wide, with an estimated weight of 300 pounds, placed on three roughly triangular supports of approximately the same size, about one foot at their base. The larger stone appears to have been artificially shaped to a distinct point on one side and a flat back on the other for a specific purpose, as Scherz discovered when he surveyed the structure in the context of its surroundings. A line of sight from a perched rock in the distance to the little dolmen points to a notch in a ridge a few miles to the west.

"When the Sun set south of this line," he explained:

The fall or autumnal equinox had arrived. From the large boulder to the dolmen, the Sun set in line with a very prominent notch on the horizon. The Sun goes down along this line on about October 30th. It signifies a propitious moment to leave this northern land, and relocate to a place where the winters are less severe. Interestingly, the date of about October 30th also corresponds to what is called the "fall cross-quarter day" period in the solar calendar, midway between the autumnal equinox and the winter solstice. Although the cross-quarter days were far more important to ancient people than in our time, we still honor the ancient fall-cross quarter period with Halloween (Hallows Eve), and All Saints and All Souls Day in the Catholic Church calendar.

It was at this time that ancient Europeans honored the memories of their dead ancestors. Interestingly, the natives of the New World also had a ceremony to honor their dead ancestors at the same period. This "Feast of the Dead" is still celebrated in Mexico and corresponds to the fall cross-quarter day ceremonies. If a hiker on the south shore of Lake Superior lost his calendar, he knew when these old ceremonies would be due to take place by watching the setting Sun from near the dolmen atop Huron Mountain.[11]

Other lithic timekeepers have been found thirty-two miles from shore, on the largest island in Lake Michigan, thirteen miles long and six miles across. Beaver Island is mostly flat and sandy, providing an ideally unobstructed platform for its seven circles of stone to complete their alignments with the sky. Their high number for such a small location testifies to its use as a celestial observatory staffed by a small community of astronomers, who were well-fed by a sophisticated system of local garden beds producing abundant yields of squash, corn, and other crops. Beaver Island's largest astronomical arrangement is 397 feet across, composed of thirty-nine stones ranging from two feet to ten feet in diameter.

Like virtually all other megalithic configurations in both the Old and New Worlds, it is not truly circular, but oval, reflecting its heavenly orientations. A 4-foot-wide, 2.5-foot-high round stone at the precise midpoint features a depression atop its center to accommodate an alignment post (known as a gnomon), serve as a bowl for signal fires for sacrificial offerings, or some other unknown function. Similarly cupped stones were used by the Incas and their predecessors in far-off Peru, supposedly to reflect starlight or moonlight when filled with water for observational purposes.

In any case, Beaver Island appears to have been the hub of an astronomical complex that ancient mariners and miners depended on for vital sailing and seasonal timetables. This celestial network spread over the entire Upper Great Lakes Region wherever the valuable copper was being excavated, and into Central Ontario, where another dolmen stands in Algonquin Provincial Park, located between Georgian Bay and the Ottawa River. Two Canadian dolmens in the remote Caneopiscou area of Quebec were accidentally discovered by a pair of caribou hunters during 2005, although several more dolmens at the Melville Peninsula in the Northwest Territory have been known since at least the mid-twentieth century.

Also in Quebec, a pointed megalith has been perched upright at a specific angle atop Mt. Eternity, overlooking the Saguenay Fjord and Eternity Bay. From here, the Pierre Hexagonal Stone indicates sunrise and sunset on the vernal and autumnal equinoxes, and on the summer and winter solstices. The same solar orientation the Pierre Hexagonal Stone shares with Huron Mountain's dolmen and other megaliths in North America and Western Europe demonstrates a cultural identity common to them all.

*Fig. 12.3. Quebec's Pierre Hexagonal Stone is aligned to various solar orientations. Photo from* Ancient American *magazine.*

While the special relationship between these two continents began with hunting-fishing abundance off the Eastern Seaboard, followed by copper transported from the Upper Peninsula, the seafaring megalith-builders expanded their influence westward into the plains and foothills of the Rocky Mountains from Colorado, Wyoming, Montana, and North Dakota into Alberta and Saskatchewan. Throughout this broad region, they laid out at least seventy stone circles, known to Native Americans in their vicinity as "Sacred Hoops" or "Medicine Wheels."

These are typically large circular arrangements of stones marked by small rock piles connected to spokelike lines of more stones radiating outward from a central cairn. Their physical resemblance to ancient Old World counterparts and time frame contemporaneous with Western Europe's Megalithic Age complements tribal accounts describing construction of the oldest Medicine Wheels by non-Indian "sky worshippers" in the deep past.

Similar venerable oral traditions have been confirmed by archaeoastronomers, who found numerous orientations among prehistoric Sacred Hoops to the stars Aldebran in the constellation Taurus, Rigel in Orion, and Sirius in Canis Major. Rigel rises just past dawn, twenty-eight days after Aldebran, as Sirius does following Rigel. So too, each Medicine Wheel is typically made of twenty-eight spokes, which compute the stellar cycle and correspond to the number of days in a single lunation. Dr. David Zink marveled how such stone arrangements "reveal the surprisingly sophisticated consciousness behind their construction."[12]

Gerald Hawkins concurred that they constituted "unwritten evidence for astronomical knowledge of a high order in a prehistoric culture."[13] Found high in the mountains, such structures seem out of place to materialist scholars unable to understand them as anything more than agricultural calendars. Instead, no population centers or even small village sites lay close to the circles, positioned as they are in barren, often virtually inaccessible locations. Remarkably, many (if not most, or all) Medicine Wheels, although usually separated by hundreds of miles, are aligned with each other. Wyoming's Bighorn Medicine Wheel and Saskatchewan's Moose Mountain Sacred Hoop are identical, though nearly 500 miles of mountainous territory lie between them. They are both approximately seventy-five feet across and feature twenty-eight spokes (the Rigel-Aldebran Cycle). Composed of rounded boulders, central cairns at both sites are thirty feet in diameter. From each radiate five lines of smaller stones forming circles six feet wide. A sixty-two-by-fifty-foot ellipse surrounds either cairn.

*Fig. 12.4. Wyoming's Medicine Wheel in Bighorn National Forest. Photo courtesy of the U.S. Forest Service.*

Just inside the border with Alberta, due east of Empress, sitting on the northern rim of the South Saskatchewan River Valley, is the Roy Rivers Medicine Wheel. It is entirely configured to represent a sunburst, appropriately enough, because the formation is aligned with sunset on the summer solstice.

Another singular Sacred Hoop was laid out in the image of a dog atop a knoll overlooking the Big Muddy River Valley in south-central Saskatchewan, just west of the town of Minton. The unique bioglyph is 130 feet long, with a thirty-foot-wide circle of stones in the center and a sunburst design at its left side. Even more remarkably, the Minton Medicine Wheel's primary axis is aligned to the rising of Sirius, famous throughout pre-Classical Western Europe and the Near East as "the dog star." Appropriately, its appearance heralded New Year's Day for dynastic Egyptians. That they and the ancient inhabitants of Canada should have especially referenced Sirius is intriguing enough, but their identical association of the star with canine imagery is proof of contact.

As such, direct connections in the form of shared astronomy between Saskatchewan's stone circle and the ancient Old World are self-evident.

Those connections are made all the more apparent by relative time frames. In 1971, partial excavations at Alberta's Majorville Medicine Wheel showed it was laid out just when megalith-building was flourishing in Brittany and the British Isles—4,500 YBP. "Radio-carbon dating of bone from the bottom of the central cairn confirmed this date," writes sacred sites encyclopedist, Brad Olsen.

East of the village of Milo, Majorville covers sixteen square miles, making it not only the oldest, but greatest Sacred Hoop in Canada; only Wyoming's Bighorn Medicine Wheel, which it closely resembles, is slightly larger. Majorville measures "29 feet in diameter, and 5.3 feet high," Olsen continues, "a surrounding stone ring eighty-eight feet in diameter, and twenty-eight stone lines connecting the two features. The twenty-eight spokes of the Majorville wheel may represent the twenty-eight days in a lunar month, suggesting this site was likely a ceremonial center, as well as an astronomical calendar."[14]

The site's central cairn atop one of a series of low hills overlooks the Bow River, about forty-five miles east of Calgary. Retired University of Alberta professor Gordon Freeman, who is intimately familiar with the site, has stated that Majorville "marks the changing seasons and the phases of the Moon with greater accuracy than our current calendar."[15]

Like their European counterparts, North American megaliths served multiple purposes. Sometimes they memorialized the honored dead, or indicated a specific direction. Others were astronomical computers. Occasionally, all three functions combined in a single site. Every surviving example, however, stands as irrefutable testimony to the enduring greatness of a vanished people.

# 13

# Little Hell

*The value of history is that it teaches us what Man has
done and thus what Man is.*

R. G. COLLINGWOOD (1889–1943),
BRITISH HISTORIAN

The prehistoric purveyors of astronomical knowledge embodied it in permanent structures from New England and the Upper Middle West to the West and Northwest. Their impact on ancient America, however, spread far beyond the Rocky Mountains. Listed by the National Register of Historic Places in 2002, the so-called Florida Stonehenge was discovered by accident four years earlier during excavation for a Miami apartment building. The prehistoric structure was cut four feet down into the limestone bedrock to form a thirty-eight-foot diameter, perfectly circular platform. Around its perimeter, twenty-four identical uniformly spaced oval holes, from six to twelve inches in width, originally held as many posts—corresponding to hours of a single day.

The site's astronomical character is emphasized by its two holes facing due north with single holes at the other cardinal points. One hole not only faces east, but has a discernable "eye" with stone pupil carved in it, underscoring the structure's identification as an observatory. Its position on the south bank of the Miami River, which empties into Biscayne Bay and connects directly with the Atlantic Ocean, suggests the maritime provenance of its builders. Excavation of the Miami Circle yielded numerous shell tools, axheads, shark teeth, a dolphin's skeleton, and other items of aquatic origin.

Charcoal from fires and human teeth were radiocarbon dated to around 200 BCE, a period when south Atlantic coastal Florida was inhabited by the Tequesta Indians, who lived there from 500 BCE until they were virtually wiped out by disease and wars in 1763 CE. While their habitation of the site more than 2,000 years ago is certain, they were not responsible for its construction—it represents a level of cultural sophistication they never attained. They were nomadic hunter-gatherers unfamiliar with the kind of settled existence required by the Miami Circle, nor exhibited the considerable organized labor required to raise it. They did not build in stone, nor were they astronomers. Their own domiciles were actually inferior to those set up by other tribes, and if they did build the Miami Circle, it was their only such construction—an unlikely proposition—and far superior to anything else they ever made, before or after.

Additional examination of the location should reveal an antiquity deeper than debris left by visiting Tequesta in the third century BCE. Some physical evidence already points away from them: They were not known to have traded much beyond their immediate area, yet chert from the state's upper west coast, Georgia basalt, and galena from Illinois-Missouri at the Mississippi River have been recovered from the site. More revealingly, the Miami Circle has yielded copper ingots excavated by the ancient miners of Michigan Upper Peninsula. None of these materials, moreover, appear to have ever been used by the Tequesta.

From Florida, the megalith-builders sailed southward to leave their mark on South America. In Colombia, 109 menhirs carved from pink sandstone stand in two rows—fifty-four in the north, fifty-five in the south—outside the Boyacá Department's Villa de Leyva, ninety-four miles from Bogotá, in "Little Hell." The name was occasioned by mid-sixteenth-century Spanish conquistadors suffering from the tropical savannah climate's intense heat, which seemed appropriate for the "diabolical" monuments they encountered. Like Michigan's Huron Mountain dolmen, a seventeen-foot-high central column, now missing, was oriented to the vernal and autumnal equinoxes. As early as 1845, the renowned German naturalist and explorer Alexander von Humboldt stated in his five-volume work, *Kosmos,* that El Infiernito was an astronomical observatory.[1] He wondered, too, if it was an entirely aboriginal complex, or imported, at least conceptually, from Stone Age Europe— and not solely for its physcal resemblances to European megaliths.

*Fig. 13.1. Lined up like soldiers standing at attention are the monoliths of Colombia's El Infiernito.*

The indigenous U'wa people, who had virtually no contact with the outside world until the 1970s, believe Little Hell's menhirs are their ancestors, who were turned to stone during the ancient past after landing on the shores of Colombia as survivors from a great flood. Remarkably, their oral tradition is a rendition of the Greek myth of Deucalion, the deluge-hero, who, following his escape from the natural catastrophe, repopulated the devastated Earth by throwing rocks over his shoulder; as they struck the ground, they turned into men and women, the ancestors of all subsequent peoples.

Archaeologists believe El Infiernito parallels a calendar used by the Muisca, a native people who take their name from Muyscas, the "Civilizer." When a wicked goddess caused the world to flood, he compelled Huitaca to forever hold up the sky. Thereafter, the bearded "White One" laid down ground rules for Colombia's first civilization, then departed, leaving behind four chiefs to govern through his authority and example.[2] This native myth parallels Plato's fourth-century BCE dialogue, the *Kritias*, listing Musaeus, "Of the Muses," as the fifth king of Atlantis, which perished in a cataclysm; Muisca means, literally, "the Musical Ones."[3] Elsewhere in Greek myth, Atlas, the first monarch of Atlantis (which derived its name from him) was portrayed supporting the heavens on his shoulders as eternal punishment for rebelling against the Olympian gods. "On the common interpretation of mythic traditions," concluded the late nineteenth-century British mythologist, W. S. Blackett, "these Atlantides ought to be provinces or places in South America."[4]

The earliest carbon-14 date obtained at El Infiernito so far is 2,880 ± 95 Years Before Present, about three centuries after the close of the Megalithic Age in Europe. Although further deeper testing with improved dating techniques may find older levels, Little Hell's menhirs could have been moved from an earlier location. Sacred stones were occasionally transported from one place to another in various parts of the ancient world. Examples include Bangkok's Lak Muang column, previously set up at the fabled Thai capital, Ayutthaya; and the Lia Fáil, or "Stone of Destiny," removed from Ireland's old capital, Tara, where it was the "Coronation Stone," taken to the Hebredean island of Iona, thereafter carried to the Scottish city of Scone (pronounced "skoon"), then London's Westminster Abbey, and back again to Scotland. Alternatively, Little Hell's lithic technology, previously introduced elsewhere in Colombia, was subsequently transplanted near Villa de Leyva.

Either possibility is worth considering within the context of San Agustín, the largest collection of megalithic sculpture in all South America. Located 340 miles from Bogotá, it includes several dolmens indistinguishable from Western European types. Archaeologists Julio Cesar Cubillos and Luis Duque Gomez have developed a credible time frame for San Agustín, beginning with an Archaic Period from around 3300 BCE to 1000 BCE, which roughly embraces the late half of the Megalithic Age. While the precise number of Colombian standing stones has not been determined, others in the Boyacá Department occur at Chita and Chiscas. Still more are found in Sutamarchán, Tunja, Ramiriquí, Tibaná, and Paz de Río, pushing their total number into the low hundreds, at least.

As recently as 2006, archaeology was turned on its head by discovery of the "Brazilian Stonehenge." Until then, Amazon prehistory was regarded as nothing more than an incrementally inclined flat line of hunter-gatherer development from earliest human arrivals in South America 11,000 years ago to present levels of aboriginal tropical forest horticulture. Nothing there approaching an advanced society was believed to have ever existed. That paradigm was rendered abruptly obsolete when a series of monumental formations came to light outside the village of Calcoene, in Amapa state, near the border with French Guyana, in far-northern Brazil.

They consist of 127 well-preserved granite blocks, each weighing several tons, standing uniformly upright as tall as ten feet in an open field on a hilltop overlooking the bank of a river. The five crownlike circles are evenly spaced from each other and average ninety feet in diameter. Long known to generations of farmers and fishermen in the region, geographers and geologists accidentally encountered the location while conducting a socioeconomic survey by foot and helicopter of the area. They noticed almost at once that one of the larger menhirs evidenced a solar orientation.

"It is this block's alignment with the winter solstice that leads us to believe the site was once an astronomical observatory," said Mariana Petry Cabral, an archaeologist at the Amapa State Scientific and Technical Research Institute. The upright was deliberately positioned to allow the disappearance of its shadow when the sun is directly over it on December 21. "Transforming this kind of knowledge into a monument," Cabral stated, "the transformation of something ephemeral into something concrete, could indicate the existence of a larger population and of a more complex social organization. We may be also looking at the remnants of a sophisticated culture."[5]

Rough estimates at determining its age range from only 500 years to more than two millennia, although such subjective guessing based on no real physical evidence must eventually yield to radiocarbon and stratigraphic examination of the area. Already, however, early limited excavation around the stone circles has yielded numerous ceramic fragments, whole urns with charred bones, and, far more revealingly, the same kind of red ochre used by North America's Maritime Archaic builders of standing stones and contemporaneous megalith-builders from Western Europe. These foreign influences at the Amapa site are underscored by its close proximity to the Atlantic coast, where the Red Paint people would have made their landfall.

Moreover, location of the circles does not suggest they were arranged by native beginners experimenting for the first time in celestial mechanics, who coincidentally raised their menhirs just north of the equator. Quite the contrary, sophistication of Brazil's Stonehenge and its emplacement at this astronomically crucial position argue strongly in favor of the site's deliberate choice of geography and its construction at the hands of outside professional observers already well-versed in the applied principles of calendrical astronomy.

Apparent foreign influences at work among South American megaliths were suspected as long ago as the 1860s, when the renowned American archaeologist E. G. Squier visited a pair of stone formations on the south shore of Peru's Lake Umayo (please see plates 16 and 17 of the color insert). After examining the approximately ninety-foot diameter feature, together with its 150-foot wide companion encompassed by a platform of square-cut blocks, he remarked on "the close resemblance, if not absolute identity of the primitive monuments of the great Andean plateau, elevated thirteen thousand feet above the sea, and fenced in with high mountains and frigid deserts, with those of the other continent."[6]

Squier reported that both structures were known locally as *Intihuatanus,* or "sun circles," reflecting their function as solar observatories. The larger of the two—which has since been obliterated by an early twentieth-century mountain slide—uniquely enclosed a single upright not near the midpoint, but more off-center. Together with its still-surviving counterpart, these "primitive monuments" are in stark contrast to far more sophisticated mortuary towers thirty feet tall and built of skillfully cut blocks that share the immediate vicinity of Silustani, as the area is known. Both obviously belong to radically different cultures separated by thousands of years; the latter chullpas contained deceased royalty of the early fifteenth-century Colla people, while the former Intihuatanus appear to date back millennia earlier to the megalith-builders, whose own "sun circles" they identically resemble.

Whatever comparable associations or astronomical alignments may have once applied to the standing stones of north-central Argentina were lost beginning in 1897. At that time they were progressively removed from their original location in the Calchaquíes Valley—named after the area's extinct native tribe—for study by the Italian archeologist and naturalist Juan Ambrosetti. From 1976 to 1983, 114 scattered monoliths were painstakingly tracked down and collected in the El Mollar District's Parque Los Menhires, an area the size of a football field. Standing twelve to fifteen feet tall, averaging three feet in diameter, and weighing four tons, they were made of granite, like virtually all megaliths elsewhere.

Archaeologists assume the menhirs date to circa 820 BCE, although no evidence for stonework undertaken by the Tafi-I culture of that period exists. In fact, virtually nothing is known about the structures due to Ambrosetti's unfortunate removal from their original settings. According to a *Science* article published in the same year he began investigating them, "some of the decoration [on the menhirs] shown in his cuts [lithographic illustrations] is strikingly like that on the stone pillars of Hatuncolla [capital of the Colla people], two leagues [six miles] from Lake Titicaca, portrayed in Squier's Peru, pages 385 to 386."[7]

This comparison is particularly important to our discussion because it connects Peru's sun circles to the Argentine standing stones. They share a yet more surprising relationship with 11,600-year-old pillars on the other side of the world. Similar to Göbekli Tepe's monoliths, some of the El Mollar District menhirs are represented with engraved faces, arms, and hands to give them a human appearance. Zoomorphic or astronomical motifs, likewise found at the southern Turkish site, decorate other monoliths. Many of the abstract or geometric patterns covering them also suggest designs found at Göbekli Tepe and Neolithic sites or artifacts.

The Parque Los Menhires' specimens additionally recall chapter 7's examination of a possible affinity between Anatolia's "Navel Hill" and Polynesia's "Navel of the World," where similarly anthropomorphic standing stones were likewise created. That Argentina may have served as a link connecting South American and Pacific megalith-building is suggested by surviving Calchaquí pottery adorned with line drawings of birds, reptiles, and human faces duplicating Peruvian and Malay themes. But Easter Island's more famous moai do not comprise sole evidence for standing stones in the Pacific.

Almost impossible on which to make landfall for its boulder-strewn coasts and high seas, with neither trees nor fresh water, thirty-nine-acre Neckar Island—unknown even to Polynesian mariners until its European discovery in 1789—is a highly unlikely location for human civilization of any kind. Yet, it is covered with thirty-four archaeological zones, including two prehistoric cemeteries, together with fishhooks, sinkers, fiber fishing lines, cowery shell lures, hammerstones, grindstones, adzes, and innumerable other tools—physical proof for large, settled populations in an environment unable to support life. P. V. Kirch, who visited the islet during the early 1980s, reported that the "*marae* [ceremonial stone stages] are amazingly consistent in plan and architectural style, and consist basically of a low, narrow, rectangular platform adjoining a paved rectangular court or terrace. Arrayed along the platform are a series of upright stone slabs, while other slabs are positioned at certain points in the court."[8]

Menhirs in Fiji are sometimes engraved with the same kind of concentric circles found at megalithic sites from the shores of Lanzarote, in the Canary Islands off the Atlantic coast of North Africa, to Colombia's San Agustín. Tahiti features its own marae enclosing ten monoliths irregularly positioned for specific celestial alignments. Rarotonga, in the Cook Islands, is encompassed by an ancient road, known as the Ara Matua, that skirts a marae measuring twenty-five feet by fifty feet, likewise with ten monoliths. The 711 miles of open water separating Tahiti from Raratonga suggest that both islands belonged to a common megalithic culture. Tahiti derived its name from the Hiti, antediluvian giants in Samoan myth, who ruled the world and built the marae before "the heavens fell down" to set their island aflame.

Due east from Australia, 'Esi Makafakinanga is a six-foot-tall, ten-ton stone driven into the ground at Niutoua, on Tonga. In its immediate vicinity are two more monoliths, plus a dolmen. Among the most obscure islands in the vast Pacific Ocean is Babeldaob, largest of 343 in the Palau cluster. At Bairulchau, on the northern end of the island, several sets of standing stones, averaging thirteen feet tall and three tons apiece, have been arranged in rows. One arrangement on a hilltop overlooking the sea comprises fifty-two menhirs, just two short of an otherwise identical collection in far-away Colombia's Little Hell. The Micronesian inhabitants neither claim responsibility for Babeldaob's hundreds of orderly positioned monoliths, nor preserve any folk traditions associated with them.

An eight-foot-high obelisk fronting the rising sun in New Guinea is surrounded by a circle of smaller uprights. Similar formations are found on remote islands off Wewak, among the Schouten Group. Atop a mountain in New Ireland was discovered an outstanding example of standing stones engraved with concentric illustrations apparently representing the sun. How the circle's eleven-foot-long blocks, each weighing in excess of five tons, were hauled up to the summit of Mount Kambu's twenty-five-hundred-foot peak is not known.

"They are so ancient," writes Australian author Keith Willey in

*Assignment: New Guinea,* "that the natives do not even have legends about them."[9] Although broken, a beautifully carved menhir inexplicably alone in the jungles of Malekula still stands about thirteen feet tall and weighs approximately fifteen tons. A specialist in Melanesian megaliths, John Layard, found a twelve-foot-tall example in the mainland village of Tolamp. "Another at the same location," writes archaeologist Dr. David D. Zink, "originally stood over thirty feet. The breadth at the base was over three-and-a-half feet. Broken into three pieces, only eight-and-one-half feet of this coral monolith stood at Layard's arrival."[10]

Kai natives claim New Guinea's oldest megalithic centers were erected by a race of giants who ruled the world before a cataclysmic flood changed their bodies into immense stone blocks. This Kai version is essentially the same transformation Colombia's U'wa people used to explain the megaliths of El Infiernito, and the mechanism by which the Greek Deucalion repopulated the world after the Deluge. It was also repeated in Palau to explain the presence of ancient monoliths at Bairulchau, on Babeldaob. The Kai, however, refer to the extinct giants as the Ne-Mu. More than sixty of their naturally mummified remains were found during the mid-1930s, sitting chin-to-chin in a limestone cave located at New Guinea's goldfield district of Morabe. According to an article in *Science Newsletter,* "The most remarkable feature of these mummies is their light skin."[11] Mixed descendants of the Ne-Mu survived at least into the early twentieth century.

An *Australian Geographer* article told of the relatively fair-complected Tarifyroro, who dwelt in the country's virtually inaccessible hinterland. "At one time," according to the resident magistrate of New Guinea, Jack Hides, "these light-skinned people inhabited the whole of this tableland and were driven back westward by the more virile Papuans."[12]

More than 600 menhirs originally made up New Zealand's large Waitapu circle before they were deliberately thrown down by Maori tribesmen, perhaps during the early seventeenth century. "Nothing was left 'standing' after the site was destroyed by the warriors," according to local leading authority, Martin Doutré. "The stones, thankfully, lie very close to their original positions, and need only to be stood up again. The site has delivered up its former geometric layout through careful surveying," which reveal its "stone components laid out in recognizable, geometric patterns."[13]

Today's sole surviving megalithic cultures inhabit remote parts of the Indonesian archipelago, although their existence was unknown to the outside world until the late nineteenth century. On Nias, an obscure island off the coast of western North Sumatra, aboriginal handlers were photographed conveying a very large stone block using only ropes and logs to a construction site in 1915. Other similar communities can be found in interior North Sumatra, Sumba island in East Nusa Tenggara, and interior South Sulawesi. It should be pointed out, however, that these native peoples are less megalith-builders than megalith-movers. They never astronomically orient their blocks, which invariably lack the multiple arrangements of very much older monoliths. Their big stones have no celestial or directional qualities, but only represent ancestral spirits, which, if not properly appeased, become vengeful ghosts for the people of Nias and their fellow Austronesians.

Herbert William Krieger (1889–1970), archaeologist and curator of the Division of Ethnology for the United States National Museum of the Smithsonian Institution, served for many years in New Guinea, where he became a leading authority on its natives. "The New Hebridean," he observed, "is actually most concerned with obtaining and slaughtering pigs, with problems of social prestige, which is dependent on wealth, and with the obtaining and keeping of women." Krieger described the *Maki,* a fifteen-year-long ceremony, in which the participant pays homage to his ancestors "with the erection of stone monuments; they (and later he) hover about these monuments. The potential wrath of all ancestors, personified in the devouring Guardian Ghost, who guards the cave through which his ghost must later pass en route to the Land of the Dead, is also evoked in the Maki."[14]

The ceremony concludes with human sacrifice in the more remote areas of New Guinea, but elsewhere pigs are substituted for the benefit of paying tourists too squeamish for total authenticity. Although this ritual behavior forms a connection with the ancient megalith-builders, it soon degenerates into unrelated cultural activities belonging entirely to the Austronesians. They nevertheless self-evidently carry on the megalithic tradition, however diminished.

The authentically ancient menhirs are still referred to throughout Indonesia as a different class of structures distinguished from more recently erected specimens. These Punden Berundak are found in Java, Sumatra, Sulawesi, Lesser Sunda Islands, Pagguyangan Cisolok and Gunung Padang, West Java. Western Europe's characteristic dolmen appears in several examples at Laonatang, a village in the Kanata district; in the jungles around Lambanapu and "in front of the house of a chief of Lewa" who lived there; and many other locations throughout the archipelago.

According to Rex Gilroy, a leading authority on Stone Age sites in the Western Pacific, the highest number of standing stones occurs in Australia, although they are virtually unrecognized by the outside world due to their extremely remote locations.[15]

Many hundreds of better-known megalithic sites were scattered from Hokkaido in the north down thorough the Ryukyus in the extreme south southern islands of Japan. Most were dismantled and used by farmers in the construction of wells or fences. As the American archaeologist Edward Sylvester Morse reported for *Popular Science Monthly*, "I am told by Japanese scholars that their early records call attention to these megalithic chambers existing in different parts of the country. Many of them have been destroyed, either for the purpose of securing the stone they contained for building materials, or to gain ground for cultivation."[16]

But some survived because they were revered as *iwakura*, dwelling places for animistic deities, or concentrations of spiritual energies referred to as *mononoke*. Among the most venerated iwakura today is Takimatsuri-no-kami, at Naiku, in the precinct of the Shrine at Ise. Although few of these places have been professionally investigated, archaeologists were nonetheless able to determine that Japan's earliest stone circles were laid out as long ago as the Early Jōmon Period. It stretched from 7,000 to 4,000 Years Before Present, just when Western Europe's Red Ochre People and North America's Red Paint People were sailing the seas in search of deep-sea game. The Jōmon were not only equally skilled maritime hunters, but identically covered their dead with red ochre. Jōmon, "cord marks" or "cord-patterned," refers to their characteristic pottery designs made by using sticks wrapped with cords. The proper term is *Jōmon doki,* or "rope pattern," signifying earthenware resembling patterns made by rope pressed into the clay.

The Jōmon also raised megalithic structures. Among the last and best known is the 4,000-year-old Oyu specimen in northeastern Japan, Akita Prefecture. It comprises two stone circles referred to as Manza—measuring 144 feet across—and Nonakado, with a 126-foot diameter. At the center of Manza is a three-foot tall upright, generally known as a sundial. According to the official Heritage of Japan web page, "stone circles are often located at a site, usually a mountain location, from which the sunset or stars such as Polaris could be viewed at the time of the equinox or solstice . . . the place of the sunrise over Mount Tsukuba on the morning of the winter solstice was marked by extending a line from the central marker of the stone circle at the Terano Higashi Site of Totigi."[17]

Oyu bears a closer resemblance to North America's mountainous Medicine Wheels, as do most other Japanese stone circles. An example with obvious astronomical orientation is Oshoro, near Otaru, Hokkaido, which is constructed in an ellipse ninety-nine feet by sixty-six feet. One of Japan's largest stone circles is also in Hokkaido, the Morimachi, near Hakodate city, at 111 feet across. Iwate prefecture's Monzen site was built with 15,000 pieces of granite rock carried from the beach about one mile away. Nearby, the Mawaki circle shares a commonality with Florida's Stonehenge in the dolphin bones both entombed.

As in Western Europe, neither menhirs nor dolmens are missing from Japan. "The dolmens are found in the villages Hattori Gawa and Kori Gawa, which lie at the base of a low chain of mountains," Morse

*Fig. 13.2. Remains of a dolphin skull; dolphins were ritually interred at Florida's Miami Circle.*

reported in 1880. "They are widely scattered in groups of several along the slopes of the mountains for a considerable distance; and their general appearance is not unlike the mounds of Upsala, Sweden."[18] Many more dolmens may be found further south, throughout the mountainous region of Tokushima prefecture, around Kyūshū and Shikoku. (Please see plate 18 of the color insert.)

Genetic mapping studies conducted by the foremost population geneticist, Luigi Luca Cavalli-Sforza, documented human expansion across the Sea of Japan into the Korean Peninsula and throughout eastern Asia during the early Jōmon period.[19] This mass movement resulted in the appearance of megalith-building in Korea, where an estimated 30,000 dolmens—comprising 40 percent to 50 percent of the world's total—still survive, in addition to another 70,000 standing stones of various kinds. They are distributed, with a few exceptions, north of the Han River, often in groups, and spread out in lines parallel to the direction of streams, like those found in the Upper Middle Western Great Lakes region of North America. But the Korean structures are primarily burial monuments, a function that accounts for their great numbers. Megalithic formations at Gochang, Hwasun, and Ganghwa have been designated World Heritage sites by the United Nations. (Please see plate 19 of the color insert; a photograph of the megalithic formation at Gochang.)

Dolmens and menhirs appear in far less profusion at Liaoning, Shandong, Zhejiang, and Chou-Chou-Che' in northeast China. As recently as 2003, however, Chinese archaeologists unearthed a 4,100-year-old megalithic site in the northern part of their country, at Shanxi province. According to the official Xinhua News Agency, it is "a semicircle one hundred twenty feet across in the main observation platform, with a one hundred eighty-foot diameter in the outer circle." Standing on the foundation of the first circle, thirteen menhirs formed twelve gaps between them.

"The ancient people observed the direction of sunrise through the gaps and distinguished the different seasons of the year," said He Nu, a spokesman for the Institute of Archaeology at the Chinese Academy of Social Sciences. Both twelve and thirteen were highly significant numbers to ancient astronomers, most often applied to the zodiacal houses, months of the year, hours of the day, and the thirteen lunations, respectively. He and his colleagues "spent a year and a half simulating the observations of the findings at the site. To their surprise, the seasons marked by observation at the site are only one or two days different from the seasonal division of the traditional Chinese calendar."[20]

Dr. Foster writes of the Yan Yuen Shek dolmen in the Wanchai district of Hong Kong: "Its axial tip points to both the Midsummer sunrise and the Midwinter sunset, caught in the notch of a hill."[21] Yan Yuen Shek's orientation is reminiscent of New Jersey's Tripod Rock, which sights in the summer solstice sunset and (probably) winter solstice sunset on the crest of a far ridge. (Please see plate 20 of the color insert.)

Other standing stones have been discovered in Vietnam's Dong Nai province and in the Liao River basin of Manchuria. They marched into India, where "dolmens dot the land from the Nerbuddha River to Cape Comorin. At the latest count [1977], the Neermul jungle of central India has yielded at least two thousand of the monuments," according to science writer Rene Noorbergen, "and another twenty-two hundred have been located in Dacca."*[22] An interesting specimen near Madras stood on four supports atop a hill at Pallicondah, where it was encircled by two concentric rings of smaller stones. The late nineteenth-century French anthropologist, Jean-François-Albert du Pouget, wrote of 2,129 dolmens in the district of Bellary (Deccan) alone.†

Approximately eighty menhirs, some as tall as fourteen feet, and several hundred smaller standing stones are scattered across the agricultural fields of Mudumala, in the Mahabubnagar District of Andhra Pradesh. During early 2006, University of Hyderabad historian Dr. K. P. Rao and his team of investigators, with financial assistance from the University Grants Commission, observed several rows of menhirs aligned to the rising and setting of the sun on both sets of solstices and equinoxes. "This suggests the megalithic community here was aware of the solar trajectories," he said.[23]

Among the greatest and least known mysteries of the Megalithic Age are an estimated 3,000 standing stones—mostly dolmens—that cover approximately 8,000 square miles on both slopes of the Western Caucasus Mountains through Russia and Abkhazia. Although little studied and more often vandalized and destroyed, new specimens are being found every year. Their time parameters range from the late

---

*Noorbergen produced the Netherlands Radio Network, was a reporter for the *London Daily Mail* newspaper, Managing Editor in the Publications Department of the Ford Motor Company, and prolific writer during the mid- to late-twentieth century.
†du Pouget, Marquis de Nadaillac (1818–1904) was a French anthropologist and pale-ontologist; correspondent of the Institut de France; a member of learned societies in every part of the world, including several in the United States; he held decorations from half a dozen governments, besides being a chevalier of the Légion d'honneur. He was among the earliest explorers of the caves in southern France.

fourth millennium BCE to the early second millennium BCE, according to carbon-14 dating of pottery and human remains found at some of the monuments, which lay within the middle and late phases of the Megalithic Age.

While they seem stylistically related to Western European counterparts, Russian versions are distinct for their exceptionally fine workmanship of exactly dressed and fitted slabs and blocks shaped into 90-degree angles to form corners for a rectangular or curves for a circular structure. Most belong to the former kind, with a minority of round dolmens that are particularly attractive. Floor plans are square, trapezoidal, rectangular, and round. In the center of their facade, all the dolmens have been pierced by a large hole executed with a precision remarkable for Neolithic stonework. Most have round portholes, but a few are almost perfect squares. The dolmens sit inside rectangular courtyards usually outlined by large, occasionally three-foot-high stone walls enclosing the court. Their most common decorative motifs are identical to the vertical and horizontal zigzags, hanging triangles, concentric circles, and animal themes adorning contemporaneous structures in Western Europe.

Not found anywhere else, however, are the Western Caucasian structures' large stone spheres. The only similar existing structures are a world away, in the jungles of Costa Rica—which, far from elucidating the mystery in any way, only add to it. While approximately 330 Central American stone balls—some of them more than six feet in diameter and in excess of sixteen tons—have been unearthed since 1940, nothing has been ascertained about their age or human origins. Any connections they might have to the Russian spheres are entirely speculative.

Until the 1950s, an untypical trio stood in a row on the Black Sea coast atop a hill above the Zhane River. The smallest dolmen, at twelve feet across, is rectangular. It was flanked on either side by round dolmens, fifteen feet wide, until Soviet authorities bulldozed them. Many other megalithic structures still stand in Mamed Canyon, and along the shores of the White Sea and the Barents Sea.

Another important location is the Central Ural island of Vera, in Lake Turgoyak. "The isle has so many different ancient constructions that it can be turned into one of the most interesting open air museums, ranking next to Stonehenge, in England," according to the Senior Research Scientist of the Chelyabinsk Research Center at the Institute for History and Archeology of the Urals, a department of the Russian Academy of Sciences.

"Among the most interesting monuments of the isle are its megaliths," says Stanislav Grigoryev. "The largest of them is about eighteen meters [twenty-five feet] long, and weighs about seventeen tons. Most likely, it is a temple complex related to the sun calendar cult. These megaliths average six thousand years old. Their further study may possibly change the history of the mountain forest zone of the Urals in the end of the Stone Age."[24] But who built so many of them in these often remote locations, and why, eludes researchers like Grigoryev.

Further southward from the Western Caucasian Mountains brings our brief survey into Armenia, where megalith building began with Karahunj. Dolmens are found throughout the Middle East and Near East, from northern Lebanon to southern Jordan. They are profusely concentrated in a broad area on either side of the Great Rift Valley, primarily on the east, mostly on the Golan Heights and the Hauran. Jordan may own the highest number of dolmens in the Middle East; Saudi Arabia, in the Hejaz, has the least; and Yemen not many more. About ten miles from the Sea of Galilee's eastern coast, hundreds of dolmens cover the middle of a large plateau. The walls of some are perforated with the same kind of precisely cut portal found more commonly at Russian dolmens in the Western Caucasian Mountains.

Among those in the Syrian region of the Golan Heights is a formation of more than 42,000 rocks arranged in concentric rings 8 feet and 6.6 feet high, 520 feet across, enclosing a mound 65 feet wide. Growing progressively thinner as they near the center, the four embankments are composed of 37,500 metric tons of partly worked basalt. Their northeast entrance follows a 20-foot-long accessway to the circles' midpoint, where a post mounted atop the 15-foot-high tumulus was oriented to sunrise of the summer solstice around the turn of the fourth millennium BCE. This alignment helped investigators determine the age of Rujm el-Hiri, a name referring to the Rephaim. This was a race of "giants," tall megalith-builders exterminated by invading Israelites on orders of Yahweh to seize "the promised land" from its original inhabitants in the Golan Heights.

Egypt's Nabta Playa has been discussed in some detail, although it is not the only megalithic site in North Africa. During 1880, the renowned French anthropologist Girard de Rialle saw "fifteen covered avenues distributed without apparent order," near the Tunisian village of Ellez, on the road from Kef to Kerouan. "The upright stones vary from about ten to thirteen feet, and are surmounted by huge slabs. The chief dolmen has within it as many as ten chambers." Another one hundred or so, "and in excellent preservation," were still standing during his visit to Enfida.

Du Pouget told of approximately 600 dolmens on the slopes of Algeria's Mount Redgel-Safia. He described "a cromlech consisting of a number of concentric circles of large stones set upon an elliptical tumulus, more than fifty-four square yards in area. Quite close is a workshop of flint weapons, probably in use at the time of the erection of the megaliths. In Midjana, the number of megaliths exceeds ten thousand, and General Faidherbe* counted more than two thousand in the necropolis of Mazela, and a yet larger number in that of Roknia," a necropolis in the Guelma region of northeast Algeria consisting of 7,000 dolmens spread over an area of more than a mile.[25]

At Bou-Merzoug, stated M. Feraud [French anthropologist, Berenger-Feraud] in a radius of three leagues [more than ten miles], on the mountain as well as on the plain, the whole country about the springs is covered with monuments of the Celtic [sic] form,

---

*Louis Léon César Faidherbe (1818–1889) was the French colonial administrator of West Africa.

such as dolmens, demi-dolmens, menhirs, avenues, and tumuli. In a word, there are to be found examples of nearly every type known in Europe. For fear of being taxed with exaggeration, I will not fix the number, but I can certify that I saw and examined more than a thousand in the three days of exploration, on the mountain itself, and on the declivities wherever it was possible to place them. All the monuments are surrounded with a more or less complete enceinte [a structure protected by an encircling fortification] of large stones, sometimes set up in a circle, sometimes in a square.[26]

Less than twenty miles from the Atlantic coast, 168 menhirs out of possibly 175 original stones stand in an extremely remote, difficult to find backwater of northern Morocco. Like other celestially oriented megalithic sites, they form an ellipse, with a major axis of 195 feet and a minor axis of 185 feet. More than fifteen feet in height, the tallest monolith is referred to by local inhabitants as El Uted, "the Pointer," suggesting a celestial orientation. At the center of the oval is a large tumulus, badly damaged by archaeological excavations of the mid-1930s, which left a great X-shaped scar still very much in evidence at the location. Forty years later, Mzora, as the structure is known, was surveyed for the first time by the same James Watt Mavor Jr. of the Woods Hole Oceanographic Institution in Massachusetts who investigated New Jersey's controversial dolmen.

"It is this survey," observes Graham J. Salisbury, a well-traveled authority on megaliths, that

revealed Mzora to be not only remarkable in its own right, but to have implications for the history of megalithic sites in Britain. Incredibly, Mzora appears to have been constructed either by the same culture that erected the megalithic sites in France, Britain and Ireland, or by one that was intimately connected with them. The ellipse is constructed using a Pythagorean right-angled triangle of the ratio twelve, thirty-five, thirty-seven. This same technique was used in the construction of British stone ellipses. Furthermore, it appears that the same unit of measure, the megalithic yard (or something remarkably close) used in the construction of the British sites surveyed by Thom, was also used in the construction of Mzora.*[27]

Alexander Thom (1894–1985) was a Scottish engineer who discovered a Stone Age unit of measurement (about 2.72 feet) found at megalithic sites in Western Europe and elsewhere. Mavor's survey showed that the Moroccan structure computes sunrise and sunset on the summer and winter solstices, together with those on both equinoxes. These parallels echo Geoffrey of Monmouth's mid-twelfth-century statement, "The giants of old brought them (the monoliths) from the farthest coasts of Africa, and placed them in Ireland, while they inhabited that country."[28]

The same story was fundamentally retold on the other side of the world, throughout Micronesia and Polynesia, where the Hiti were known as "white-skinned giants" who raised standing stones from Samoa to New Guinea. The virtual universality of this myth materializes in thousands of similar megaliths encircling the Earth. Are they and their legendary builders remnants of humankind's first global culture?

---

*A skillfully made scale model of Mzora is on display at the archaeological museum in the city of Tétouan, much farther to the east.

# 14

# Secret of the Stones

*The only true knowledge of things is the knowledge of their causes.*

ROBERT LEIGHTON (1611–1684),
SCOTTISH PRELATE AND SCHOLAR

With Mzora and its apparent relationship to the British Isles, our round-the-world review of megaliths comes full circle. Although exact figures are unavailable, their total number approximates 70,000 menhirs and dolmens, a conservative estimate.

"Their construction is unparalleled in human history," writes Gilroy, "surpassing even the more sophisticated structures of the later civilizations of Mesopotamia, the Middle East or the Americas."[1] Today's archaeological consensus admits, at most, only isolated, regional similarities among a few, neighboring clusters out of this enormous assembly. All the rest are totally unrelated to each other. They must have been independently set up by numerous cultures mostly unaware of one another's existence as a kind of an irrational, natural human impulse to erect big stones. Although surrounded by thousands of examples, mainstream scholars insist that a European megalithic culture never even existed.

"No one has ever been rash enough to claim a nation-wide unity of all aspects of Neolithic archaeology," affirms Euan Wallace MacKie, a British anthropologist who coined the term "archaeo-astronomy."[2] He believes prevailing doctrine should be changed if evidence appears to contradict it. Nor should official opinions be used to question the relevance or reliability of such evidence.

MacKie's commendable stance seems at odds with his disdain for Grafton Elliot Smith (1871–1937), who saw in the worldwide scope of standing stones self-evidence for a global megalithic culture. The Australian anatomist pioneered the application of new technologies in archaeology—such as his x-raying, the first ever, of an Egyptian mummy. Too many commonalities shared by menhirs everywhere, he observed, argued on behalf of Stone Age seamanship that long ago circled the Earth.

Although his conclusion won support from prominent colleagues, such as the influential anthrolopogist Sir Arthur Keith (1866–1955), Smith was later denigrated as a "hyper-diffusionist," whose ideas no longer merited consideration. Even before his time, leading scholars could not help but notice so many details in common with numerous megaliths widely separated by geography. Du Pouge confessed, "it is impossible to look upon these close resemblances as the result of an accidental coincidence."[3] Those "resemblances" still persist, despite the tendency of majority archaeologists to dismiss them as almost entirely circumstantial and insignificant.

An important dissenter was Dr. David D. Zink (1927–2008), named "Explorer of the Year" in 1976 by the International Explorers Society (Miami, Florida), for spending decades seeking out hundreds of megalithic sites around the world. His personal survey was perhaps the most comprehensive of its kind ever undertaken by a single researcher, and at his own expense. Although a university-trained investigator, he admitted that the societies responsible for erecting the standing stones raised

> unsettling questions with respect to the generally accepted version
> of human prehistory. They suggest a past marked by a mobility and
> an intellectual and technological sophistication that approaches or

even equals our own. . . . But, at the same time, these cultures are spread over a considerable time-span, and they are widely separated geographically. These facts would argue against a single, worldwide culture, unless the local cultures known today at each site are actually built over various centers of an earlier, single, worldwide culture, which is now forgotten.

Did various cultures develop essentially in isolation, or did many worldwide migrations lead to cross-fertilization? In other words, did human culture diffuse from some ancient center, or did it develop in many, separate locations, evolving through independent invention? . . . The suggestion that some elements of prehistoric culture might have been transmitted (diffused) over even a few hundred miles of open sea seems to cause something like an allergenic reaction from many scholars. Specialists who work on a particular culture seem to develop a vested interest that impels them to see all local cultural evolution as totally autonomous. . . . Such chauvinism leads to cognitive filters (blinders), which protect the investigator from any evidence that does not fit his own beliefs, in this case, about the evolution of man and his culture.[4]

The megalithic sites are unrelated, mainstream archaeological opinion holds, because they are separated by too many centuries. Yet, the monoliths of North America's Maritime Archaic, New Hampshire's Mystery Hill, Alberta's Majorville Medicine Wheel, the Colombian menhirs of San Agustin, Brazil's "Amazon Stonehenge," Japan's Oyu circles, the Chinese standing stones of Shanxi province, thousands of dolmens in the Western Caucasian Mountains, and many more have all been dated by standard radiocarbon procedures to the European Megalithic Age. Others exhibiting later periods signify only that they have not yet been subjected to those same procedures; or that the tradition of raising great stones, begun much earlier, was carried forward by successive generations, just as the Astronesians still do.

Red ochre burials found in context with megalithic sites throughout

Western Europe, North America, South America, and Asia are extremely revealing and nothing less than cultural fingerprints left by their builders. Transoceanic connections—such as Canada's dog-shaped stone structure at Minton deliberately pointing at Sirius, the most important stellar orientation in the Nile Valley—are abundant. That many if not most of these megalithic structures share the same celestial alignments should at least give skeptics pause for reconsideration. The envisioned but true-life spectacle of many thousands of deeply ancient monuments—all flashing around the world in concert with the rising sun while the Earth turns on each winter solstice—does not seem likely as the result of pure chance or disassociated independent invention.

Quite the contrary, these worldwide orientations powerfully affirm an affiliated continuity no less self-evidently demonstrated by identical or virtually identical physical resemblances among megaliths everywhere. The standing stones of Tokoshima, Japan are indistinguishable from counterparts in Brittany, just as no archaeologist could tell the difference between New Jersey's Salem tripod and a typically Western European dolmen. So too, Quebec's Pierre Hexagonal Stone planted atop Mt. Eternity in conjunction with equinoctal sunrises and sunsets finds its mirror image in a comparable block on the Isle of Lewis among the Outer Hebrides, where the lithic formation of Callanish features the same orientation. Dr. Zink points out that "the number of these alignments, as well as their appearance in many cultures over the planet's surface, clearly indicate purpose."[5]

In locations as far removed from each other as Classical Greece, Colombia's Little Hell, and the Kai natives of New Guinea, a strange, oral tradition is repeated describing the megalith-builders as Deluge survivors who tossed stones over their shoulders to repopulate a flood-ravaged Earth. Our brief, global overview of megalithic sites provides an objective perspective from which their fundamental oneness emerges.

While mainstream scholars still balk at recognizing such apparent unity, Classical Greek writers often mentioned an *ecumene*, or "universal" culture known worldwide shortly after the beginning of time. In his early-seventh-century BCE cosmological work concerning the origins of the world, the poet Hesiod described the first of four "ages of man" as a Golden Age. But the "gold" he cites was not the precious metal associated with material wealth, but a metaphor for the life-giving rays of the golden sun. Early civilized humans did not worship shiny coins, he stated, but rather light, a veneration suggesting the solar calendars found among so many remarkably similar menhirs, dolmens, and stone circles.

Appropriately, Hesiod was himself a founder of archaic Greek astronomy and ancient time-keeping. Moreover, the divine patron he associated with that tranquil epoch was Astraea, "star-maiden," yet another not-so-subtle hint at the big stones' celestial orientations. In his *Theogony,* we learn how the Golden Age was an era of peace, harmony, stability, and prosperity—qualities archaeologists apply to the Megalithic Age, citing its general absence of military artifacts or ruined fortifications.

Nor was this primordial epoch an exclusively Greek convention. India's Hindu Satya yuga was a golden age corresponding to Hesiod's Chrýseon Génos, which had additional counterparts from pharaonic Egypt, Keltic Europe, and Atlantic North Africa to pre-Columbian America, the pre-Christian Pacific islands, and Southeast Asia, areas corresponding to a preponderance of menhirs and dolmens. That accounts of a golden age were not only known in so many of these unrelated and often unconnected cultures around the world—but similarly described by them—bespeaks a common experience each shared independently.

Given that a megalithic culture flourished during some global golden age during the deep past, why did its creators go to the profound trouble of sailing great distances and erecting 70,000 immense stones, often on mountain tops and other physically challenging locations? Archaeoastronomers might argue that celestial alignments shared by many standing stones suggest they were sacred structures erected to orient with and pay homage to the gods and goddesses of the sun, moon, and stars, as part of a Neolithic cult.

Envisioning the megalith-builders as transoceanic missionaries may be their most convincing interpretation, because economic or other mundane alternatives can explain neither the appearance nor profusion of the same kind of structures in so many radically different environments. Their imagined role as astronomer-priests may be only partially correct, however, because the megaliths themselves imply something additional, something else. It would be wrong to think of the tens of thousands of standing stones encircling the planet as astronomical markers only. Nor are they just the monuments or ruins of the first global culture.

The megaliths are all these things, but were envisioned and originally set up for combined purposes. As Dr. Zink succinctly stated from personal experience, "the ancient stones speak." That is, close yet objective scrutiny of everything about them—their regional and immediate vicinity, dimensions, material compositions, positions, environmental relations, weathering, color, and so on—when viewed as component parts of an archaeological puzzle, begin to disclose a bigger picture. Their most revealing characteristic is location.[6]

During 1982, geologist Paul McCartney discovered that virtually every British stone circle and menhir was located either within a seismic fault zone or positioned above an intrusion of mineral enhancement (i.e., the intense compression of various minerals, especially igneous granite, in a concentrated area to generate high levels of magnetism). When his map of all known megaliths was overlaid on a plat of the country's mineral enhancement and seismic zones, he discovered that the man-made and geologic regions correlated almost exactly.

How the megalith-builders could have suspected the presence, much less determined the exact subterranean distribution of these seismic areas with enough precision to insert their stones between the faults, baffle scientists. Paul Devereux, a Research Fellow with the International Consciousness Research Laboratories group at Princeton University in New Jersey, and leading authority on European standing stones, wondered, "If we are not dealing with some bizarre coincidence, what could the ancients have been seeking at fault zones? The first, obvious answer is that these parts of the Earth's crust have been subjected to considerable tectonic forces; they are natural 'energy zones.' Faults tend to have high mineralization around them affecting local electric and magnetic fields, and to be points of weakness where stress and strain in the crust can manifest, causing energy effects within and above the ground."[7]

Zink similarly and independently observed, "These structures of massive stone are found all over the world—often in places of intense seismic activity—in locations, which, after thousands of years of occupation by changing cultures with changing beliefs, continue to evoke in those who visit them some instinct for the sacred."[8] Their perennial evocation is generated by natural construction material deliberately selected for virtually all these monuments: either granite or metamorphic rock thickly veined with quartz.

"A well existed that has proven to be a source of quartz crystals" at America's Stonehenge, according to Bruce Scofield. "There is a vertical fault in the rock, about twenty-two feet down, from which the crystals were mined."[9] The existence and discovery of this crystal-rich vertical fault may have been the determining factor in choosing the New Hampshire site. "Choice of stone did not respond merely to what was readily available," Dr. Foster points out, "the builders would transport stones for hundreds of miles, evidently choosing them for specific qualities or properties."[10]

Quartz crystals react to external pressures exerted on them by accumulating electrical charges. These produce electricity that takes the form of a luminous vapor, itself caused by massive concentrations of negative ions (atoms or molecules) suddenly released into the atmosphere. During these concentrations of energy, the total number of electrons is not equal to a total number of protons, resulting in a positive or negative electrical charge. When negatively charged en masse, they electrically connect with each other in an effect known as piezoelectricity, from the Greek *piezo,* or *piezein,* which means to "squeeze" or "press," and *electron* for "amber," whose color it sometimes resembles.

As an example of the process, early crystal radio sets were activated by turning a knob connected to a vise that exerted sufficient pressure on an internally mounted quartz to "jump the spark," as a popular expression went during the early 1920s. Today, common fireplace-starters ignite by pulling a trigger that drops a trip-hammer on a crystal; this mehanical pressure on the stone causes it to emit a sufficiently hot flash. Accordingly, granite or any crystalline rock will react to pressures high enough for the accumulation of electricity, until mechanical energy changes into electrical discharge in the form of an incandescent haze, usually blue, but occasionally red, yellow, or white, depending on the mineral composition of the stone being thus subjected.

The megalith-builders appear to have understood and applied piezoelectricity by intentionally positioning their standing stones specifically at geologically active locations, where seismic activity would exert the mechanical stress necessary to squeeze clouds of glowing, negative ions from the quartz-veined monuments. For time out of mind, menhirs have been and still are associated with ghostly illuminations, traditionally known across the British Isles as "fairy lights." Illumination known as *das blaue Licht* ("the blue light") is most often reported at the Externsteine, a famous Neolithic site in Lippe, northwestern Germany, near the town of Horn. The same phenomenon is referred to in Scandinavia wherever ancient standing stones are found as *haug-eldir*, or "the lambent flame." As confirmed by geologists from the University of Lyons and reported by Devereaux, "The greatest megalithic complex in the world, around Carnac, in Brittany, France, is hemmed in by fault systems, and occupies France's most volatile tectonic region."[11]

It is here, too, that local oral traditions have long spoken of the Feux Follets dancing among Carnac's hundreds of aerostats, and still occasionally witnessed by modern tourists. "The known placing of certain types of megalithic sites in northwestern Europe in geological areas suitable for earth lights occurrence," Devereux observes, "is quite possibly a result of the use of this environmental method of causing mind-change effects."[12] He knew whereof he spoke.

A fellow Briton, Kenneth Shaw, demonstrated that quartz does indeed interface with human consciousness. During the summer of 1980,

*Fig. 14.1. Germany's Externsteine, a Stone Age mecca for ritual activity and still host to "earthquake lights." Photo by Daniel Schwen.*

he participated in a controlled experiment that required him to position the palms of his hands six inches above a crystal connected to a molecular resonance meter. It was designed to detect changes in the way molecules in minerals bond together. Digital readouts indicated no change. But when Shaw was instructed to visualize healing energy streaming from his hands into the crystal, the meter registered a powerful reaction. As soon as he suspended his visualization, the readings immediately fell back to normal. The experiment was repeated numerous times, always with the same result. Shaw's scientific testing demonstrated crystal's sensitivity to external energies, even individual human energies. But it was and is the capacity of stressed quartz to produce quantities of concentrated negative ions sufficient to incandesce into a cornonal discharge.

The ponderous standing stones were not painstakingly sited directly over concentrations of seismic energy just to create dramatic light shows, however. Their real purpose in producing luminous mists or clouds of negative ions was to evoke spiritual euphoria from celebrants of a megalithic cult. During the early 1990s, the acceptance grew for ion therapy, or negative air ionization as an alternative to pharmacologically induced procedures; patients reported a surge of spiritual intensity. While thus sedated, they claimed to have undergone a broad variety of psychic phenomena, such as their conscious mind separating from its physical body;

live encounters with deceased relatives, friends, or pets; meeting a Christ-like figure and long-dead celebrities; hovering high above the Earth or some other world; transcending space and time as fast as thought; receiving advanced knowledge about healing; visiting celestial parks and libraries; seeing past and future lives; or being bathed in the clear light of a cosmic love.

Investigators were surprised to learn that these visions were not confined to religious persons, but equally shared with patients indifferent to metaphysical questions, even hardcore atheists. Indeed, their convictions or lack thereof could not be isolated as a determining factor. As the relationship between such experiences and the application of ion therapy became more prevalent, medical practitioners traced the visionary experiences to both hippocampi, one in each side of the brain, where these important component parts play important roles in the consolidation of information from short-term memory to long-term memory and spatial navigation.[13]

They form one part of the limbic system—a group of brain structures that surround the brain stem. The hippocampi play an important role in the experience of certain emotions—such as fear and anger—motivations, and memory. They are also associated with religious and aesthetic emotions. When stimulated by negative ions, the hippocampi respond by flooding the entire neurological system with otherworldly sensations and imagery. Why this happens is unknown, though sharply debated between scientists and metaphysicists. In any case, only high, sustained concentrations of negative ions, such as those generated by quartz-veined standing stones, are capable of eliciting such a response. It would seem, then, that our megalith-building ancestors understood the correlation between crystalline rock and seismic activity to produce a piezoelectric effect on human consciousness. Such a discovery would not entail modern scientific research, but require only simple observation of natural processes. For example, one could look to "earthquake lights," fiery colored, usually dark blue clouds that sometimes appear in conjunction with seismic activity.

As the pressures that produce a quake squeeze subterranean minerals, electrical currents are generated to break down underground water molecules, thereby releasing charged ions of oxygen and hydrogen into the air. The process chemically separates electrons from their paths around atomic nuclei, transmuting their energy into light. Effected water molecules are thereby condensed into statically charged mists or clouds that appear glowing or incandescent. As a growing earthquake exerts stress on granite and/or other crystalline rock in the planet's crust, a visual, piezoelectric charge is emitted. The same phenomenon takes place in the mountains of South America—from whence the term "Andes Glow" derives—although the phenomenon occurs all over the world, wherever quartz-rich rock is in place.

The Andes Glow is a brilliant discharge of electrical energy into the atmosphere, sometimes hundreds of miles long, generated by tectonic activity. It was undoubtedly witnessed as often by humans during pre-history as it is today by modern tourists. That the former also observed the relationship between these earthquake lights and altered states of human consciousness is exampled by towerlike formations heavily embeded with quartz—the eroded leftovers of long-extinct volcanoes in central California's Salinas Valley—about forty miles inland from the Pacific Ocean, some eighty miles south of the San Francisco Bay Area. Resident Chalone and Mutsun Indians on a vision quest climbed to the top of what has since become Pinnacles National Monument, where they would become enveloped in a blue haze (please see plate 21 of the color insert).

In 1973, David Kurbin, a British historian, photographed a massy but amorphous light-form hovering directly over the monument before it rotated and vanished in midair. The formation sits on its own "Pinnacles Fault," a closely connected spur of the more notorious San Andreas Fault, which, in fact, gave birth to the local volcanic extrusions a million years ago. The combination of frequent seismic activities with crystalline concentrations and their resulting earthquake lights induced the Chalone's and Mutsun's sought-for altered state of consciousness.

Ute Indian shamans still go up into the Wasatch Mountains for the collection of clear quartz crystals, which are sewn into filmy-thin pouches for nighttime ceremonial dances. As the bags whirl about, their crystals collide with one another, emitting piezoelectric sparks.

Our Stone Age ancestors were no less intellectually capable than their twenty-first-century descendants; in at least some aspects, they may have been our superiors, because they were far more in tune with and sensitive to an environment unpolluted by toxins, artificial noise, and bright lights. Observing the visual and psychological effects associated with natural locations such as Pinnacles National Monument, they learned that these phenomena were generated by a special relationship between quartz crystal and seismic activity.

The most famous example is England's Stonehenge. Its inner ring is composed of so-called blue stones, which the Neolithic builders went to a great deal of trouble transporting from the Prescelly Mountains in Wales some 240 miles away. These dolerites were selected because they are a species of crystalline rock. Other construction components at the Salisbury Plain monument are made of rhyolite, a sandstone likewise chosen for its high crystal content. Accordingly, mysterious lights are still witnessed there, as documented by author Mollie Carey in her book, *The Ley Hunter.* Stonehenge thus joins Germany's blaue Licht at Externsteine, Sweden's haug-eldir at the Snarringe dolmen, Brittany's Feux Follets at Carnac, and so many other megalithic sites around the world where the luminous phenomenon is experienced.

The negative ion effect made by these structures on the human brain's hippocampi was undoubtedly their chief purpose around which a Neolithic cult developed. Additional functions as tombs, directional indicators, and astronomical observatories were component parts and variations of the mystical encounters afforded by the standing stones. Their transcontinental-transoceanic distribution might have been the result of seafaring megalith-builders-cum-missionaries driven by religious fervor to share their ion-induced spiritual experiences with the rest of humankind.

Something of their unwritten theology may have survived in the Hermetic tradition of "As above, so below," referring to the patriarchal influences of the cosmos combined with the matriarchal powers of the Earth, a principle embodied in the structures' celestial alignments and tectonic sensitivities. As such, the Megalith Age may have occasioned not only the earliest worldwide religion, but the first global culture, remembered by Classical Greeks as the ecumene of humanity's prehistoric Golden Age.

Its demise was brought about by global climate change. "During the megalithic period," writes Dr. Foster, "the British Isles were blessed with sunny skies, calm seas, and ample, but not excessive rainfall—a climate conducive to sea trade, cosmic observations and exterior gatherings. About 1500 B.C., the cold, wet Sub-Atlantic period began. As the climate continued to change, megalith building ceased."[14]

These deteriorating conditions excceded themselves and climaxed dramatically in 1198 BCE, when the periodic comet that ushered in the low-temperature phase returned for a closer passage, raining down a barrage of meteoric destruction around the Northern Hemisphere. Work at Stonehenge terminated, and the site was abandoned. For centuries thereafter, its celestial alignments could no longer be made, due to persistent cloud cover. Heavily overcast skies rendered inoperable the astronomically oriented monoliths wherever they were erected.

Following eighty-four centuries during which they stood and unerringly performed their duties, all at once these tens of thousands of megalithic timekeepers encircling the globe stopped. They would not resume counting the solstices or equinoxes until the climate restabilized itself and the heavens cleared after another 500 years. But by then, no one was left to observe them, nor to fathom their significance.

# 15

# The First Atlantean

*What, after all, do we know of the ancient world so far,*
*so as to permit us to adopt an attitude of negation to*
*the deep-rooted traditional statement, so oft-repeated*
*in the most venerable chronicles, that in a period almost*
*transcending the imagination, a civilization of a high*
*order, from which all the cultures of this planet proceeded,*
*shone, flickered, and, like a shattered sun, cast its broken*
*lights upon the dark places of our world? If we can discover*
*no material proof of that civilization, is it not because it*
*remains asleep beneath the Atlantic? But we can surely*
*infer with confidence from its last fragments in Europe,*
*Africa and America, appearing suddenly, and having no*
*roots therein, as well from its well-authenticated tradition,*
*that it assuredly existed.*

LEWIS SPENCE, *THE HISTORY OF ATLANTIS*

The earliest complete (more or less) and best-known account of
Atlantis was part of a philosophical dialogue written around 360
BCE by the Greek philosopher Plato. As a prominent mathematician
and founder of the Academy in Athens, he was not likely—contrary

to modern skeptics—to have fabricated a major historical event or anything else in his Atlantean dialogue, the *Kritias*. It is named after Plato's uncle, who learned about Atlantis from Solon—the influential Athenian constitutionalist—following a visit to Egypt where temple records documented the lost civilization.

Although Plato's critics accuse him of inventing the story, he was not the first Greek scholar to write about it. He was preceded by the early fifth-century BCE historian Hellanicus of Lesbos, with an otherwise lost work quoted in part by subsequent writers. Atlantis survives in fragmentary form in the Oxyrhynchus Papyri (11, 1359). It was composed about twenty-five years before Plato was born, and discovered during 1882 at el-Bahnasa, the ancient Oxyrhynchus, a city in Upper Egypt, located approximately 100 miles south-southwest of Cairo.

Plato's account tells of "a large island" (*nesos,* the Greek word for "island," not "continent") "beyond the Pillars of Heracles," or outside the Straits of Gibraltar, in the Atlantic Ocean, named after Atlantis, just as the Indian Ocean derives from India, the China Sea from China, and so on. We are not told the original name of the island, only that its precivilized inhabitants were rather primitive, "for there were still no ships or sailing in those days."[1] Later, when the Olympian gods began to divide up the Earth among themselves, Poseidon's allotment included the anonymous nesos. He found a mortal woman residing atop "a hill of no great size," which he improved "by enclosing it with concentric rings of sea and land. There were two rings of land and three of sea, like cartwheels, with the woman's hill, now an islet, at their center, and equidistant from each other."[2] The first son she bore him was Atlas, after whom the whole island was named, and the city that grew up on Poseidon's alternating circles became "Atlantis," literally, "the daughter of Atlas."

In the *Kritias,* Plato appears to be repeating a very old myth going back to Neolithic big-stone construction engineers—who, like the Olympians, were in charge of a worldwide culture. Since Poseidon's concentric configuration resembles the circlular layouts common to

Western European sites, the sea god may have been intended to personify the maritime megalith-builders—who arrived at the Atlantic island during prehistory, intermarried with its aboriginal residents, and fashioned the same kind of ringed structures they left elsewhere. Many, if not most, were aligned with specific celestial phenomena, a feature underscored by Atlas himself, because he was depicted in classical myth as the founder of astronomy and astrology.

According to the *Kritias,* Atlantis (Atlanikos) grew to become a military power that declared war on the kingdoms of Greece and Egypt in 9600 BCE, shortly thereafter succumbing to a fatal natural catastrophe. The dialogue tells how a hieroglyphic pillar in the temple of the goddess Neith, the divine patroness of history at the city of Sais near the south end of the Nile Delta, documented the rise and fall of the Atlantean Empire. This version was translated for Solon, the famous Athenian legislator who was visiting Egypt around 590 BCE. It was then he was told that Atlantis (Etelenty, in Egyptian) was defeated and destroyed nine millennia earlier.

But an Atlanto-Athenian War would not have been possible, because Athens did not exist at that time, while contemporaneous levels of human population and cultural development in the Lower Nile Valley were far too low to constitute anything approximating Pharaonic Civilization. Plato's tenth-millennium BCE date nonetheless coincides with the earliest Neolithic hilltop sanctuary in southeastern Turkey, where the site's lowest strata (Layer III) has been dated to $9559 \pm 53$ BCE. Moreover, Göbekli Tepe bears at least a faint—if radically downsized—resemblance to Atlantis, in that both were characteristically arranged in concentric circles. The latter city, as portrayed in detail by Plato, developed into the capital of an unmistakably Late Bronze Age civilization (1500 BCE–1200 BCE), identified by its citadel, temple, armed forces, advanced metallurgy, and so on.

These contradictions play havoc with the account, and may only be reconciled by what Desmond Lee, a mid-twentieth-century British translator of the *Kritias,* referred to as "a bad sense of time. . . . And though the Greeks, both philosophers and others, were interested in origins, they seem to have been curiously lacking in their sense of the time-dimension," a fault made obvious by numerous anachronisms that plague the mid-fourth-century BCE dialogue, as pointed out by the German scholar Eduard Gottlob Zeller (1814–1908).[3] As such, Plato's dating of the destruction of Atlantis to the mid-tenth millennium BCE is more incongrous than placing the September 11 destruction of New York City's World Trade Towers back in the Roman Era. His concept of time was not the same as ours, so it is impossible to know just what he meant by stating that the lost capital flourished more than 9,000 years before he discussed it.

In truth, we have no idea what Plato meant by "9,000 years," because he and his fellow Greeks used many different simultaneously employed calendrical systems, which were additionally confused by numerous, albeit necessary, modifications—the precise significance of which bewilder classical scholars. These various timekeeping systems included the Attic, or "Hellenic" calendar; a state calendar of ten arbitrary months; an agricultural calendar; a sidereal calendar; and a complex, cumbrous luni-solar calendar of twelve lunar months adding up to around 354 days, eleven days or so shorter than the solar year, and was, as a consequence, in need of readjustment from time to time. Our current Gregorian calendar's "9,000 years," directly carried over into any one of these systems, would not come close to Plato's date for Atlantis, as presently understood as having flourished in the mid-tenth millennium BCE.

We do know that the Egyptian priests who translated the Atlantean story for Solon used a lunar calendar. When they told him that Atlantis existed 9,000 years before his day, they meant lunar years. This information is no assistance, however, because it is not known into which of the Greeks' five different nebulous and contradictory calendars those years were recalculated, if at all. No one ever shall. If we suppose that Solon directly quoted the Egyptian priest, without bothering to transpose his Atlantean period into any equivalent Greek calendar, then the

"9,000 years" he mentioned dates to around 1200 BCE. This year fits Plato's account perfectly, because it signified the cultural zenith of the Late Bronze Age, when citadels like the capital of Atlantis he describes epitomized the era, which climaxed at that time with a global natural catastrophe.

He tells of a ceremonial center laid out by seafaring visitors from the European continent during the Megalithic Age, when such structures were being raised in many other parts of the world. Over the following centuries, subsequent generations continued to build upon Neolithic foundations, giving Atlantis its concentric appearance. In view of their standing stones' seismic-energy relationships, its ocean-going founding fathers were right to worship Poseidon, who was not only the divine patron of sailors, but the god of earthquakes. His name means, literally, "earth-shaker," an otherwise inexplicable title for a deity whose domain is the sea. It was in his kingly ritual, however, that he may have preserved the secret of Atlantean origins.

The *Kritias* (4f) recounts how the ten monarchs of Atlantis, representing various regions within their imperial network, convened together in the Temple of Poseidon alternately every fifth and sixth year during the late afternoon of an unspecified holy day—presumably the sea god's feast day. Alone and without the assistance of priests, guards, or advisors, they "consulted on matters of mutual interest"—in other words, the diplomatic, commercial, and military concerns that foremostly concerned the Empire. In all their decisions related to these issues they were guided by Poseidon's ancient laws engraved on a ceremonial column at the center of his sacred precinct. These injunctions were accompanied by "an oath invoking horrible curses on anyone who disobeyed it."[4]

But before any judgments could be passed, a special sacrifice was required to sanctify them. The ten kings began by forming a circle around the column, beseeching the sea god to bless the offering they were about to make him. They then repaired to an outside corral where sacred bulls were allowed to roam freely, and subdued one of them with staves and nooses only, because custom forbade the use of any metal utensils. Dragging their prey into the Temple, they used a sharp flint or obsidian blade to slit the beast's throat atop the ritual pillar, allowing the blood to flow over its inscription.

Into a bowl of wine one clot of blood was dropped for each of the monarchs, who disposed of the carcass, lighted an altar fire, washed the pillar, and bathed themselves. Thus refreshed, they drew golden cups into the bowl, poured a libation over the fire, swore by Poseidon's oath to give judgment according to his laws, and neither give nor obey any order contrary to them. With that, they drank to consecrate their pledge, each man dedicating his golden cup to the Temple.

The kings' ceremony appearing in Plato's dialogue has a ring of authenticity beyond his power to invent, if only because it was unlike the religious practices of his times. In fact, two of the golden cups—or something very much like them—were discovered in a beehive tomb for royalty known as a *tholos* at Vapheio, a region near Sparta in southern Greece. Both date from the Late Bronze Age (the sixteenth to thirteenth centuries BCE), and depict a shared scene: a man attacking a bull with staff and rope (please see plate 22 of the color insert).

Whether these cups were carried by survivors of the Atlantean catastrophe or colonizers from Atlantis in the Aegean is not known. The cups nonetheless portray the same hunt described by *Kritias,* but nowhere else in Classical antiquity. Moreover, the manner in which the Atlantean hunt was conducted seems to have derived from a remote, precivilized era prior to the introduction of metallurgy, as indicated by the proscription of any metal tools in the ritual slaughter. This is in sharp contrast to Plato's Atlantis, characterized in his dialogues as a copper-, bronze-, silver-, and gold-rich economy.

The ritualistic use of staves and nooses harkens back to a very early time—Neolithic, Lower Paleolithic, perhaps even 16,000 years ago to the cave painters at places like Lascaux and Trois Freres—where images of the bull predominate, and when Poseidon's laws, which the ceremonial hunt was meant to commemorate, may have been first propounded, possibly even engraved on the *Kritias'* pillar over which the creature's blood was spilled. This monolith itself seems to have been less a free-standing "column" than a less-refined standing stone of the kind megalith-builders erected along the Atlantic coastal regions of Brittany, beginning in the early fifth millennium BCE.

Bull sacrifice implies astrological significance, and uniquely fits the Atlantean kings' sacrifice, because to them the victim was an astral bull, whose slaughter meant the end of the Age of Taurus. In numerous other cultures—Minoan, Mycenaean, Hittite, Trojan, Assyrian—bull sacrifice was regarded as a prelude to renewal in the rhythm of growth. Taurus himself signified rejuvenation and revival. In much later Mithraism, Taurus assisted in the creation of life by having his own throat cut, thereby enabling plants and animals to spring from his shed blood.

His myth was reenacted in a rite called the *taurobolium* to commemorate the death and resurrection of the hero, Mithras, who impersonated the next age, and baptized initiates into his cult. Drinking wine clotted with bull's blood also occurred among other peoples. As late as the fifteenth century CE, Turkish soldiers, following an ancient tradition, drank red wine mixed with bull's blood before battle to imbibe strength and resistance. Clearly, the Atlantean kings celebrated a *tauroctony*, in which bull sacrifice marked the close of the Age of Taurus in 1658 BCE, as calculated by Max Heindel (1865–1919), Denmark's classic authority on the Zodiac.[5]

His mid-seventeenth-century BCE date is an insignificant thirty years off from the penultimate destruction of Atlantis in 1628 BCE. Geophysicists now recognize that a series of major natural catastrophes beset the Earth in that year, from a historically unprecedented eruption of Thera—known today as Santorini, a volcanic island in the Aegean Sea—to its nuclearlike equivalent on the other side of the world in New Zealand. If, as it would appear, that the Age of the Bull was synonymous with the Age of Atlantis, then Taurus and Atlantis were simultaneous affairs. Heindel gave the start of the Age of Taurus at 3814

BCE. The arrival of Neolithic seafarers and their establishment of a megalithic culture on the island could not have come at a more propitious time.

From his vantage-point in the early twentieth century, Lewis Spence correctly deduced that Atlantis began as a Stone Age society. "If we are to judge her condition," he stated in his first of four authoritative books on the subject, "we must in the event assess her culture . . . as a typical Paleolithic or Upper Old Stone Age culture."[6] To him, the Stone Age originated in Atlantis, from whence it spread to Western Europe, the same conclusion arrived at by the equally praised American scholar, Mary Settegast, much later in the same century.

Their supposition appears to have been contradicted, however, by Plato's depiction of the earliest Atlanteans as primitive, isolated land-lubbers. They were later visited, he stated in the *Kritias,* by overseas' mariners in the collective guise of their sea god, Poseidon, who built the island's first circular structure at the height of Western Europe's Megalithic Age. Paleoanthropologists know this same era coincided with a climatic period of intense aridification that triggered worldwide migration to river valleys and coastal areas, resulting in an outward population expansion, stimulating fundamental change and dramatically spreading Neolithic culture beyond continental Europe on a hitherto unprecedented scale.

Certainly, the most profound innovations occurred in food production. Cattle were domesticated and wheat was cultivated for the first time. The earliest known recipe—for brewing beer—comes from this era. "The transition from hunting to farming societies in Northern Europe took place in a very short time, between 4000 and 3800 B.C.," observes paleoagriculturalist, Theron Douglas Price.[7] It was as seafaring farmers that they came to the Mediterranean island of Malta, where they raised the world's oldest freestanding structure (until Göbekli Tepe's discovery) in a temple known locally as Ggantija, in 3800 BCE (please see plate 23 of the color insert).

A chambered tomb and subterranean shrine at the Xaghra Circle shares the same date. Maltese funeral objects from this period (Mgarr) are typically coated in red ochre, that cultural fingerprint of the megalith-builders from Europe to America. Refined, polished flint axes, which granted a distinct technological edge over previous versions, were simultaneously developed, along with the earliest earth long barrows, extensive burial tombs for the illustrious dead.

The world's first engineered road, referred to today as the Post Track, extended 6,600 feet across the Somerset Levels, today a sparsely populated coastal plain and wetland area of central Somerset in south-west England, dates from 3838 BCE, according to test results of dendrochronology (tree-ring dating). Another in the area, the Sweet Track, followed thirty years later, as part of an interconnecting network of crossed wooden poles of ash, with lime and hazel posts spaced along nine-foot intervals, and driven into the waterlogged soil to support a walkway consisting mainly of oak planks laid end-to-end. Meanwhile, in Brittany, construction began at the world's largest megalithic complex, Carnac; and a discovery that would become a leading feature of Atlantis took place at various sites in Iran, where copper was extracted from ore by smelting for the first time.

The cultural surge and outward expansion Neolithic Europe experienced 5,800 years ago magnificently coincide with the Age of Taurus and its birth in 3814 BCE, just when the concentric foundations of Atlantis would have been laid. Civilization had a head start there, due to its relative isolation from outside conflicts; the fecundity of its rich, volcanic soil; a year-round temperate climate that allowed, according to Plato, twice-annual growing seasons; natural mineral wealth; abundance of fresh water; and close approximation to the challenging sea, which invariably stimulates cultural growth and innovation. These nurturing environmental conditions promoted population growth, itself a prod for social and technological development.

Before the fourth millennium BCE was over, Atlantis had grown to become the first modern civilization, and was poised to bequeath its greatness to the outside world, igniting similarly high cultures in the Valley of Mexico, the Nile Valley, the Indus Valley, and Mesopotamia's Fertile Crescent.

The questions remain: If Western Europeans, as signified by Poseidon, brought a megalithic culture to the Atlantic island some fifty-eight centuries ago, who were the native inhabitants waiting for them when they arrived? When and how did these first humans reach what would much later develop into a high civilization? The *Kritias* inadvertently provides a hint when it describes "numerous elephants" that roamed there.[8] Until the mid-twentieth century, Plato's skeptics cited the appearance of these ridiculously out-of-place animals in the middle of the ocean, hundreds of miles beyond the nearest landfall and farther still from the beast's African homeland, as proof that his account was fiction.

But in 1967, oceanographers dredging the ocean floor some 250 miles off the Portuguese coast unexpectedly hauled up hundreds of elephant bones from more than forty different locations. Bottom-profiling subsequently revealed a submerged land bridge extending from the Atlantic shores of Morocco into formerly dry land.[9] These important discoveries not only tended to verify the *Kritias,* but showed that a peninsula once extended from the coast of northwest Africa, over which herds of elephants crossed far out into the Atlantic Ocean. What seismic violence did not eventually collapse in this geologically unstable region, rising sea levels inundated, leaving the animals stranded on surviving dry territories, now islands, one of them much later known as Atlantis. An identical process took place in the Mediterranean, when Malta was connected to North Africa by a land bridge until it too sank at the end of the last ice age. At a place called the "Cave of Darkness," Ghar Dalam, the skeletal remains of not only elephants, but hippopotami, deer, and bear testify to their arrival in Malta before 15,000 years ago.

More than thirty years before the mid-twentieth-century discovery of abundant elephant bones in the near-Atlantic, a prescient Lewis Spence stated:

It has always seemed to me probable that the passage relating to the elephant (Kritias, 114) is one of those which serves to reveal the historical value of Plato's account . . . it is not improbale that it was still wandering to and fro between the European continent and the island-continent [*sic*] over a still-existing land-bridge, and that, after this land-bridge disappeared, it became extinct in Europe, but continued to flourish in Atlantis, where it was marooned. . . . In any case, there is nothing extravagent in the supposition that elephants actually existed in Atlantis. If they did not, it is most unlikely that the Egyptian tradition, as handed down by Plato, would have alluded to them at all. The elephant was an animal by no means familiar in Egypt, although known to the Egyptians to exist in Central Africa. It is, therefore, unlikely that it would have been dragged in by the priest of Sais merely to render his tale still more highly coloured.[10]

Previous to the contemporaneous disappearance of an Afro-Atlantis land bridge at the close of the last glacial epoch, when sea levels rose steeply, the migrating elephants were pursued by early hominid hunters. They, too, were rendered islanders via the combined forces of rising seas and tectonic upheavals provoked by the seismically overactive Mid-Atlantic Ridge, a great gash on the ocean bottom, torn between the contrary drift of the European and American continents.

Spence's supposition of an Atlantean land bridge based on Plato's elephants, followed by the discovery of their bones on the ocean floor in the 1960s, was by then regarded as geologically self-evident by earth-scientists in Russia. Emmet Sweeney, an Irish historian from the University of Ulster, quoting Nikolay Zhirov (1903–1970), chief chemist at the Kiev Polytechnic Institute, tells how the leading Soviet geologists G. B. Udintsev and A. V. Zhivago determined that much of the Mid-Atlantic Ridge stood above sea level before the end of the last ice age, when "the summits of these ranges were evidently in a sub-aerial (dry-air) position; this fits in excellently with paleozoological [i.e., pachyderm skeletal remains] and paleobotanical data. Quite recently, many of these ranges were bridges linking up continents and the route for migration of flora and fauna."[11] Zhirov went on to write that the conclusions reached by Udintsev and Zhivago concerning preglacial land bridges from the Mid-Atlantic Ridge to northwestern Africa and southwestern Europe represented consensus opinion among their Russian colleagues.

But more than flora and fauna crossed over these ice age connections. In the fourteenth century, when Portuguese explorers discovered the Canary Island of Tenerife, 185 miles from Morocco, they found it already inhabited by an aboriginal people in possession of a low-level material culture. The Guanches, or "men," as they called themselves, abhorred the surrounding sea, and, like the precivilized natives of Atlantis Plato described, knew neither shipbuilding nor sailing, unusual for islanders. Yet, their ancestors had obviously arrived in the Canaries somehow; most likely by wandering over the former peninsula that extended from northwest Africa into the Atlantic Ocean before its demise.

During his examination of Guanche mummies, Carleton Stevens Coon (1904–1981), a Harvard lecturer and leading physical anthropologist of the mid-twentieth century, determined that they were Cro-Magnons, perhaps the last survivors of the earliest modern humans. Similarly, Markku Niskanen of the Department of Anthropology at the University of Oulu, Finland, claimed the "strong cheekbones and flaring zygomatic arches of many Finno-Ugrians, commonly and erroneously assumed to be Mongoloid features, are actually inherited from European Cro-Magnons."[12]

"Like many of the animals and plants of the vestigial lands," Spence wrote, "Cro-Magnon Man was cut off and marooned on them by some great natural cataclysm."[13] Although the Cro-Magnons, like us, were *Homo sapiens sapiens,* they were still markedly different: with a more robust physique, slight browridges, and a larger brain capacity. They were also distinguished by their rectangular orbit, the cavity or socket of the skull in which the eye and its appendages are situated; our orbit is conical. As the prominent Atlantologist R. Cedric Leonard points out, "All Cro-Magnons are modern, but all moderns are not Cro-Magnon."[14]

*Fig. 15.1. This standing stone, preserved at Tenerife's Archaeolgical Museum in Santa Cruz, California, testifies to the arrival of New Stone Age visitors via the Atlantic Ocean.*

Over time, under the stimulus of dramatic climate changes accompanying the end of the last glacial epoch, the Cro-Magnons gradually lost their distinctive characteristics, morphing into the Caucasian race. Parallel with Cro-Magnon was an eastern branch paleoanthropologists refer to as Brünn Man, Combe Capelle, or Predmost, names derived from locations were remains were found. More gracile, with less brain capacity, this was a shorter type that migrated from Europe, settling throughout the Orient, where it evolved into the various Asian races.

But in Tenerife, the Cro-Magnons, isolated from the outside world, retained their Upper Paleolithic traits. Something similar must have happened on another Atlantic island, where Plato's precivilized inhabitants suggest they, like the Canary Island Guanches, were Cro-Magnon remnants, and, like their elephant companions, were stranded in the middle of the ocean after the inundation and collapse of the peninsula their ancestors used as a land bridge out of northwest Africa.

Spence, as mentioned above, believed that the earliest Atlanteans were Aurignacian, belonging to the cave-painters of Old Stone Age Europe. Since his time, however, fresh clues have emerged to suggest that they were not, after all, the first Atlanteans, but had been preceded by a far more ancient, premodern hominid that played a decisive role in human evolution. Appropriately, "Atlanthropus" was the name originally applied to an advanced example of *Homo erectus,* the cranial remains of which were discovered on the Atlantic shores of Morocco.

In 1933, part of an *Atlanthropus* skull was found in the vicinity of Rabat, and, twenty-one years later, at Sidi 'Abd ar-Rahman, researchers uncovered mouth parts belonging to what appeared to be an intermediate stage between *Homo erectus* and early *Homo sapiens.* "The jaw bones are massive," observed Russian paleoanthropologists in the 1970s, "and the chin is not prominent. The teeth are large, but fully human in structure. The parietal bone is relatively thick."[15] Though similar to late *Homo ergaster,* a direct ancestor of later hominids, *Atlanthropus* was a discernibly advanced improvement—possessing more features in common with European *Homo sapiens* than *Homo erectus* contemporaries in Africa or Asia.

Moroccan *Atlanthropus* appeared identical to late *Homo erectus,* early *Homo sapiens,* according to remains of an adult and child with milk teeth discovered in 1965 at Vertesszoelloes, thirty miles east of Budapest. The Hungarian site was dated to a warm phase within the second Mindel glaciation (200,000 to 380,000 years ago), which means these early humans were on the move, having relatively recently come up from North Africa when the Straits of Gibraltar connecting southern Spain could have been crossed on foot. Fluctuations in sea level occasionally cut off access to the Atlantic Ocean, transforming the Mediterranean into a lake. The Vertesszoelloes' remains were classified *Homo* [*erectus seu sapiens*] *paleohungaricus* to reflect the same mixed *Homo erectus* and *Homo sapiens* characteristics displayed by *Atlanthropus.*

The date for *Atlanthropus*—Middle Pleistocene, about 360,000 years ago, according to the Russians—also made sense. The oldest known *Homo erectus*—from Swartkrans, South Africa—migrated northwest to Morocco (*Atlanthropus*), into Western Europe (*Atlanthropus* and *Homo* [*erectus seu sapiens*] *paleohungaricus*), and northeast across Asia to become the latest examples of *Homo erectus* in Lan-T'ien, China, at Java's Sangiran and Modjokerto, and at the Djetis fossil beds. But the Hungarian find's occipital bone from the rear part of the skull told a different story.

David Pilbeam, curator of paleoanthropology at the Peabody Museum of Archaeology and Ethnology in Cambridge, Massachusetts, observed how it "does not resemble that of *H. erectus,* or even Archaic Man, but instead that of earliest Modern Man. Such forms are dated elsewhere no older than 100,000 years."[16] Hungary's foremost anthropologist, Andor Thoma (1928–2003), took precise measurements of the Vertesszoelloes' skull, and found they were radically different from those belonging to *Homo erectus,* being instead "fairly close to the modern average."[17] It was virtually a mirror image of a 90,000-year-old skull discovered during 1932 in a Palestinian cave near Mount Carmel.

The "forbidden archaeologist," Michael A. Cremo, writes that Skhul V:

is considered to be among the earliest anatomically modern human skeletal remains. One hundred thousand years is the age currently favored for the very first anatomically modern human (*Homo sapiens*). . . . Another sign that the Vertesszoelloes hominid was probably *Homo sapiens* rather than *Homo erectus* is the presence of evidence for campfires. The deliberate building of campfires is an activity that most researchers do not attribute to *Homo erectus*. Many stone tools and broken animal bones were also found at Vertesszoelloes.[18]

*Homo [erectus seu sapiens] paleohungaricus* did not, moreover, have the thick cranial vault lines, large brow and occipital ridges, or the oversized teeth typical of early *Homo erectus*. While the Central European and northwestern African *Atlanthropus* were both the same hominid, their parallels demonstrate he stood at the leading edge of evolutionary change from late *Homo erectus* to early *Homo sapiens*. This crucial transition concerns us most, because it suggests that the final upgrade from premodern to modern humans took place within the Atlantean realm.

In addition to his more refined physical features—and as revealed at Morocco's Ternifine site—*Atlanthropus* had progressed from a primitive tool-pebble industry worker to the producer of hand axes, the same step achieved successively and separately by *Homo erectus* in South Africa during the Late Developed Oldowan Phase (named after the Tanzanian site discovered by the famous archaeologist, Louis Leaky, during the 1930s).

But as more related finds came to light thirty years later, it was apparent that *Atlanthropus,* though perhaps the most advanced form of *Homo erectus* embodying many characteristics of *Homo sapiens,* did not seem different enough from *Homo erectus* to warrant its own generic name. Evolutionary scientists learned a variable type of *Homo erectus* appeared in Mid-Pleistocene, combined with *Homo habilis* and other presapiens in a mingling of genes to create various subspecies: *Homo erectus-erectus, Homo erectus pekinesis,* and *Homo erectus mauritanicus,* the former *Atlanthropus*.

It was this *Homo erectus mauritanicus* that somehow got to Europe as the *Homo [erectus seu sapiens] paleohungaricus* immediately preceding the evolution of *Homo sapiens*. Paleoanthropologists speculate the trek was made from North Africa into Iberia across the Straits of Gibraltar when it was a land bridge to Spain. Physical evidence of an *Atlanthropus* connection between the Atlantic isles and Central Europe during the Mid-Pleistocene does indeed exist in four jadeite hand axes from the French Alps found in the Canary Islands' Gran Canaria, where the Cro-Magnons were to later make their appearance.

A temperate climate created by a prolonged warm phase in the second Mindel glaciation, together with the challenging abundance of the surrounding sea, were stimulating factors for evolutionary change on the Atlantic island, where mankind conceivably took the penultimate step toward modern humans. The simultaneous occurrence of this warm phase in the second Mindel glaciation and the birth of *Homo sapiens* 200,000 years ago was not coincidental; the latter was, to a large extent, made possible by the former.

Although scientists seem to have missed the connection, the Oranian stone tool industry created by the Mechta-el-Arbi race—a North African branch of the seafaring Solutreans, about 16,000 Years Before Present, during the Late Würm Glaciation—appears to have been directly descended from *Homo erectus mauritanicus*' hand ax production, which it almost identically resembles. If, as seems likely, *Homo erectus mauritanicus* was a local ancestor of the Mechta-el-Arbi Solutreans, then we may postulate an origin for protocivilized cultures in the region of the Atlantic island. Even today, some residents of the Canary Islands display muted Solutrean features that are more pronounced in the Guanche aboriginals of Gran Canaria.

According to Peter Lemesurier, a Cambridge-educated linguist, "the percentage of 'O'-group blood has found to be as high as ninety four per cent among exhumed mummies of the Canary Islands."[19] O-type blood characterized the Paleolithic peoples, but mostly not modern Europeans. The high percentage of O-type blood among the prehistoric Guanche is also cited by Canary Island histtorian John Mercer.[20] "Apart from Iceland, the northwestern British Isles and the

Cotentin peninsula (in Normandy, forming part of the northwestern coast of France)," Lemesurier continues, "only Crete, Sardinia and a small area of Tunisia around what used to be Carthage exhibit comparable percentages of 'O'-group blood. In fact, the area where this group is most prevalent may be summed up as comprising the more mountainous Atlantic coasts of Europe and Africa and the shores of the Mediterranean basin—within which its distribution corresponds to an uncanny degree with the areas listed by Plato as having been specifically colonized by the Atlanteans."[21]

North Africa's Oranian industry bore a close resemblance to the Cro-Magnons' Magdalenian culture, as it developed in Iberia—a later parallel with the apparent relationship between *Homo erectus mauritanicus* in Morocco and *Homo [erectus seu sapiens] paleohungaricus* in Central Europe. In fact, the Oranian was often referred to by anthropologists as "Ibero-Maurusian," reflecting its combined Iberian and Mauritanian (Moroccan) features.

This Ibero-Maurusian—or Oranian—culture was not some Stone Age society confined to the shores of Rabat. It dominated the Moroccan coasts all along the Atlantic and the Mediterranean littorals of North Africa to the Cyrenaica region of Libya and—between 26,000 and 18,000 years ago—spread down the length of the Nile Valley as far south as Nubia, where it was referred to as the Halfan Culture, known primarily for its stone tools and profusion of vibrant rock art. This very ancient racial (*Homo erectus mauitanicus*) and cultural (Ibero-Maurusian) connection from the Atlantic shores of Morocco, including the Canary Islands, across Libya and into Egypt—and from the Atlantic through Iberia into Central Europe—ties in vitally with the story of Atlantis. Their relationship shows a deeply prehistoric, cultural commonality linking Western Europe and North Africa through an Atlantic source.

It also helps clarify the early migrations from Atlantis in 3100 BCE, when the island was wracked by geological upheavals that prompted many of its inhabitants to leave. They fled mostly over temporarily surviving land bridges to Iberia and North Africa. But their trek across the latter continent was not a prolonged wandering in search of some unknown Promised Land. For more than 7,000 years previous, the Mechta-el-Arbi had formed a continuous, cultural bond (the Oranian) from the Atlantic shores of Morocco into the Nile Valley. The Atlantean émigrés and culture-bearers followed the earlier blazed trails eastward to finally settle at the Nile Delta and in southern Mesopotamia to spark Egyptian and Sumerian civilizations. The story was much the same in Western Europe, where the Atlantean refugees were not pioneers, but followed the cultural trails opened up long before by ice age Solutreans, their direct ancestors.

There was, moreover, a genuine affinity between Euskara, the language of the Basque—whose O-type blood they inherited directly from their Paleolithic ancestors—Moroccan Berber, and Tamatschaq, as spoken by the Tuaregs of the Sahara. Luigi Luca Cavalli-Sforza, Italy's renowned population scientist mentioned in chapter 13, combined these comparative blood types with cranial morphology and genetics to suggest that the Basque people may be partly descended from the original Cro-Magnons. His research appeared to have been confirmed in 2006, when a study of Basque DNA discovered a 1 percent incidence of the Cro-Magnons' mtDNA haplogroup U8a.[22]

Some colleagues were unimpressed with the percentage rate, arguing it is too low to prove that the current Basque population comprises Cro-Magnon descendants. Combined with related blood types and common cranial morphology, however, the presence of any mtDNA haplogroup U8a among modern-day Basque makes for persuasive evidence of their Upper Paleolithic roots. The ancestry of some Guanche mummies goes back even further: the pentagonal form of the cranium when viewed from above caused by the prominent parietals (roughly quadrilateral bones, which, when joined together, form the sides and roof of the cranium) is an unmistakable Solutrean trait. Both Guanche and Solutrean caves were similarly decorated in ceremonial red ochre, diagnostic of Stone Age seafarers around the world. Evidence for human evolution in North Africa and Europe within an Atlantean context is scanty, but clear.

It suggests that, about 360,000 years ago, early hominids (*Atlanthropus,* or *Homo erectus mauritanicus*) followed herds of game from northwest Africa (Morocco) over a peninsula extending westward by several hundred miles into the Atlantic Ocean. There, the primitive hunters found conditions particularly stimulating throughout subsequent millennia for continuous genetic development, which was additionally influenced by contact with seafaring Solutreans, who arrived around 22,000 Years Before Present.

About 7,000 years later, sea levels occasioned by the Keg Mountain Oscillation rose over 300 feet, inundating Europe's coastal populations and submerging most of the Afro-Atlantean peninsula. Only its higher territories were left as remote islands above the swelling tide. On the largest and most naturally prosperous of these, its human inhabitants— already in possession of the most advanced Upper Palaeolithic culture— were able to sustain its development through the coming centuries in more or less continuous peace, far from the pressures of dangerous megafauna.

Thanks to their remote location, they were also spared the violent close of the last glacial epoch, when Magdalenian domination of the European continent was abruptly terminated. Increasingly arid conditions and a return to hard winters during the early fourth millennium BCE prompted Western European expansion, which reached the Atlantic island in 3814 BCE. Visiting megalith-builders raised a characteristically Neolithic ceremonial center of concentric circles, upon which descendants of liaisons between newcomers and natives eventually built a walled citadel. Seven centuries later, it had grown into a city, followed by the rise of Bronze Age civilization, with which the urban center began its cultural denouement as the capital of a thallasocracy, an oceanic empire.

If our interpretation of the foregoing evidence is valid, then the story of Atlantis is as old as our own evolution, and its transition on that

Blessed Isle from premodern *Atlanthropus* to Bronze Age imperialist is nothing less than our long development from early hominids to present civilizers. That this most critical transformation in the history of the human species may have occurred on the island Plato described twenty-four centuries ago renders Atlantis more significant than its most imaginative champions ever dreamed possible.

# 16

# Stone Age Déjà Vu

*A likely impossibility is always preferable to an
unconvincing possibility.*

ARISTOTLE

Archaeological evidence suggests that the seafaring Solutreans became
proto-Atlanteans after they made an Upper Paleolithic landfall at the
island. So too, their impact on America 16,000 years ago is documented
by a growing abundance of related discoveries. But the very nature of
inquiry is to seek out its ultimate limits, to push beyond the barricades
erected by defensive dogmatists. As the Clovis line mainstream paleoanthropologists drew in the sand has been forever crossed, so even the
older Solutrean threshold is being breeched by no less persuasive proofs.

One of these paradigm-shattering finds was made at a remotely
inhospitable place, 130 miles north of the Arctic Circle. During summer 1938, a pair of university-trained archaeologists found telltale
signs of an old settlement faintly outlined on the Alaskan permafrost,
about 325 miles north of Nome. They assumed the site did not differ from other small, primitive communities occupied by local fishing
peoples—the direct ancestors of Alaska's Eskimos—dating back no further than five centuries ago. Returning in June 1940 to complete their

excavations at Ipiutak on the Point Hope peninsula, Magnus Marks and F. G. Rainey felt blessed by the unseasonably warm temperatures that allowed for greener grass and moss, against which the outlines of the subsurface hamlet could be discerned for the first time. But as the scientists followed its outlines, they could distinguish features of an urban center greater than anything associated with ancestral Eskimos. Long boulevards of square foundations spread east and west along the shore of the Arctic's Chukchi Sea. "We became aware of the astonishing extent of the ruins," Rainey told Natural History magazine.[1] He and Marks traced the figures of large square structures regularly arranged in five main avenues and down shorter cross blocks, where smaller foundations, suggestive of family domiciles, stood at right angles to the thoroughfares.

Their finished survey identified more than 600 buildings, but incomplete test pits indicated at least another 200. The archaeological zone is less than a quarter-mile across and nearly one mile long, with an estimated original population of some 4,000 residents, larger by far than anything known to the Eskimos—who, in any case, never built such structures, nor laid out the kind of urban planning apparent at the site. Moreover, in the twenty-three buildings excavated during 1940, nothing resembling anything similar to local native culture was found.

"One of the most striking features of the Ipiutak material," Rainey stated, "is the elaborate and sophisticated carving and the beautiful workmanship, which would not be expected in a primitive, proto-Eskimo culture ancestral to the modern."[2]

The absence of any large refuse deposits covering the buildings, which were not superimposed over older structures, showed that the town was simultaneously settled by its inhabitants, and did not slowly develop over time. Every indication of the physical evidence demonstrated that Ipiutak was raised at once and occupied by the same people that built it. As such, they seemed to have arrived as one group, en masse, on the Chukchi coast already in possession of their construction technologies and skills, which they applied to building their city the moment they arrived. Excavators of their cemetery found the remains of tall, slender-built individuals with strands of blond hair and Cro-Magnon-like skulls. Clearly, they were not related to the shorter, squat, black-haired Eskimos.

An artistic design preferred by the ancient inhabitants of Ipiutak was a spiral composed of two elements carved in the round. The motif appears nowhere else in the Arctic region, but is found on the other side of the Pacific Ocean among the Amur River tribes in northeastern Asia and the aboriginal Caucasoid Ainu of Japan, renowned for their amber-colored eyes. Thus, it would appear that northern Alaska's ancient metropolis was imported by the Jōmon-jin people, the globe-trotting megalith-builders, as they were known in prehistoric Japan. But when could they have possibly built it?

Rainey found the Point Hope town "buried beneath so much sand from the beach" that it must have flourished many thousands of years ago. Ipiutak could only have been inhabited when warmer conditions permitted its higher culture to survive and prosper there. Around 14,000 Years Before Present, a sudden warm phase interrupted the last glacial epoch for another 3,200 or 2,500 years, before the sudden return of cold temperatures with the Younger Dryas stadial. Following this "Big Freeze" 1,300 years later, the Arctic settled down to its present climate, referred to as the Holocene. While the onset of Japan's Jōmon culture closely coincides with the 14,000-year-old warm phase, paleoclimatologists are doubtful that northern Alaska benefited much or was even affected during this period.

According to the National Snow and Ice Data Center, "The last time that scientists can say confidently that the Arctic was free of summertime ice was one hundred twenty-five thousand years ago, during the height of the last major interglacial period, known as the Eemian. Temperatures in the Arctic were warmer than now and sea level was also four to six meters (thirteen to twenty feet) higher than it is today, because the Greenland and Antarctic Ice Sheets had partly melted."[3]

If Jōmon-jin people settling along the Point Hope peninsula between

14,000 to 12,800 years ago appears unlikely, their arrival 125,000 years ago seems utterly impossible. Yet, how are we to account for the Ipiutak ruins "buried beneath so much sand from the beach," a deposition giving every indication of extreme antiquity? Moreover, the Younger Dryas stadial and Holocene that followed the warm phase brought sea levels down from the archaeological zone on the Chukchi Sea coast by as much as twenty feet. The original dry-land site was once covered by water that later retreated, a process that fits the Eemian Period, not the Younger Dryas. Current evolutionary theory states that *Homo sapiens* migrating out of Africa 125,000 years ago only got as far as the Near East. Humans did not reach Alaska until more than 105,000 years later by following herds of bison across the Bering land bridge from Siberia.

"Located in the Arctic Circle," Dr. Gunnar Thompson explains, "this strait was an effective barrier to migration for most of antiquity. However, the barrier is not a permanent geological feature. During cyclical temperature extremes called 'Ice Ages,' the sea level drops by hundreds of feet, and the bottom of the Bering Strait lies exposed. At maximum glaciation, the sea level can drop nearly four hundred feet. . . . When this happens, retreating seas expose enormous areas of the continental shelf, including a land-bridge of habitable territory between Siberia and Alaska. Geographers call this transcontinental passageway, 'Beringia.'"[4]

Although mainstream scholars insist that this was the only conceivable route used by the first humans crossing from Siberia into Alaska 13,000 years ago, their paradigm was laid to rest when researchers found abundant physical proof that Beringia flooded into the Arctic Ocean at that time. Funded by the National Science Foundation, scientists from California's Woods Hole Oceanographic Institution, Scripps Institution of Oceanography at the University of California (San Diego), and the University of Massachusetts (Amherst) analyzed deep-sea cores collected from three different sites along the Bering Strait during a 2002 cruise by the U.S. Coast Guard Cutter Healy. These were radiocarbon dated at the National Ocean Sciences Accelerator Mass Spectrometry facility at Woods Hole to show that no one used the "transcontinental passageway," because it was inundated 11,000 years ago, effectively closing off the land bridge that supposedly facilitated human migration from Asia.[5] The first Americans had to have made their way to our continent by some other means, at some other time.

Not to be outdone by these revelations, orthodox archaeologists came up with a new alternative, arguing that Siberians must have migrated into North America during the twelfth millennium BCE through a hypothetical passage that opened up through the Wisconsin Glacier, an enormous stretch of ice spread over west and central Canada.

"Geologist D. R. Crandell cast doubt on a 'corridor' through the Wisconsin Glacier, inhospitable to man or beast," stated Dr. Covey, "along which no artifacts have been found, and large, pro-glacial lakes that dominated the environment would haved presented insuperable deterrents during both advance and retreat of the glacier. He doubted firstcomers were big-game hunters, with the attraction of marine-littoral resources for simple watercraft."[6]

Our examination of the Solutreans in chapter 6 shows they arrived 6,000 years prior to any migrations from the north. But even these ice age Western Europeans were long preceded in America by other visitors. Although conventional archaeologists still insist that the first humans crossed the Rio Grande River no earlier than 11,000 years ago, strong, profuse physical evidence to the contrary came to light during seventeen professional excavations undertaken in as many years beginning in 1956. These excavations focused on the base of Tlapacoya, a hill at the shore of the former Lake Chalco, in the Valley of Mexico.

Piles of disarticulated butcher-bones of bear and deer, plus 2,500 flakes and blades presumably from the butchering activities, together with a nonfluted spearpoint were recovered from the same stratum containing three circular hearths filled with charcoal and ash for easy carbon-14 dating. Nearby, obsidian blades were found in contemporaneous strata. All materials dated between 21,250 and 25,000 Years Before Present. Despite these paradigm-shattering finds, official indifference allowed Tlapacoya to be mostly covered by highway construction in 1973.

Chapter 6 described the discovery of 16,000-year-old microflints and hammerstones by Albert C. Goodyear III, a professor at the South Carolina Institute of Archaeology and Anthropology, who began digging at the Topper Site during the 1980s. Shocked but intrigued by these finds, he dug deeper into the ground and the past. He came to yet another cultural strata in November 2004, when a cache of stone tools dated to 38,000 years ago came to light. Important as his find may have been, it was neither the first nor oldest of its kind.

The same time frame was independently matched and substantially magnfied thousands of miles to the south, when Niède Guidon and her colleagues unearthed more than 800 prehistoric habitation sites at Brazil's Serra da Capivara National Park, in Piauí, where she is the chief archaeologist and conservator. This is the same researcher who, in 1978, proved that Pedra Furada's 1,150 wall paintings were 17,000 years old. Guidon explained how abundant carbon-14 samples from several burned out hearths at Serra da Capivara yielded firm dates of occupation between 32,000 and 48,000 Years Before Present.

Professor Covey describes how Guidon beheld "two hundred seventy-five rock-shelters in towering cliffs for one hundred twenty miles along the Rio Piauí, one hundred eighty-six bearing murals in red, yellow, black, gray and white, often on ceilings, as well as walls, and more art engraved or pecked, than painted. She tabulated fifteen thousand motiffs—animals, including armadillos, caybara (the world's largest rodent), ostrich-like rheas, et al; trees, people, crabs, and abstract symbols. . . . Its murals appeared to follow styles from Aurignacian [Neanderthal] to Spanish-Levantine Mesolithic [Middle European Stone Age], in tandem with France and Spain."[7]

Although Guidon's *Nature* magazine article appeared as long ago as 1986, mainstream archaeologists still teach that the first humans in South America did not arrive until just 9,000 years ago. Five years after the publication of Guidon's work, Dr. Richard MacNeish

(1918–2001), director of the Andover Foundation for Archaeological Research in Massachusetts, announced the discovery of numerous paradigm-shattering artifacts found at New Mexico's Pendejo Cave in the Tularosa Basin mountain range, near Orogrande. Physical evidence he retrieved and tested proved the site, located 200 feet below on the valley floor, had been occupied on and off for millennia as a shelter from enemies and for butchering animals. The objects his team collected included the 25,000-year-old bone of an extinct horse; a clay-lined fireplace with a human handprint 3,000 years older; a bone spear point that lodged 1.6 inches into a horse's hoof in 34,400 BCE; and the bone of an extinct bison dated to 51,000 years ago.

*Ancient American* reporter Barbara Holley Rock wrote that "fourteen of the twenty-two stratified levels at the cave date from 350 to 50,000 Years Before Present."[8] Dr. MacNeish was no fringe archaeologist but "revolutionized the understanding of the development agriculture in the New World, the prehistory of several regions of Canada, the United States and Central and South America," according to his National Academy of Sciences biography. "He pioneered new methods in fieldwork and materials analysis and brought attention to the importance of interdisciplinary collaboration. His legacy also includes an influence on generations of archaeologists."[9] These credentials notwithstanding, MacNeish's work at Pendejo Cave has been ignored by his mainstream colleagues.

The level of antiquity he found there had already been reached during the previous century, when Whiteside County construction laborers near the eastern banks of the Mississippi River, in Illinois, inadvertently unearthed a large copper ring in company with a metal rod resembling a boat hook from 120 feet beneath the surface of the Earth. Earlier, at shallower depths from ten to fifty feet, the workers found an iron spear-shaped hatchet embedded in clay, together with stone pipes and pottery.

About 100 years later, in September 1984, Michael Cremo was informed by Illinois' State Geological Survey that the deposits at 120 feet in northwestern Illinois varied from 50,000 to 410 million years old; the former date corresponds with cultural levels at Pendejo Cave. For the sake of comparison, Europe was dominated by Neanderthals at the time, and Cro-Magnon, or modern man, would not appear for another 10,000 years. More challenging, metallurgy of the type in evidence at Whiteside County was otherwise unknown until invented by the Hittites of Asia Minor during the fourteenth or thirteenth centuries BCE.

Yet, the same time frame was cited during 1969 by *Tulsa World* (Oklahoma), which told how "amino-acid dating of a human skull found in California indicates human habitation of North America fifty thousand years ago."[10] Douglas C. Wallace, cited earlier as the geneticist who pioneered human mtDNA as a molecular marker, documented fourteen-thousand- to fifteen-thousand-year-old Western European influences on Native American populations. On the PBS television program NOVA, he further stated, "All of the papers that have been published have come to a very similar conclusion: that the first migration was in the order of twenty thousand to thirty thousand years ago. Mitochondrial DNA analysis has found that some members of some native North American tribes have an Old World heritage going as far back as 50,000 Years Before Present."[11]

Doubling this profound antiquity to parallel the founding fathers of Alaska's Ipiutak is surprisingly supported by a variety of contemporaneous finds. At the northern end of Lake Huron and Georgian Bay, Ontario, the National Museum of Canada's T. E. Lee labored at an archaeological precinct known as Sheguiandah, on Manitoulin, the world's largest freshwater island. Between 1951 and 1955, he dug up finely made stone tools and worked fragments of quartzite at strata consistent with 100,000 Years Before Present.

For attempting to overthrow anthropological dogma with new information, Lee "was driven from his government post into eight years of unemployment," writes Cremo, "blacklisted and unemployable in his own country," even though the Sheguiandah site had been confirmed as anciently authentic by "four prominent geologists."[12]

Forty years later, chipped quartzite cobbles were found at another Canadian dig near Calgary. "It is undeniable that these cobbles look artificially worked," observed the American physicist and great compiler of anomalous scientific information, William R. Corliss (1926–2011). "In fact, they closely resemble the human-made 'choppers' from Early Paleolithic sites in Asia and Europe. The Alberta 'tools' could be over one hundred thousand years old, completely upsetting the accepted timetable for human activity in North America."[13]

The same period belongs to finely made pottery, together with stone arrowheads and knives, discovered in profusion by Dr. Charles C. Abbott at New Jersey's Trenton Gravels. After examining Abbott's collection, Alfred Russel Wallace, codiscoverer of evolutionary theory with Charles Darwin, remarked that many specimens were "almost identical in size and general form with the well-known Paleolithic implements of the valley of the Somme [France]. These have been found at depths of from five to over twenty feet from the surface, in perfectly undisturbed soil, and that they are characteristic of this particular deposit is shown by the fact that they are found nowhere else in the same district. . . . Dr. Abbott found a well-chipped spear-shaped implement immediately beneath a stone weighing at least half a ton."[14]

Although these objects came to light under unimpeachable conditions as long ago as the 1880s, generations of paleoanthropologists have refused to discuss them. Principal investigator at California's Mission Ridge site in the San Diego River Valley, B. Reeves, from the University of Calgary, has retrieved dozens of scrapers, choppers, and worked flakes his stratigraphic analysis dated to 120,000 Years Before Present, making them more closely contemporaneous with Ipiutak's proposed time scale.

The cause for this apparent proliferation of Stone Age discoveries in North America may have been the onset of the Abbassia Pluvial. This was an extended wet and rainy period that lasted until about 90,000 years ago. The North African Desert bloomed with abundant vegetation fed by lakes, swamps, and river systems, nourishing wildllife now associated with grasslands and woodlands south of the Sahara. These lush conditions also triggered a surge in human cultural development that shifted Lower Paleolithic society into a more sophisticated Middle Paleolithic era, as reflected in surviving examples of more advanced stone-tool workmanship. Paleoanthropologists believe that the first mass movement of modern *Homo sapiens* from Africa and into the outside world was sparked by the Abbassia Pluvial, although they deny any migrations entered America during this period.

But dramatic climate change cannot explain material evidence for much older traces of humans in the New World, such as a collection of implements that surfaced during the 1950s along Wyoming's Black Fork River. Corliss stated that "morphologically, they nicely matched the tools made by *Homo erectus*. . . . Great antiquity for the Black Fork River objects was also suggested by their strongly abraded surfaces. They appeared to have been water-worn. But the high river terraces from which they had been collected had not supported rivers for over 150,000 years."[15] Similar artifacts from California's Calico site, better known because of Louis Leaky's involvement in the 1960s, are dated 50,000 years older still.

The quarter-million-year barrier for humans in America was broken during the early 1960s, when prehistorian Juan Armenta Camacho began finding some very old-looking lithic implements at Hueyatlaco, seventy miles southeast of Mexico City. He had assembled an impressive collection by the time geologist Dr. Virginia Steen-McIntyre arrived to assist in excavating the Valsesequillo region project as an expert in the field of dating materials associated with fire evidence.

"The stone tools were roughly of two types," she said.

Those in the older, lower layers were blades and flakes with edges retouched to make them sharp. Those from the upper layers were well-made, bifacially-worked artifacts. That is, stone flakes were chipped off both faces of the tool. Both the upper and lower layers contained projectile points—spear-heads—which showed that the hunters actually pursued game and did not just cut up a dead carcass that they had happened across. . . . radiometric dates using methods identical to those used in Africa to date the early sites there place these ancient hunters way back in time, to slightly over a quarter of a million years ago.[16]

Establishment resistance to her findings was ferocious.

Steen-McIntyre continues: "A branch of the [Mexican] government descended on Juan and confiscated his entire fossil bone and artifact collection—those discovered during the Valsequillo Project and the bone collection of the anthropology department, University of Puebla—and all his equipment. All was moved up to Mexico City. He was forbidden by law to do any more field work there, ever."

Steen-McIntyre was snubbed by colleagues for decades, despite persistent efforts to have her data peer-reviewed, until she was forced out of archaeology. "So there I was at the end of 1981," she confessed, "no job, tarnished reputation, stone-walled, discouraged, crushed emotionally. I pretty much turned my back on science and went in other directions. From 1987 to 1994, I cared for elderly relatives and became a professional flower gardener."[17] As Michael Collins, a University of Texas archaeologist, laments, "The best way in the world to get beaten up, professionally, is to claim you have a pre-Clovis site."[18]

More than professional jealously stood against Steen-McIntyre, however. Her arguments on behalf of Upper Paleolithic artifacts were hard enough for mainstream scholars to accept, but the Valsequillo Project's quarter-million-year-old period dated 150,000 years before the supposed evolution of *Homo sapiens sapiens,* rendering Steen-McIntyre's dating of the site, however incontrovertible, dangerous to consensus reality and hence unworthy of consideration. Aside from application of state-of-the-art dating techniques, Dr. Covey observed that the site's "artifacts lay in association with extinct fauna."[19] The hunters at Hueyatlaco preceded the arrival of Christopher Columbus a bit too much for official acceptance.

But complimentary evidence began to surface around the turn of the last century in Brazil, where stone and bone tools found in a cave at Toca da Esperanza were dated by the uranium-thorium method between 204,000 to 255,000 Years Before Present. Even the quarter-million-year-old barrier has been transgressed one mile north from the Oklahoma town of Frederick, at a ten-mile-long, half-mile wide ridge. Ten to twenty-five feet from beneath the surface of this gravel deposit are found dozens of well-crafted stone implements cemented in place in common strata with the bones of extinct animals firmly dated to 750,000 years ago.

C. N. Gould, Director of the Oklahoma Geological Survey, reported, "There can be no doubt that the artifacts occur in the pit near the basal portion, on the same level as the fossil remains. An examination of the undisturbed face of the pit, immediately above the position of the finds, showed unbroken, nearly horizontal strata above it. . . . As the case stands, it looks very much as though the artifacts are of the same antiquity as the fossil animals. At the same time, it would be well to reserve final judgment until we are certain that the artifacts are not secondary inclusions."[20]

Since Gould released his report in 1929, subsequent investigations of the Holomon Pit, as it is locally known, repeatedly confirmed that the stone tools are not later inclusion, but were indeed laid down at the same time the animal bones were stratified, three-quarters-of-a-million years ago. At that time, Peking Man, one of the earliest versions of *Homo erectus,* was just emerging in China. Although *Homo erectus pekinensis* made tools, they were vastly inferior to stone specimens retrieved from the Holomon Pit.

This technological discrepancy combines with the implements' anomalous appearance near Frederick to push their very existence beyond the comprehension of conventional paleoanthropologists. To be sure, the implications such objects suggest are difficult for even broad-minded investigators to accept; namely, that contemporaneous North Americans more advanced than Old World *Homo erectus* were already established as far inland as Oklahoma. Yet, even this event-horizon would be crossed as recently as late 2005.

Earlier that year, archaeologist Silvia Gonzalez of Liverpool's John Moore's University in England discovered a line of human footprints dating back 40,000 years ago near Puebla, in Mexico. Mainstream scholars sought to debunk the heretical period she assigned the evidence by dispatching a team of leading geologists led by Paul R. Renne, director of California's Berkeley Geochronology Center, to the site. Once there, they undertook repeated argon testing to investigate the magnetic imprint of the foot-printed rock, together with other state-of-the-art dating procedures. Renne announced their results in the scientific journal *Nature,* stating that the rock featuring the footprints was not 40,000 years old after all. It was, instead, 1.3 million years old. "We conclude," he said, "that either hominid migration into the Americas occurred very much earlier than previously believed, or that the features in question were not made by humans on recently erupted ash."[21]

When anatomists subsequently confirmed that the impressions were indeed human, orthodox archaeologists still rejected all claims for the footprints' objectionable antiquity, theorizing that they were only look-alikes that had been caused by vibrations from a nearby highway and an active quarry. Sadly, the desperate scholars were unable to reproduce a single human footprint with any degree of anatomical correctness by subjecting rock to vibration from a highway and/or quarry. They were thus hoisted on their own petard, because the basic axiom of science holds that the validity of a proposition is acceptable only if it can be repeated.

In any case, the discovery of 1.3-million-year-old footprints in Mexico is troubling, because only then did protohumans arrive in Europe for the first time. The remains of *Homo antecessor,* a possible ancestor of Neanderthals, have been found at several locations in Spain and England. Plausible explanations for the simultaneous appearance of early man in the New and Old Worlds may be elusive, but the nearness of footprints at Puebla to the stone tools of Hueyatlaco should at least give us pause. Indeed, there seems to be no limit to human antiquity in the Americas.

During the early twentieth century, archaeologist Carlos Ameghino

(1865–1936) led teams of excavators along the Argentine coast south of Buenas Aires after detecting clues to an early habitation site at Miramar. By 1914, he discovered numerous stone tools cemented within Pliocene Era strata. As Silvia Gonzalez experienced in the following century, Ameghino's critics commissioned a group of professional geologists to debunk his assertion. Instead, they verified it, stating that the artifacts had been laid down between 2 million and 3 million years ago. Although their analysis was released by the prestigious Anales del Museo de Historica Natural de Buenas Aires, it has since been ignored by archaeologists in the outside world.

To put the implications of Ameghino's finds into perspective, the earliest human ancestor is 2 million years old. Fossilized bones of a South African male child and adult female were found in Malapa, near Johannesberg, as recently as 2008. Three years later these fossils were confirmed as intermediary between ape and homind, defined as when *Australopithecus sediba*'s combination of both physical features in the first step toward the *Homo* genus became apparent.

"It's as if evolution is caught in one, vital moment," said Richard Potts, director of the human origins program at Washington, D.C.'s Smithsonian Institution, "a stop-action snapshot of evolution in action."[22] Texas A&M University anthropologist, Darryl J. DeRuiter, stated, "This is what evolutionary theory would predict, this mixture of Australopithecene and Homo. It's strong confirmation of evolutionary theory."[23]

DeRuiter and his coleagues believe, moreover, that the first stone tools were invented in East Africa, at Tansania's Olduvai Gorge, about half-a-million years after the debut of *Australopithecus sediba*. Contrary to their conclusion, hundreds of stone artifacts—mostly well-crafted mortars and pestles—have been "extracted from Tertiary gravel deposits located under Table Mountain," located in the Sierra Nevadas of Tuolumne County, in east-central California. Corliss goes on to describe how "Table Mountain is capped by a thick layer of lava. . . . The lava cap implies that these artifacts were buried and lava-capped more than nine million years ago."[24]

Florentino Ameghino (1854–1911) made an even more controversial discovery than his younger brother, Carlos, mentioned above. Florentino amassed one of the late nineteenth-century's largest fossil collections when he was a paleontologist, professor of zoology at the University of Córdoba, and director of the Bernardino Rivadavia Natural Sciences Museum, in Buenos Aires. One of modern history's greatest scientists, Ameghino has a moon crater named after him, and *Ameghiniana,* Argentina's leading palaeontology journal, is still among the most important periodicals in the world of science. These enduring honors are cited to contrast Florentino Ameghino's most significant, neglected discoveries made while excavating at Monte Hermosa, thirty-seven miles northeast of the city of Bahia Blanca, on the north-central coast of Argentina, during March 1887.

In the process of examining part of the skeleton of a long-extinct camelid, he saw among its bones a yellowish red piece of quartzite, "displaying positive and negative bulbs of percussion, a striking platform, and eraillure [small, secondary flakes]. These features indicated in an irrefutable manner that I had found a stone object worked by an intelligent being during the Miocene period. I continued my work, and soon found several, similar objects. Doubt was not possible."[25] Earlier, and also at Monte Hermosa, Ameghino unearthed man-made hearths of the same age as its quartzite tools dated 10 million to 20 million Years Before Present. Today, even in his native Argentina where he is remembered as that country's premiere scientist, his discoveries near Bahia Blanca are given short shrift.

How are we to account for these examples of extreme human antiquity in the Americas? The circumstances that brought them to light, usually under controlled environments guided by university-trained professionals, are credible, even convincing. Their discovery does not necessarily imperil current archaeological understanding of our species, but rather expands it. The picture presented by mainstream scholars is not incorrect; just limited in scope and distorted by their reluctance to consider all the evidence. Mexico's 1.3-million-year-old footprints; the profusion of 9-million-year-old mortars and pestles at California's Table Mountain; stone tools in Argentina going back 20 million years, and all the other, similarly disturbing finds, may be reaching for something beyond archaeology itself.

Our own pedigree seems at least fundamentally clear. Some 100 million years ago, a common genetic ancestor of mice and humans appeared. *Australopithecus afarensis,* what may have been the earliest human ancestor, was born 3.9 to 2.9 million Years Before Present. Anatomically modern humans originated in Africa about 200,000 years ago, reaching full behavioral modernity about 160,000 years later in Europe. But this is an oversimplification. The tree of humanity has had numerous branches, and unknown numbers of them undoubtedly remain to be discovered. As the popular historian Will Durant (1885–1981) stated, "Immense volumes have been written to expound our knowledge and conceal our ignorance of primitive man. Primitive cultures were not necessarily the ancestors of our own. For all we know, they have been the degenerate remnants of higher cultures that decayed when human leadership moved in the wake of the ice."[26]

Those artifacts and skeletal remains that seem to contradict consensus archaeology may, in fact, have belonged to others from whom we are not descended. In other words, ours might not have been the only human evolution. Man may have evolved, reached some level of cultural maturity, then died out more than once, perhaps several times— sometimes parallel to our line, sometimes before it—over the past 100 million years, leaving no traces behind, save in the puzzling discoveries made throughout the Americas. Whatever future conclusions may be drawn from these anomalous finds, they together suggest a past deeper and richer than we currently realize.

# 17

# After Atlantis

*To be ignorant of the past is to remain a child.*

Cicero (106–43 BCE)

History is popularly avoided and even despised today, because it is improperly presented. What happened long ago is over and dead, with no relevance to the living. Hence, trying to convey something of what has come before us is shunned as a tedious imposition on our time. Interest in the past is nothing more than a sure sign of advancing old age, with its vain regrets for missed opportunities and lost youth, because, according to the influential British statesman, Lord Chesterfield (1694–1773), history is nothing more than "a useless heap of facts."[1]

Such indifference or aversion represents an alarmingly tragic state of affairs—it is the condition of a people cut off from their own sense of self-identity, and a critical benchmark in their precipitous decline. Author Robert Penn Warren (1905–1989) went so far as to conclude, "The lack of a sense of history is the damnation of the modern world."[2] General rejection of history is a kind of second childhood societies suffer as symptomatic not of early youth, but approaching senility. Because we have no interest in history, we blindly blunder from one catastrophe to another, belatedly grasping for explanations as desperate as they are incredible. "History isn't really about the past, settling old scores," said filmmaker Ken Burns. "It's about defining the present and who we are."[3] A people without history is a people ignorant of itself. A people without a history is a people without a future. Or, as the Spanish philosopher, George Santayana (1863–1952), put it more bluntly, "A country without a memory is a country of madmen."[4]

An anodyne to the civilized world's national dementia lies in understanding that the past never dies, but is alive in us, its inertia inexorably carrying us into the future. Both individually and as a species, we are the sum total of everything that has led up to what and who we are and what we must become. Accordingly, our foregoing panorama of human origins and earliest cultural development spans some 4 million years. It began with our ancestral transition from a safe—if relatively unstimulating—and hence, unchanging existence in the trees to a more perilous, though motivational, life of evolutionary progress on the ground. During the hundreds of millennia that followed, our species gradually mastered increasingly sophisticated levels of technology, resulting in the birth of protocivilization.

From this overview two generally applicable conclusions proclaim themselves. First, our entire history, from premodern beginnings to the advent of all higher cultures, is fundamentally a result of the natural environment on human population. Climate change prompts evolutionary and social change. Our ancestors would have never voluntarily exchanged their static arboreal habitat for the stimulating savannah had they not been driven out of the trees by prolonged aridity that blighted the forests of East Africa. Then, as later, they were compelled to either adapt or die: a choice that came to not only characterize their evolution, but power it. Only those who successfully completed the transition lived to pass on their modified genetic heritage to subsequent generations.

The next species challenge arose when massive flooding forced our ancestors into the water, where their adaptation skills made the most of marine resources in the first of an unknown number of aquatic phases that punctuated human development. The greatest environmental impact on this development was made 75,000 years ago, when the eruption of Indonesia's Mount Toba simultaneously pushed our existence to the very brink of extinction, while boosting our evolution beyond *Homo sapiens* toward *Homo sapiens sapiens*. Some of us escaped to the Mediterranean good life for the next several millennia, until evicted by North Africa's climatic deterioration. Then, we invaded the European continent, where more hardships in the form of bad weather and hostile Neanderthals comprised our coming of age.

The most recent glacial epoch, with its alternating warm and cold periods, continuously provoked human adaptabilities, thereby engendering more genetic changes for improved survival. Ocean levels rose and fell, then rose again, often catastrophically, in our challenging relationship with the sea. The onset of milder conditions 8,000 years ago made possible a Neolithic age of peace, prosperity, and cultural betterment. But this era too, was brought to a sudden close by the 8.2 Kiloyear Event that converted the deifiers of Mother Earth into the worshipers of Father Sky. Over the subsequent millennia, human response to environmental change continued to mold society, culminating in the modern, industrialized world.

Assuming that this immemorial struggle between humankind and Nature no longer affects us—because our present technological society has somehow immunized ourselves against it—represents an unjustified faith and defiance of that old proverb, "Pride comes before a fall." If anything, the human story affirms that we have become what we are because we learned how to survive by intellectually and physically adjusting to envirnomental changes. Our success was not achieved by striving to overcome or negating Nature's demands, but by adapting to them. This is the Great Lesson prehistory has for our time. Upon our willingness to learn and apply it depends, obviously enough, our own survival. Whether or not we do so, however, is all the same to Nature, who invariably wins in the end, because she, not us, holds all the cards in the game of life and death.

We are preceded by innumerable species no longer among the living. Our destruction, while everything to us, would be just another extinction event in the many thousands that make up Earth's history. Human die-off means nothing to an eternal process perpetually renewing itself with fresh life, remorselessly discarding flawed examples for improved performers. Flying in the face of this stark reality is to court Nature's wrath, which has already begun to show in more than disturbed weather patterns, however ultimately symbolic they may be. Our own evolutionary track record is filled with a rich variety of hominids that no longer exist, although they lasted longer than we have so far, leaving us the only human type still standing.

The second conclusion forced upon us by consideration of the past is that the success of any society depends on a proper balance between population and environment. Happily, we are provided with the spectacle of several, true Golden Ages, such as the Neolithic, made up of small settlements near each other for mutual cooperation, but far enough apart to avoid excessive competition. This social arrangement grew from the natural instinct for keeping one's distance in personal relationships. It thereby allowed the good will inherant in humans to thrive.

Left behind is no evidence of armies, wars, kings, prisons, pandemics, famines, civil disorders, economic exploitation, or terrorism, neither foreign nor domestic. Instead, its material legacy includes agricultural abundance, commercial expansion, social harmony, artistic florescence, and spiritual richness. These conditions were by no means static, but became increasingly sophisticated with improved techniques or refined methods, uninterrupted in their upward development over the course of 1,800 years. New Stone Age culture was not subject to the common cycle of birth, growth, youth, maturity, decline, and death subject to every urban civilization from Sumer to the Soviet Union and beyond.

The Neolithic secret of success was keeping its population numbers within a proper living space. The individual's natural desire for human contact was and is as deeply rooted as his or her innate requirement for mutually respectful distance. A healthy combination of these two needs resulted in the same kind of psychological well-being expressed by positive personal behavior, as found among an entire community of individuals committed to the same balance. The Golden Ages arising from this primeval, if eminently sensible, realization and its application demonstrate inherant fellowship, social cooperation, and preference for peacefully productive activity.

This instinctual amiability contradicts "the strong, aboriginal propensity to kill" that Winston S. Churchill (1874–1965) believed was "inherent in all human beings."[5] He lived during and importantly contributed to human history's most violent century—in the glaring light of which many others came to share his gloomy conclusion, borne out ever since, it would appear, by current events. But this is a misleading illusion. If, as Churchill's fellow countryman, Edward Gibbon (1737–1794), stated, history is "little more than the register of the crimes, follies and misfortunes of mankind,"[6] then that is because all urban societies, which have characterized civilization since the mid-fourth millennium BCE, are too populous for the broader living spaces people require for psychological well-being. Nowhere is this imbalance more obvious than in the middle of New York City, with its huge Central Park, where urbanites seek natural refuge. So too, small towns experience proportionally less crime than metropolitan areas.

The First Law of Economics similarly applies to humans: the more there are of them, the cheaper their lives are individually valued. Witness the traditional indifference to suffering in overpopulated lands like India or China; scarcity equals value. Joseph Stalin (1878–1953), who certainly knew first hand about such things, observed that "when one person dies, it's a tragedy, but when a million people die, it's a statistic."[7] In other words, the process of depersonalization begins with population increase. The greater that increase, the deeper and broader depersonalization becomes.

The Roman republic performed admirably from its inception, but faltered when too many of the eternal city's burgeoning masses sought evermore representation from a growing number of senators, who learned to their political advantage that something an individual citizen would never do privately he could be made to publicly champion in a mob. Corruption, tyranny, terror, incompetence, deceit, coercion, unwarranted ambition, and psychological manipulation—endemic to governments everywhere throughout time—are far less effective and not easily concealed in small communities, where residents are acquainted personally with one another and more alert to demagoguery.

"History cannot give us a program for the future," said Robert Penn Warren, "but it can give us a fuller understanding of ourselves, and of our common humanity, so that we can better face the future."[8] More specifically, the foregoing chapters have enumerated certain forces that have led up to our present condition and identified the causes that prevent our civilization from maintaining an accord with Nature. Whether or not we shall achieve social harmony by rediscovering that lost equilibrium of population and environment is the difference separating the fulfillment of our higher destiny from human extinction. Between these two outcomes there lies no middle path. We must either get on with our higher evolution, or vanish.

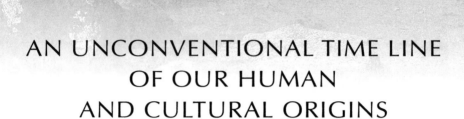

# AN UNCONVENTIONAL TIME LINE
# OF OUR HUMAN
# AND CULTURAL ORIGINS

| | |
|---|---|
| **20 Million Years Ago** | Humans working with quartzite tools reside at Monte Hermosa, on the north-central coast of Argentina. |
| **+9 MYA** | At Table Mountain, in east-central California's Sierra Nevada Mountains, a human community manufactures hundreds of well-crafted mortars and pestles. |
| **+4 MYA** | Arid climate conditions force some primates from their arboreal existence to survival on the ground, setting in motion the long, evolutionary process leading directly to modern humans. |
| **-4 MYA** | *Australopithecus* is forced by environmental changes in East Africa to adapt to watery surroundings, thus initiating the first hominid aquatic phase. |
| **3.2 MYA** | *Australopithecus afarensis* emerges from the first hominid aquatic phase as an upright-walking human ancestor. |

| | |
|---|---|
| **3 MYA** | Stone-tool users arrive on the Argentine coast, near Miramar. |
| **1.7 MYA** | *Homo erectus* debuts; perhaps originally in Indonesia. |
| **1.3 MYA** | *Homo antecessor,* the predecessor of Neandertal man, arrives in Europe. Humans leave their footprints near Puebla, Mexico. |
| **850,000 Years Before Present (YBP)** | *Homo erectus* mariners cross eighteen miles of open water to settle in the Malay island of Flores. |
| **750,000 YBP** | Stone-tool users are busy near Frederick, Oklahoma. |
| **700,000 YBP** | Seafarers arrive in Crete. |
| **400,000 YBP** | *Homo sapiens* debuts in East Africa. |
| **360,000 YBP** | *Atlanthropus* migrates out of northwest Africa across a peninsula extending into the mid–Atlantic Ocean. |
| **250,000 YBP** | Humans settle around campfires at Hueyatlaco, Mexico. |
| **125,000 YBP** | The Abbassia Pluvial causes an extended warm period throughout the Northern Hemisphere. An urban center is founded at Alaska's Ipiutak, above the Arctic Circle. |
| **120,000 YBP** | Mission Ridge, in California's San Diego River Valley, becomes the site of Stone Age artisans. |
| **100,000 YBP** | Stone tool makers are at work at Canada's Manitoulin Island and near Calgary. |

| | |
|---|---|
| **75,000 YBP** | Indonesia's Mount Toba erupts, killing off all but a few thousand breeding pairs of *Homo sapiens*. Some survivors flee to Pacific and Indian Ocean islands, where—isolated from the outside world—they pursue their own evolutionary path toward becoming Lemurians, creators of the first high culture. |
| **55,000 YBP** | The owners of stone and bone tools enter Brazil's Toca da Esperanza cave. |
| **51,000 YBP** | New Mexico's Pendejo Cave is the site of a rock shelter and abattoir. |
| **38,000 YBP** | Stone-tool users occupy the Topper Site, in South Carolina. |
| **22,000 YBP** | Solutreans arrive along the northwest African peninsula extending into the mid–Atlantic Ocean. In Europe, the Neanderthals die out. |
| **17,300 YBP** | Cave artists create mural masterpieces on the walls of Lascaux, in France. |
| **17,000 YBP** | Artists decorate Pedra Furada, in Brazil. |
| **15,000 YBP** | The Keg Mountain Oscillation inundates coastal Western Europe and most of the Afro-Atlantean Peninsula, the highest remnants of which survive above sea level as islands, stranding human populations there. |
| **14,220 YBP** | Seafarers settle at Monte Verde, Chile. |
| **12,700 YBP** | The Yonger Dryas "Big Freeze" strikes the Northern Hemisphere. |
| **9600 BCE** | Construction of the first permanent building structure at Göbekli Tepe, in Turkey. |

| | |
|---|---|
| **8000 BCE** | The collision of comet Kronos with the Earth brings the last ice age to a catastrophic end. Göbekli Tepe is abandoned. |
| **7500 BCE** | Mu, the first city, becomes a thriving urban center. |
| **6200 BCE** | The 8.2 Kiloyear Event ushers in drastically low temperatures, abruptly terminating the Neolithic Age. Mu is submerged by rising waters in the Gulf of Cambay, off the northwestern coast of India. |
| **5500 BCE** | Arrival, in Labrador, of North America's Red Paint people coincides with florescence of the Red Ochre People in Northern and Western Europe. Armenia's Karahunj astronomical observatory becomes operational. |
| **4900 BCE** | Germany's Goseck Circle and Egypt's Nabta Playa are built. |
| **4800 BCE** | The Grand Menhir Brisé is erected on the coast of Brittany. |
| **3814 BCE** | Mariners from Western Europe arrive on what would later become the island of Atlantis, where they build a megalithic ceremonial center and intermarry with the native Atlanthropus-Solutrean inhabitants. Their offspring comprise the Atlantean population of the Neolithic and Bronze Ages. |
| **3100 BCE** | Copper mining begins in the Upper Great Lakes Region of North America. |
| **1628 BCE** | The final destruction of Lemuria by a succesion of tsunamis, the result of meteoric debris from a passing comet impacting the Pacific Ocean. |

| | |
|---|---|
| **1198 BCE** | The final destruction of Atlantis signifies the sudden end of the Megalithic Age. |
| **590 BCE** | Solon learns the story of Atlantis from an Egyptian priest while visiting the Nile Delta. |
| **360 BCE** | Plato composes the *Kritias.* |
| **1868 CE** | Cro-Magnon skeletal remains are identified for the first time. |
| **1871** | Charles Darwin's *The Descent of Man* is published. |
| **1879** | The Altamira cave is discovered in Spain. |
| **1882** | First evidence of North America's Red Paint People is found at the Penobscot River, in Maine. |
| **1926** | At Austria's Anthropological Congress in Saltzburg, Dr. Max Westenhöfer publicly describes his aquatic ape theory for the first time. |
| **1940** | The cave at Lascaux is discovered. |
| **1942** | Dr. Max Westenhöfer's *Das Eigenweg Des Menschen* (The Singular Way to Mankind) is published. |
| **1960** | Sir Alister Clavering Hardy publishes his version of the aquatic ape theory for the first time in England's *New Scientist* magazine. |
| **1982** | Elaine Morgan's book, *Aquatic Ape: Theory of Human Evolution,* is published. |
| **2001** | The sunken ruins of Mu are discovered in the Arabian Sea by oceanographers from India's National Institute of Ocean Technology. |

# Notes

## CHAPTER 1. EVOLUTIONARY BAPTISM

1. DeWitt, "Greater than 98% Chimp/Human DNA Similarity? Not Anymore," www.answersingenesis.org/articles/tj/v17/n1/dna (article dated April 1, 2003; accessed September 21, 2012).

2. William Donato, personal correspondence, November 9, 2010.

3. Westenhöfer, *Der Eigenweg des Menschen,* 144.

4. Hardy, "Was Man More Aquatic in the Past?" 643.

5. Hardy, "Was There a Homo Aquaticus?," 6.

6. Hawkes, "The Achievements of Paleolithic Man," 186.

7. E. Hernandez, book review. Go to www.amazon.com and search on "Morgan Aquatic Ape," then search customer reviews for "Swim a little faster" (accessed September 21, 2012).

8. Langdon, "Umbrella Hypotheses and Parsimony in Human Evolution: A Critique of the Aquatic Ape Hypothesis," 479.

9. Morris, "Desmond Morris on the Aquatic Ape Hypothesis," www.youtube.com/watch?v=mFRYtPQfyCk (undated video; accessed September 21, 2012).

10. Morgan, "Aquatic Ape Theory," www.primitivism.com/aquatic-ape.htm (undated article; accessed September 21, 2012).

11. Ibid.

12. Ibid.

# CHAPTER 2. HOMO AQUATICUS

1. Morgan, *The Aquatic Ape,* 14.

2. *Science Daily,* "Human Gland Probably Evolved From Gills," www.sciencedaily .com/releases/2004/12/041206205216.htm (article dated December 7, 2004; accessed September 21, 2012).

3. Morris, "Desmond Morris on The Aquatic Ape Hypothesis," www.you tube .com/watch?v=mFRYtPQfyCk (undated video; accessed September 21, 2012).

4. *National Geographic,* April 1975; article on Tierra Del Fuego, 12.

5. Morris, "Desmond Morris on the Aquatic Ape Theory," www.youtube.com/ watch?v=mFRYtPQfyCk (undated video; accessed September 21, 2012).

6. Henneberg, "Über die Bedeutung der Ohrmuschel," 22; see Duchenne, *Physiology of Motion Demonstrated by Means of Electrical Stimulation and Clinical Observation and Applied to the Study of Paralysis and Deformities.*

7. Verhaegen, message to online forum, http://groups.google.com/group/sci .anthropology.paleo/msg/b5eb7aa0d05e7360?hl=en, and search topics on "Verhaegen Jan 10 1999" (accessed September 21, 2012).

8. Ibid.

9. Westenhöfer, *Der Eigenweg des Menschen,* 58.

10. Emerson, *Emerson,* 208.

11. Burke, "Swimmers: Body Fat Mystery," www.sportsci.org/news/compeat/fat .html (article dated November 16, 1997; accessed September 21, 2012).

12. Morgan, *The Aquatic Ape,* 163.

13. Morris, "Desmond Morris on the Aquatic Ape Theory, www.youtube.com/ watch?v=mFRYtPQfyCk (undated video; accessed September 21, 2012).

14. Verhaegen, message to online forum, http://groups.google.com/group/sci .anthropology.paleo/msg/b5eb7aa0d05e7360?hl=en, and search topics on "Verhaegen Jan 10 1999" (accessed September 21, 2012).

15. Hardy, "Was there a Homo Aquaticus?" 4–6.

16. Wind, "Human Drowning: Phylogenetic Origins," http://dx.doi.org/10 .1016/0047-2484 (76) 90040–3 (accessed September 21, 2012).

17. Morgan, *The Aquatic Ape,* 177.

18. Morgan, "Aquatic Ape Theory," www.primitivism.com/aquatic-ape.htm (undated article; accessed September 21, 2012).

19. Ibid.

20. Hardy, "Was There a Homo Aquaticus?" 4–6.

21. Morris, "Desmond Morris on the Aquatic Ape Theory, www.youtube.com/watch?v=mFRYtPQfyCk (undated video; accessed September 21, 2012).

22. World Records Academy, "Deepest Free Immersion Dive—World Record Set by William Trubridge," www.worldrecordsacademy.org/sports/deepest_free_immersion_dive_world_record_set_by_William_Trubridge_101665.htm (article dated April 25, 2010; accessed September 21, 2012).

23. Westenhöfer, *Der Eigenweg des Menschen,* 88.

24. Bell, "On Syndactyly and Its Association with Polydactyly," 110.

## CHAPTER 3. THE CRADLE OF LIFE

1. Morris, "Desmond Morris on the Aquatic Ape Theory, www.youtube.com/watch?v=mFRYtPQfyCk (undated video; accessed September 21, 2012).

2. Odent, "Birth Under Water," 1476.

3. Garland, *Waterbirth,* 142.

4. Coila, "Why Are Babies Comforted by Rocking?" www.livestrong.com/article/515361-why-are-babies-comforted-by-rocking (article dated August 18, 2011; accessed September 22, 2012).

5. Willard, "Rocked In The Cradle Of The Deep," http://womenshistory.about.com/library/etext/poem1/blp_willard_cradle_deep.htm (accessed September 22, 2012).

6. Coila, "Why Are Babies Comforted by Rocking?" www.livestrong.com/article/515361-why-are-babies-comforted-by-rocking (article dated August 18, 2011; accessed September 22, 2012).

7. Preston, *The Wild Trees,* 167.

8. Morgan, *The Aquatic Ape,* 55.

9. Gorton's Inc., "Seafood is Brain Food!" http://gortons.com/smartnutrition (undated article; accessed September 22, 2012).

10. Ibid.

11. *Science Daily,* "Fish Really Is Brain Food: Vitamin D May Lessen Age-Related Cognitive Decline," www.sciencedaily.com/releases/2009/05/090521084832.htm (article dated May 22, 2009; accessed September 22, 2012).

12. Morris, "Desmond Morris on the Aquatic Ape Theory, www.youtube.com/watch?v=mFRYtPQfyCk (undated video; accessed September 21, 2012).

13. Hardy, "Was Man More Aquatic in the Past?" 644.

14. William Donato, personal correspondence, November 9, 2010.

15. Morgan, *The Aquatic Ape,* 77.

16. Briggs, "Elephant Had an Aquatic Ancestor," http://earthisours.blogspot .com/2008/04/elephant-had-aquatic-ancestor.html (undated article; accessed September 22, 2012).

17. Morgan, *The Aquatic Ape,* 148.

18. *Daily Star,* "New View of Human Evolution," www.thedailystar.net/new Design/news-details.php?nid=174208 (article dated February 15, 2011; accessed September 22, 2012).

19. William Donato, personal correspondence, November 9, 2010.

20. Thorpe et al., "Origin of Human Bipedalism as an Adaptation for Locomotion on Flexible Branches," 1330.

## CHAPTER 4. GENES DON'T LIE

1. Chesner et al., "Eruptive History of Earth's Largest Quaternary Caldera (Toba, Indonesia) Clarified," 201.

2. Nietzsche, *Twilight of the Idols,* 157.

3. Ambrose, "Late Pleistocene Human Population Bottlenecks, Volcanic Winter, and Differentiation of Modern Humans," 644.

4. Oppenheimer, *Eden in the East,* 185.

5. Churchward, *The Lost Continent of Mu,* 211.

6. Melville, *Children of the Rainbow,* 94.

7. Knappert, *Pacific Mythology,* 183.

8. Oppenheimer, *Eden in the East,* 242.

9. Kramer, *The Sumerians,* 172.

10. Le Plongeon, *Sacred Mysteries Among the Mays and Quiches,* 231.

11. Limu Project, www.limuproject.org/why-limu (undated page; accessed September 24, 2012).

12. Heyerdahl, *The Maldive Mystery,* 147.

13. Churchward, *The Lost Continent of Mu,* 204.

14. Lippel, "Shell Beads from South African Cave Show Modern Human Behavior 75,000 Years Ago," www.eurekalert.org/pub_releases/2004-04/nsf-sbf041304 .php (article dated April 15, 2004; accessed September 24, 2012).

15. *Science Daily,* "World's Oldest Ritual Discovered—Worshipped The Python 70,000 Years Ago," www.sciencedaily.com/releases/2006/11/061130081347 .htm (article dated November 30, 2006; accessed September 24, 2012).

16. Norbu, *Drung, Deu and Boen,* 122.

17. *OL News,* "Cretan Tools Point to 130,000-Year-Old Sea Travel," www.aolnews .com/2011/01/04/cretan-tools-point-to-130-000-year-old-sea-travel (article dated January 4, 2011; accessed September 24, 2012).

18. Blumenberg, "Mankind's First Island Voyages," www.environmentalgraffiti .com/ecology/mankinds-first-island-voyages/10713 (undated article; accessed September 24, 2012).

19. Bednarik, "The First Mariners Project," http://mc2.vicnet.net.au/home/mar iners/web/index.html (undated article; accessed September 24, 2012).

20. Ibid.

21. *IB Times,* "Aboriginal Hair Reveals Two Waves of Human Migration," http://newyork.ibtimes.com/articles/218889/20110923/aborigini-hair-aus tralia-migration-africa-dna.htm (article dated September 23, 2011; accessed September 24, 2012).

22. Mathilda's Anthropology Blog, "The Evolution of Lactose Tolerance, and it's [sic] Distribution," http://mathildasanthropologyblog.wordpress .com/2008/03/08/the-evolution-of-lactose-tolerance-and-its-distribution (arti cle dated March 8, 2008; accessed September 24, 2012).

23. *Science Daily,* "Lactose Intolerance Linked To Ancestral Environment," www .sciencedaily.com/releases/2005/06/050602012109.htm (article dated June 2, 2005; accessed September 24, 2012).

24. Owen, "Stone Age Adults Couldn't Stomach Milk, Gene Study Shows," http://news.nationalgeographic.com/news/2007/02/070226-europe-milk .html (article dated February 26, 2007; accessed September 24, 2012).

25. Random FAQ, "Milk and Asians," www.randomfaq.com/facts/00595/?Milk%20 &%20Asians (undated article; accessed September 24, 2012).

26. Westenhöfer, *Der Eigenweg des Menschen,* 212.

27. Sturluson, *The Prose Edda,* 169.

## CHAPTER 5. THE ASCENT OF MAN

1. University of Copenhagen, "Center for Macroecology, Evolution and Climate," http://macroecology.ku.dk (undated website; accessed September 25, 2012).

2. *Columbia Encyclopedia,* 6th ed., s.v. "Neanderthal man," www.encyclopedia .com/topic/Neanderthal.aspx (undated entry; accessed September 25, 2012).

3. Ibid.

4. Moskowitz, "Neanderthal Brains Grew Like Ours," www.livescience .com/2856-neanderthal-brains-grew.html (article dated September 8, 2008; accessed September 25, 2012).

5. Hawkes, *Man Before History,* 160.

6. *BBC News,* "Blow to Neanderthal Breeding Theory," http://news.bbc .co.uk/2/hi/science/nature/3023685.stm (article dated May 13, 2003; accessed September 25, 2012).

7. Hawkes, *Man Before History,* 203.

8. Emile Cartailhac, quoted in Muzquiz Perez-Seoane, *The Cave of Altamira,* 276.

9. Hawkes, *Man Before History,* 202.

10. Absolute Astronomy, "Lascaux," www.absoluteastronomy.com/topics/Lascaux (undated article; accessed September 25, 2012).

11. *How Art Made the World,* hosted by Nigel Spivey. Documentary, 5 episodes. BBC Television-1, first broadcast May 9, 2005.

## CHAPTER 6. DISCOVERY AS HERESY

1. Frontiers of Anthropology Blog, "The X Factor: Best Evidence For TransAtlantic (Solutrean) Colonization of New World," http://frontiers-of-anthropology .blogspot.com/2011/02/x-factor-best-evidence-for.html (article dated February 25, 2011; accessed September 25, 2012).

2. DeGrey et al. "Lake Bonneville Flood," http://geology.isu.edu/Digital_Geology_ Idaho/Module14/mod14.htm (undated article; accessed September 25, 2012).

3. Hirst, "The Solutrean-Clovis Connection: A Theory for the Peopling of America," http://archaeology.about.com/od/skthroughsp/qt/solutrean_clovi .htm (undated article; accessed September 25, 2012).

4. Saletan, "The Mismeasure of Stephen Jay Gould," http://discovermagazine .com/2012/jan-feb/59 (accessed September 25, 2012).

5. Hirst, "The Solutrean-Clovis Connection: A Theory for the Peopling of America," http://archaeology.about.com/od/skthroughsp/qt/solutrean_clovi .htm (undated article; accessed September 25, 2012).

6. Sanford, "Immigrants from the Other Side," www.freerepublic.com/focus/ f-news/1013315/posts (article dated November 3, 2003; accessed November 28, 2012).

7. Balter, "Ancient Algae Suggest Sea Route for First Americans," www .sci encemag.org/content/320/5877.toc (accessed September 25, 2012).

8. Corliss, *Archaeological Anomalies,* 173.

9. Guidon et al, "Nature and Age of the Deposits in Pedra Furada, Brazil: Reply to Meltzer, Adovasio and Dillehay," 408.

10. *Athena Review,* "Pedra Furada, Brazil: Paleoindians, Paintings, and Paradoxes," www.athenapub.com/10pfurad.htm (article published 1986; accessed September 25, 2012).

11. Guidon et al., "Nature and Age of the Deposits in Pedra Furada, Brazil: Reply to Meltzer, Adovasio and Dillehay," 408.

12. Corliss, *Archaeological Anomalies,* 26.

13. Ibid.

14. Douglas C. Wallace, www.eupedia.com/forum/showthread.php?25951-R1*-in -North-America-South-East-Asia-and-Australia (accessed September 10, 2012).

15. Pringle, "Did Humans Colonize the World by Boat?" http://discovermagazine .com/2008/jun/20-did-humans-colonize-the-world-by-boat (article dated May 20, 2008; accessed September 25, 2012).

16. Frontiers of Anthropology Blog, "The X Factor: Best Evidence For TransAtlantic (Solutrean) Colonization of New World," http://frontiers-of-anthropology.blogspot.com/2011/02/x-factor-best-evidence-for.html (article dated February 25, 2011; accessed September 25, 2012).

17. Grotte de la Mouthe, www.culture.gouv.fr/culture/conservation/fr/grottes/ Pageshtm/89024.htm; also, Lawson, *Painted Caves.*

18. Rick Osmon, personal correspondence, August 21, 2010.

19. Boness, "World's Oldest Evidence of Deep Sea Fishing," http://scienceillustrated .com.au/blog/science/world%E2%80%99s-oldest-evidence-of-deep-sea-fishing (article dated December 6, 2011; accessed September 25, 2012).

## CHAPTER 7. STONE AGE SOPHISTICATION

1. Hawkes, *Man Before History,* 110.

2. D'Errico, "Did Humans Invent Modernity?," www.project-syndicate.org/ commentary/did-humans-invent-modernity (article dated October 24, 2012; accessed November 28, 2012).

3. Gimbutas, *The Goddesses and Gods of Old Europe,* 223.

4. Leakey, *Origins,* 92.

5. Spence, *The History of Atlantis,* 143.

6. Nogués-Bravo et al., "Climate predictors of Late Quaternary extinctions," cited by Samuel T. Turvey and Susanne A. Fritz in "The ghosts of mammals past:

biological and geographical patterns of global mammalian extinction across the Holocene," Philosophiocal Transactions of the Royal Society, Biological Sciences, London, http://rstb.royalsocietypublishing.org/con tent/366/1577/2564.full (article dated August 1, 2011; accessed November 28, 2012).

7. *Science Daily*, "Mass Extinction: Why Did Half of N. America's Large Mammals Disappear 40,000 to 10,000 Years Ago?" www.sciencedaily.com/ releases/2009/11/091127140706.htm (article dated November 27, 2009; accessed September 27, 2012).

8. Nogués-Bravo et al., "Climate Predictors of Late Quaternary Extinctions."

9. *Science Daily*, "Mass Extinction: Why Did Half of N. America's Large Mammals Disappear 40,000 to 10,000 Years Ago?" www.sciencedaily.com/ releases/2009/11/091127140706.htm (article dated November 27, 2009; accessed September 27, 2012).

10. Kennett, quoted in Hirst, "Megafauna Extinctions," http://archaeology.about .com/od/mterms/g/megaextinct.htm (undated article; accessed September 27, 2012).

11. Ibid.

12. Haughton, *Hidden History,* 238.

13. Hirst, K. Kris, "Wheat Domestication, The Origins of Wheat," *Archaeology,* http://archaeology.about.com/od/domestications/qt/wheat.htm.

14. Settegast, *Plato, Prehistorian,* 156.

15. Cahokia Mounds State Historic Site, http://cahokiamounds.org/explore/ cahokia-mounds/woodhenge (accessed September 27, 2012).

16. Murdock, "World's Oldest Observatory Found?" www.examiner.com/article/ world-s-oldest-observatory-found (article dated October 12, 2010; accessed September 27, 2012).

17. Belinskaya, "Göbekli Tepe," 24.

18. Childress, *Lost Cities of Ancient Lemuria and the Pacific,* 184.

19. Melville, *Children of the Rainbow.*

20. Churchward, *The Lost Continent of Mu.*

## CHAPTER 8. THE MOTHER OF INVENTION

1. Napier, "Evidence for Cometary Bombardment Episodes," www.stat.berke ley.edu/~aldous/157/Papers/napier.pdf (article dated October 2005; accessed September 27, 2012).

2. Zorats Karer website, collection of videos at http://wn.com/Zorats_Karer (accessed September 27, 2012).

3. Vahradyan, Vachagan, "Armenian Qarahunge Megalithic Complex Older than Stonehenge," online forum post, www.network54.com/Forum/149359/thread/1283870071/last-1285025209/Sa-na-hin-+This+Armenian+Stonehedge+Is+Older+Than+The+British+Stonehedge (accessed September 27, 2012).

4. Zorats Karer website, collection of videos at http://wn.com/Zorats_Karer (accessed September 27, 2012).

5. Stars and Stones 2010 Website, http://qarahunge.icosmos.co.uk (accessed September 27, 2012).

6. Professor Paris M. Herouni Resume, www.carahunge.com/herouni.html (undated page; accessed September 27, 2012).

7. Herouni, *Armenians and Old Armenia*, 24.

8. Manilius, *Astronomica*, 59.

9. Krapina Tourist Board, "The legend of Čeh, Leh and Meh," http://tzgkrapina.hr/en/about_krapina/about_krapina-7-legends (undated page; accessed September 27, 2012).

10. Vahradyan, Vachagan, "Armenian Qarahunge Megalithic Complex Older than Stonehenge," online forum post,www.network54.com/Forum/149359/thread/1283870071/last-1285025209/Sa-na-hin-+This+Armenian+Stonehedge+Is+Older+Than+The+British+Stonehedge (accessed September 27, 2012).

11. Alley and Ágústsdóttir, "The 8k Event: Cause and Consequences of a Major Holocene Abrupt Climate Change." http://dx.doi.org/10.1016/j.quascirev.2004.12.004 (accessed September 27, 2012).

12. Ananikian, *Armenian Mythology*, 55.

13. Khorenatsi, *History of Armenia*, 276.

## CHAPTER 9. OLDER THAN SPHINX OR PYRAMID

1. Mercatante, *Who's Who in Egyptian Mythology*, 94.

2. Malville, et al., "Astronomy of Nabta Playa," 44.

3. Brophy, *The Origin Map*, 85.

4. Gaffney, "The Astronomers of Nabta Playa," 31.

5. Schoch, Foreword to *The Origin Map*, 4.

6. *Deutsche Welle*, "Archaeologists Unearth German Stonehenge," www.dw-world.de/dw/article/0,,942824,00.html (undated article; accessed September 28, 2012).

7. Ibid.

8. Coon, *The Races of Europe,* 59.

9. Collins, *Gods of Eden,* 165.

10. Hancock and Faiia, *Heaven's Mirror,* 224.

11. Temple, *The Sphinx Mystery,* 251.

12. Nienhuis, James I., Dancing From Genesis Blog, www.google.com, and search on "Dancing from genesis lion king sphinx symbolism."

13. Schoch, Foreword to *The Origin Map,* xiv, xv, 7.

14. Ibid., 8.

15. Ibid., 7.

16. Ibid., 9.

17. Gaffney, "The Astronomers of Nabta Playa," 27.

18. Scott Creighton, "8,000 Year Old Nabta Playa Stone Circle Vandalised," post to Above Top Secret Forum, www.abovetopsecret.com/forum/thread350884/pg1 (post dated April 23, 2008; accessed September 28, 2012).

19. The Udjat, "8,000 Year Old Nabta Playa Vandalized?" http://blog.centerformaat.com/2009/05/8000-year-old-nabta-playa-vandalized.html (post dated May 28, 2009; accessed September 28, 2012).

## CHAPTER 10. STONE AGE ASTRONOMERS IN AMERICA

1. Jay Stuart Wakefield, personal correspondence, September 10, 2010.

2. Hammond, "Meaglithic Stones 'Were Navigational Aids,'" www.abc-publishing-group.co.uk/Megalithic.htm (article dated December 1, 2010; accessed September 28, 2012).

3. Thom, *Megalithic Remains in Britain and Brittany,* 102.

4. Wakefield and de Jonge, *Rocks & Rows,* 174.

5. Ibid., 173.

6. Ibid.

7. Ibid., 174.

8. Ibid., 172.

9. Scofield, *Sacred Sites,* 126.

10. Vieira, "Search for the Mysterious Stone Builders of New England," 7.

11. Zink, *The Ancient Stones Speak,* 147.

12. Foster, "Megalithic Sites Re-examined as Spacial Systems," in Swan, *The Power of Place,* 124.

13. Vieira, "Search for the Mysterious Stone Builders of New England," 8.

14. Ibid.

15. Wakefield and de Jonge, *Rocks & Rows,* 222.

16. Ibid.

17. Scofield, *Sacred Sites,* 56.

18. Ibid., 57.

## CHAPTER 11. RED PAINT PEOPLE

1. Moorehead, *The Stone Age in North America.*

2. Thompson, *American Discovery,* 67.

3. Westerdahl, "A Circumpolar Reappraisal: The Legacy of Gutorm Gjessing (1906–1979)," 36.

4. Murray, "Red Paint People and Red Ochre People, Link or Legend," 5.

5. Wakefield and de Jonge, *Rocks & Rows,* 73.

6. Fell, *America, B.C.,* 14.

7. Murray, "Red Paint People and Red Ochre People, Link or Legend," 7.

8. Covey, "The Solutrean Connection Question," cited by Sanford in "Immigrants From The Other Side," www.freerepublic.com/focus/f-news/1013315/posts (article dated November 3, 2003; accessed November 28, 2012).

9. Pepper and Wilcock, *Magical and Mystical Sites,* 95.

10. "Researchers to study Beothuk remains," CBC News, www.cbc.ca/news/canada/newfoundland-labrador/story/2009/08/14/beothuk-dna-814.html (article dated August 17, 2009; accessed November 28, 2012).

11. Quoted by Angel, "Who Built New England's Megalithic Monuments?" 9.

12. Ibid., 10.

13. Rydholm, "Michigan's Dolmen: A Stone Age Presence in America?" 31.

14. James Mavor Jr., quoted by Carol A. Hanny, "North Salem Dolmen, North Salem, New York," www.skyweb.net/~channy/NSDolmen.html (undated site; accessed September 28, 2012).

15. Angel, "Who Built New England's Megalithic Monuments?" 15.

16. Rothenberg, ed., *The Papers of Joseph Henry.*

17. Whittall, "2995 B.P. +/-180," 11.

18. Vieira, "Search for the Mysterious Stone Builders of New England," 12.

19. Whittall, "2995 B.P. +/-180," 21.

20. In Memorium: James Whittall, www.neara.org/ROS/Whittal.htm (undated page; accessed September 28, 2012).

# CHAPTER 12. SACRED HOOPS

1. Scofield, *Sacred Sites,* 79.

2. Foster, "Megalithic Sites Re-examined as Spacial Systems," in *The Power of Place;* Thom, *Megalithic Sites in Britain,* 124.

3. Geoffrey of Monmouth, *The History of the Kings of Britain,* 26.

4. Jasch, "The Tripod Rock Caper," www.njskylands.com/odhiketripod.htm (undated page; accessed September 28, 2012).

5. Fell, *America, B.C.,* 147.

6. Angel, "Who Built New England's Megalithic Monuments?" 14.

7. Scherz, "The Stone Face at Mummy Mountain," 4.

8. Foster, "Megalithic Sites Re-examined as Spacial Systems," in *The Power of Place,* 80.

9. Hansel, "Environmental Grafitti Boundary Water's Route: The Hunt for the Viking Dolmen," www.paddlinglight.com/articles/trip-reports/boundary-waters-route-the-hunt-for-the-viking-dolmen (post dated November 10, 2009; accessed September 28, 2012).

10. Scherz, "The Stone Face at Mummy Mountain," 3.

11. Ibid., 4.

12. Zink, *The Ancient Stones Speak,* 115.

13. Hawkins, "Prehistoric Astronomy: Archaeo-Astronomy, the Unwritten Evidence," 29.

14. Olsen, *Sacred Places North America,* 177.

15. Freeman, quoted in Weber, "Alberta Sun Temple has 5,000-year-old Calendar," www.thestar.com/News/Canada/article/579301 (article dated January 29, 2009; accessed September 28, 2012).

# CHAPTER 13. LITTLE HELL

1. Helferich, *Humboldt's Cosmos,* 167.

2. Engel, *Musica Myths and Facts,* 43.

3. Plato, *The Timaeus and the Kritias.*

4. Blackett, *The Lost History of America,* 158.

5. *Daily Mail Online,* "Archaeologists Discover 'Tropical Stonehenge,'" www.dailymail.co.uk/news/article-392988/Archaeologists-discover-tropical-Stonehenge.html (article dated June 29, 2006; accessed September 30, 2012).

6. Squier, 27.

7. Brinton, "Current Notes on Anthropology," 62.

8. Lilley, *Archaeology of Oceania*, 227.

9. Wiley, *Assignment New Guinea*, 54.

10. Zink, *The Ancient Stones Speak*, 135.

11. *Science Newsletter*, "Nature, Not Man, Made Mummies in Island Cave," 15.

12. Hides, 31.

13. Doutré, *Ancient Celtic New Zealand*, 52.

14. Krieger, *Design Areas in Oceania*, 13.

15. Gilroy, *Mysterious Australia*, 126.

16. Morse, "Dolmens in Japan," 38.

17. "Secrets of the Stone Circles," http://heritageofjapan.wordpress.com/just-what-was-so-amazing-about-jomon-japan/ways-of-the-jomon-world-2/did-the-jomon-have-a-calendar/secrets-of-the-stone-circles (undated post; accessed September 30, 2012).

18. Morse, "Dolmens in Japan," 73.

19. Cavalli-Sforza et al., *The History and Geography of Human Genes*, 116.

20. "Mysterious 5,000-year-old Megalith Found in E. China," www.goldenageproject.org.uk/278meganddol.php; also see Lanpo, *Early Man in China*.

21. Foster, "Megalithic Sites Re-examined as Spacial Systems," in Swan, *The Power of Place*, 99.

22. Noorbergen, *Secrets of Lost Races*, 64.

23. *The Hindu*, "Signature of the Sky in Rock," www.hindu.com/2006/04/19/stories/2006041921290200.htm (article dated April 19, 2006; accessed September 30, 2012).

24. Andy B. "Isle of Vera—Standing Stones in Russia," Megalithic Portal, www.megalithic.co.uk/article.php?sid=19208 (post dated May 9, 2008; accessed September 30, 2012).

25. du Pouge, *Manners and Monuments of Prehistoric Peoples*, 222.

26. Ibid., 119.

27. Graham J. Salisbury, "Re-discovery of Moroccan Megalithic Stone Circle," post to Lost Cities and Remote Places Blog, http://lostcities.weebly.com/1/post/2011/01/re-discovery-of-moroccan-megalithic-stone-circle.html (dated January 13, 2011; accessed September 30, 2012).

28. Geoffrey, *The History of the Kings of Britain*, 17.

## CHAPTER 14. SECRET OF THE STONES

1. Gilroy, *Mysterious Australia*, 28.

2. MacKie, *The Megalith Builders*, 139.

3. Du Pouge, *Manners and Monuments of Prehistoric Peoples*, 106.

4. Zink, *The Ancient Stones Speak*, 24.

5. Ibid., 73.

6. Ibid., 78.

7. Devereux, *Earth Lights Revelation*, 62.

8. Zink, *The Ancient Stones Speak*, 37.

9. Scofield, *Sacred Sites*, 216.

10. Foster, "Megalithic Sites Re-examined as Spacial Systems," in Swan, *The Power of Place*, 118.

11. Devereux, *Earth Lights Revelation*, 48.

12. Ibid., 112.

13. Miller, "Fear and Loathing in the Temporal Lobes," http://neurotheology .50megs.com/whats_new_9.html (article dated September 2003; accessed November 28, 2012).

14. Foster, "Megalithic Sites Re-examined as Spacial Systems," in Swan, *The Power of Place*, 27.


## CHAPTER 15. THE FIRST ATLANTEAN

1. Plato, *The Timaeus and the Kritias*, 36.

2. Ibid., 55.

3. Ibid., plus Zeller, *Über die Anachronismen*, 77.

4. Plato, *The Timaeus and the Kritias*.

5. Heindel and Foss, *The Message of the Stars*, 202.

6. Spence, *The History of Atlantis*, 132.

7. Price, *Europe's First Farmers*, 94.

8. Plato, *The Timaeus and the Kritias*, 57.

9. Whitmore et al., "Elephant Teeth from the Atlantic Continental Shelf," 1478.

10. Spence, *The History of Atlantis*, 110.

11. Sweeney, *Atlantis: The Evidence of Science*, 88.

12. Coon, *The Origin of Races*, 142; Niskanen, "The Origin of the Baltic-Finns from the Physical Anthropological Point of View," 112.

13. Spence, *The History of Atlantis*, 154.

14. Leonard, *The Quest for Atlantis,* 137.

15. *The Great Soviet Encyclopedia,* 3rd ed., 368.

16. David Pilebaum, quoted by Cremo and Thompson, *Forbidden Archaeology,* 47.

17. Andor Thoma, quoted by Cremo and Thompson, *Forbidden Archaeology,* 126.

18. Cremo and Thompson, *Forbidden Archaeology,* 38.

19. Lemesurier, *Decoding the Great Pyramid,* 79.

20. Mercer, *Fuerteventura and the Canary Islands,* 61.

21. Lemesurier, *Decoding the Great Pyramid,* 127.

22. Cavalli-Sforza, Menozzi, and Alberto, *The History and Geography of Human Genes,* 53.

## CHAPTER 16. STONE AGE DÉJÀ VU

1. Rainey, "Mystery of the Arctic."

2. Ibid.

3. National Snow and Ice Data Center, "Frequently Asked Questions About Arctic Sea Ice," http://nsidc.org/cryosphere/quickfacts (accessed October 2, 2012).

4. Thompson, *American Discovery,* 201.

5. Dawicki, "Rapid Sea Level Rise in the Arctic Ocean May Alter Views of Human Migration," www.whoi.edu/page.do?pid=39139&tid=282&cid=1652 6&ct=162 (article dated October 11, 2006; accessed October 2, 2012).

6. Covey, "The Solutrean Connection Question," cited by Sanford in "Immigrants From The Other Side," www.freerepublic.com/focus/f-news/1013315/posts (article dated November 3, 2003; accessed November 28, 2012).

7. Ibid.

8. Rock, "Pendejo Cave."

9. National Academy of Sciences, *Memoirs Of The National Academy Of Sciences.*

10. "A 50,000-Year-Old Californian," *Tulsa World,* June 29, 1969; KevinMiller50501 post to Ancient Native Heritage message board, http://groups.yahoo.com/group/ancient-native-heritage/message/2169 (post dated December 1, 2003; accessed October 2, 2012).

11. "America's Stone Age Explorers," *NOVA,* PBS, November 9, 2004, www.pbs .org/wgbh/nova/transcripts/3116_stoneage.html (accessed October 2, 2012).

12. Cremo and Thompson, *Forbidden Archaeology.*

13. Corliss, *Archaeological Anomalies.*

14. Wallace, "The Antiquity of Man in North America."

15. Corliss, *Archaeological Anomalies.*

16. Steen-McIntyre, "A Quarter Million Year-Old Human Habitation Site found in Mexico."

17. Ibid.

18. Collins, "Stone Age Columbus," www.bbc.co.uk/science/horizon/2002/colum bustrans.shtml (undated program; accessed October 2, 2012).

19. Covey, "The Solutrean Connection Question," cited by Sanford in "Immigrants From The Other Side," www.freerepublic.com/focus/f-news/1013315/posts (article dated November 3, 2003; accessed November 28, 2012).

20. Gould, "On the Recent Finding of Another Flint Arrowhead in the Pleistocene Deposit of Frederick, Oklahoma," 93.

21. Renne, quoted in Wilford, "Old, for Sure, but Human?" www.nytimes.com/ 2005/12/13/science/13find.html (accessed October 2, 2012).

22. Associated Press, "'Game-changer' in Evolution from S. African Bones," *The Daily Texan*, September 8, 2011, www.dailytexanonline.com and search on "game-changer" (accessed August 21, 2012).

23. James, K. "New Human Ancestor Will Rewrite Evolution." http://technology .gather.com/viewArticle.action?articleId=281474980232031 (article dated September 10, 2011; accessed October 2, 2012).

24. Corliss, *Archaeological Anomalies,* 96.

25. Florentino Ameghino, quoted by Cremo and Thompson, *Forbidden Archaeology,* 44.

26. Durant, *The Lessons of History,* 332.

## CHAPTER 17. AFTER ATLANTIS

1. Chesterfield, *Lord Chesterfield's Letters,* 121.

2. Good Reads, "Robert Penn Warren Quotes," www.goodreads.com/quotes/ show/41557 (undated page; accessed October 3, 2012).

3. Ysursa Family website, "History Wars," Ken Burns quote, www.ysursa.com/ history/what_is_history.htm (undated page; accessed October 3, 2012).

4. George Santayana, quoted on Student's Friend website, "The Uses of History," www .studentsfriend.com/onhist/uses.html (undated page; accessed October 3, 2012).

5. Winston Churchill, quoted in Lawson, "Rare British India Documents Surface," http://news.bbc.co.uk/2/hi/6176805.stm (article dated January 3, 2007; accessed October 3, 2012).

6. Edward Gibbon in *Bartlett's Familiar Quotations,* 248.

7. Good Reads, "Joseph Stalin Quotes," www.goodreads.com/author/ quotes/138332.Joseph_Stalin (undated page; accessed October 3, 2012).

8. Robert Penn Warren quoted in Beiswenger, "The Legacy of the Civil War: The Disparate Views of Robert Penn Warren and Allen Tate," http://spider .georgetowncollege.edu/htallant/border/bs7/beiswenh.htm (accessed October 3, 2012).

# Bibliography

Acton, John Emerich, and Edward Dalberg. "A Lecture on the Study of History: Delivered at Cambridge, June 11, 1895." New York: Cornell University Library, 2009.

Alley, Richard B., and Anna Maria Ágústsdóttir. "The 8k Event: Cause and Consequences of a Major Holocene Abrupt Climate Change." *Quaternary Science Reviews* 24, nos. 10–11 (May 2005): 1123–49. http://dx.doi .org/10.1016/j.quascirev.2004.12.004 (accessed September 27, 2012).

Ambrose, Stanley. "Late Pleistocene Human Population Bottlenecks, Volcanic Winter, and Differentiation of Modern Humans." *Journal of Human Evolution* 34, no. 6 (1998): 623–51.

Ananikian, Mardiros Harootioon. *Armenian Mythology: Stories of Armenian Gods and Goddesses, Heroes and Heroines, Hells & Heavens, Folklore & Fairy Tales.* New York: Indo-European Publishing, 2010.

Andrews, Philip. "Geology of the Pinnacles National Monument." University of California. *Bulletin of the Department of Geological Sciences* 24, no. 1 (1936).

Angel, Paul Tudor. "Who Built New England's Megalithic Monuments?" *The Barnes Review* 11, no. 5 (November 1997).

Anikovich, M. V., et al. "Early Upper Paleolithic in Eastern Europe and Implications for the Dispersal of Modern Humans." *Science* 315, no. 5809 (January 12, 2007): 223–26.

Aristotle. *Metaphysics.* Sioux Falls, S. Dak.: NuVision Publications, 2009.

*Athena Review.* "Pedra Furada, Brazil: Paleoindians, Paintings, and Paradoxes." *Athena Review* 3, no.2 (1986). www.athenapub.com/10pfurad.htm (accessed September 25, 2012).

Aujoulat, Norbert. *Lascaux: Movement, Space and Time.* New York: Harry N. Abrams, 2005.

Balter, Michael. "Ancient Algae Suggest Sea Route for First Americans." *Science* 320, no. 5877 (May 9, 2008): 729. www.sciencemag.org/content/320/5877.toc (accessed September 25, 2012).

Bednarik, Robert G. "The First Mariners Project." http://mc2.vicnet.net.au/home/ mariners/web/index.html (undated article; accessed September 24, 2012).

Beiswenger, Hugo. "The Legacy of the Civil War: The Disparate Views of Robert Penn Warren and Allen Tate." *Border States* 7 (1989). http://spider.georgetown college.edu/htallant/border/bs7/beiswenh.htm (accessed October 3, 2012).

Belinskaya, Olga. "Göbekli Tepe." *The Barnes Review* 15, no. 6 (November/ December 2009).

Bell, Julia. "On Syndactyly and Its Association with Polydactyly." *The Treasury of Human Inheritance.* Vol. 5, *On Hereditary Digital Anomalies, Part 2.* New York: Cambridge University Press, 1953.

Bender, Rebato, Marc Verhaegen, and Nicole Oser. "Acquisition of Human Bipedal Gait from the Viewpoint of the Aquatic Ape Theory." *Anthropologischer Anzeiger* 55 (1997).

Bicho, Nuno, et al. "The Upper Paleolithic Rock Art of Iberia." *Journal of Archaeological Method and Theory* 14, no. 1 (March 2007).

Blackett, W. S. *The Lost History of America.* London: Truebner and Company, 1883.

Blumenberg, Bennet. "Mankind's First Island Voyages." Environmental Graffiti. www.environmentalgraffiti.com/ecology/mankinds-first-island-voyages/10713 (undated article; accessed September 24, 2012).

Boness, Laura. "World's Oldest Evidence of Deep Sea Fishing." *Science Illustrated.* http://scienceillustrated.com.au/blog/science/world%E2%80%99s-oldest-evidence-of-deep-sea-fishing (article dated December 6, 2011; accessed September 25, 2012).

Bordes, Francois. *The Old Stone Age.* New York: McGraw-Hill Book Co., 1968.

Bourque, Bruce. *Red Paint People: A Lost American Culture.* Piermont, N.H.: Bunker Hill Publishing, Inc., 2004.

Briggs, Helen. "Elephant Had an Aquatic Ancestor." Earth Is Ours Blog. http:// earthisours.blogspot.com/2008/04/elephant-had-aquatic-ancestor.html (undated article; accessed September 22, 2012).

Briggs, L. Cabot. "The Stone Age Races of Northwest Africa." *Bulletin of the American School of Prehistoric Research,* no. 18. Cambridge, Mass.: Peaboby Museum, 1955.

Brinton, D. G. "Current Notes on Anthropology." *Science* 6, no. 155 (December 17, 1897).

Brophy, Thomas G. *The Origin Map.* New York: Writers Club Press, 2002.

Burenhult, Goran. *People of the Stone Age: Hunter-Gatherers and Early Farmers.* Vol. 2 of *The Illustrated History of Humankind.* New York: HarperCollins, 1993.

Burke, Louise. "Swimmers: Body Fat Mystery." *Sports Science.* www.sportsci.org/news/compeat/fat.html (article dated November 16, 1997; accessed September 21, 2012).

Bradley, Bruce A., and Dennis J. Stanford. *Across Atlantic Ice: The Origin of America's Clovis Culture.* Berkeley: University of California Press, 2012.

Breuil, Henri. *Beyond the Bounds of History: Scenes from the Old Stone Age.* New York: Ams Press, Inc.,1976.

Burke, John, and Kaj Halberg. *Seed of Knowledge, Stone of Plenty: Understanding the Lost Technology of the Ancient Megalith-Builders.* Oakland, Calif.: Council Oak Books, 2005.

Burl, Aubrey. *Prehistoric Astronomy and Ritual.* Oxford, England: Shire Publications, 1983.

———. *Prehistoric Stone Circles.* Oxford, England: Shire Publications, 1983.

Burroughs, William James. *Climate Change in Prehistory: The End of the Reign of Chaos.* Cambridge, Mass.: Cambridge University Press, 2008.

Cavalli-Sforza, Luca, Paolo Menozzi, and Piazza Alberto. *The History and Geography of Human Genes.* Princeton, N.J.: Princeton University Press, 1994.

Chesner, C. A., J. A. Westgate, W. I. Rose, R. Drake, and A. Deino. "Eruptive History of Earth's Largest Quaternary Caldera (Toba, Indonesia) Clarified." *Geology* 19 (March 1991): 200–203.

Childress, David Hatcher. *Lost Cities of Ancient Lemuria and the Pacific.* Kempton, Ill.: Adventures Unlimited Press, 1988.

———. *Lost Cities of Atlantis, Ancient Europe and the Mediterranean.* Kempton, Ill.: Adventures Unlimited Press, 1996.

Churchward, James. *The Lost Continent of Mu.* Albuquerque, N. Mex.: BE, Books, Brotherhood of Life, Inc., 1987. Reprint of the 1924 original.

Cicero, Marcus Tullius. *On Duties.* Cambridge, Mass.: Cambridge University Press, 1991.

Clark, J. Desmond, *The Prehistory of Africa.* New York: Praeger University Series, 1970.

Coila, Bridget. "Why Are Babies Comforted by Rocking?" Livestrong. www.livestrong.com/article/515361-why-are-babies-comforted-by-rocking (article dated August 18, 2011; accessed September 22, 2012).

Coles, John. *Sweet Track to Glastonbury: The Somerset Levels in Prehistory.* London: Thames and Hudson, 1986.

Collingwood, R. G. *The Idea of History: With Lectures 1926–1928.* Oxford, England: Oxford University Press, 1994.

Collins, Andrew. *Gods of Eden.* Rochester, Vt.: Bear and Company, 1998.

Collins, Michael. "Stone Age Columbus." *Horizon,* BBC television program. www .bbc.co.uk/science/horizon/2002/columbustrans.shtml (undated program; accessed October 2, 2012).

Coon, Carleton S. *The Races of Europe.* Westport, Conn.: Greenwood Press, 1972.

———. *The Story of Man.* New York: Alfred A. Knopf, 1954.

Corliss, William R. *Archaeological Anomalies: Small Artifacts.* Glenn Arm, Md.: The Sourcebook Project, 2003.

Covey, Cyclone. "The Solutrean Connection Question," cited by Dennis Sanford in "Immigrants From The Other Side (Clovis Is Solutrean?)" *Free Republic,* www .freerepublic.com/focus/f-news/1013315/posts (article dated November 3, 2003; accessed November 28, 2012).

Cremo, Michael, and Richard L. Thompson. *Forbidden Archaeology.* rev. ed. n.p., Calif.: Bhaktivedanta Book Publishing, 1998.

Curtis, Gregory. *The Cave Painters: Probing the Mysteries of the World's First Artists.* Harpswell, Maine: Anchor, 2007.

D'Errico, Francesco. "Did Humans Invent Modernity?" Project Syndicate, www .project-syndicate.org/commentary/did-humans-invent-modernity (article dated October 24, 2012; accessed November 28, 2012).

Daniel, Glyn, ed. *The lllustrated Encyclopedia of Archaeology.* New York: Thomas Y. Cowell Company, 1977.

———. *The Megalith-Builders of Western Europe.* Westport, Conn.: Greenwood Publishing Group, 1985.

Darwin, Charles. *On the Origin of Species and the Descent of Man.* Reissue. New York: Modern Library, 1970.

Dawicki, Shelley. "Rapid Sea Level Rise in the Arctic Ocean May Alter Views of Human Migration." Woods Hole Oceanographic Institution. www.whoi.edu/ page.do?pid=39139&tid=282&cid=16526&ct=162 (article dated October 11, 2006; accessed October 2, 2012).

DeGrey, Laura, Myles Miller, and Paul Link. "Lake Bonneville Flood." Idaho State University, Deptartment of Geosciences. Digital Geology of Idaho. http:// geology.isu.edu/Digital_Geology_Idaho/Module14/mod14.htm (undated article; accessed September 25, 2012).

De Jonge, Reinoud, and Jay Stuart Wakefield. *How the Sun God Reached America:*

*A Guide to Megalithic Sites.* n.p., Wash.: Medical Communications and Services, 2002.

Devereux, Paul. *Earth Lights Revelation.* New York: Sterling Publishing Company, Inc., 1990.

DeWitt, David. "Greater than 98% Chimp/Human DNA Similarity? Not Anymore." *Answers in Genesis.* www.answersingenesis.org/articles/tj/v17/n1/dna (article dated April 1, 2003; accessed September 21, 2012).

Dillehay, Thomas D. *Settlement Of The Americas, A New Prehistory.* New York: Basic Books, 2001.

Duchenne, Guillaume-Benjamin-Amand. *Physiology of Motion Demonstrated by Means of Electrical Stimulation and Clinical Observation and Applied to the Study of Paralysis and Deformities.* Translated by Emanuel B. Kaplan. Philadelphia, Penn.: W. B. Saunders, 1959.

Doutré, Martin. *Ancient Celtic New Zealand.* Auckland, New Zealand: De Danann Publishers, 1999.

Du Pouge, Jean-François-Albert. *Manners and Monuments of Prehistoric Peoples.* 1896. Reprint of the original, Whitefish, Mont.: Kessinger Publishing, 2010.

Durant, Will. *The Lessons of History.* New York: Simon & Schuster, 2010.

Edelstein, S. "An Alternative Paradigm for Hominoid Evolution." *Human Evolution* 2(1987): 169.

Ellis, D."Proboscis Monkey and Aquatic Ape." *Sarawak Museum Journal* 36 (1986): 251–262.

Emerson, Ralph Waldo. *Emerson: Essays and Lectures: Nature: Addresses and Lectures/Essays: First and Second Series/Representative Men/English Traits/The Conduct of Life.* New York: Library of America, 1983.

Engel, Carl. *Musica Myths and Facts.* Charleston, S.C.: Nabu Press, 2010.

Fagan, Brian. *Cro-Magnon: How the Ice Age Gave Birth to the First Modern Humans.* New York: Bloomsbury Press, 2011.

Fell, Barry. *America, B.C.* rev. ed. New York: Pocket Books, 1989.

Finlayson, Clive. *The Humans Who Went Extinct: Why Neanderthals Died Out and We Survived.* New York: Oxford University Press, 2010.

Firestone, Richard. *The Cycle of Cosmic Catastrophes, How a Stone Age Comet Changed the Course of World Culture.* Rochester, Vt.: Bear & Company, 2006.

Fitch, W. Tecumseh. "Comparative Vocal Production and the Evolution of Speech: Reinterpreting the Descent of the Larynx," in Wray, *The Transition to Language.*

Foster, Maelee Thomson. "Megalithic Sites Re-examined as Spacial Systems," in Swan, *The Power of Place*.

Freeman, Gordon, *Canada's Stonehenge: Astounding Archaeological Discoveries in Canada, England, and Wales*. London: Kingsley Publishing, 2008.

Frey, William H., with Muriel Langseth. *Crying: The Mystery of Tears*. Minneapolis, Minn.: Winston Press, 1985.

Gaffney, Mark H. "The Astronomers of Nabta Playa." *Atlantis Rising* 56 (March/April 2006).

Garland, Dianne. *Waterbirth: An Attitude to Care*. n.p., England: Books for Midwives PR, 2000.

Geoffrey of Monmouth, *The History of the Kings of Britain*. Translated by Lewis Thorpe. London: Penguin Books, 1969.

Gibbon, Edward in *Bartlett's Familiar Quotations: A Collection of Passages, Phrases, and Proverbs Traced to Their Sources in Ancient and Modern Literature*. 17th ed., New York: Little, Brown and Company, 2002.

Gilroy, Rex. *Mysterious Australia*. Kempton, Ill.: Adventures Unlimited Press, 1995.

Gimbutas, Marija. *The Goddesses and Gods of Old Europe: Myths and Cult Images*. Berkeley: University of California Press, 1982.

Goudsward, David, and Robert Stone. *America's Stonehenge: The Mystery Hill Story*. Wellesley, Mass.: Branden Books, 2003.

Gould, Charles N. "On the Recent Finding of Another Flint Arrowhead in the Pleistocene Deposit of Frederick, Oklahoma." *Washington Academy of Sciences Journal* 19 (1929): 93.

Gowland, Robert. *The Dolmens of Japan and Their Builders*. Charleston, S.C.: Nabu Press, 2010.

Guidon, N., A. M. Pessis, Fabio Parenti, Michel Fontugue, and Claude Guerin. "Nature and Age of the Deposits in Pedra Furada, Brazil: Reply to Meltzer, Adovasio and Dillehay," *Antiquity* 70, no. 268 (1996): 408.

Hadingham, Evan. *Circles and Standing Stones*. New York: Walker and Company, 1975.

———. *Early Man and the Cosmos*. New York: Walker and Company, 1984.

———. *Secrets of the Ice Age*. New York: Walker and Company, 1979.

Hammond, Norman. "Meaglithic Stones 'Were Navigational Aids.'" *The Times*. www.abc-publishing-group.co.uk/Megalithic.htm (article dated December 1, 2010; accessed September 28, 2012).

Hancock, Graham, and Santha Faiia. *Heaven's Mirror: Quest for the Lost Civilization*. New York: Three Rivers Press, 1999.

Hardy, Alister. "Was Man More Aquatic in the Past?" *New Scientist* 7 (1960): 642–45.

———. "Was There a Homo Aquaticus?" *Zenith* 15, no. 1 (1977): 4–6.

Hansel, Bryan. "Environmental Grafitti Boundary Water's Route: The Hunt for the Viking Dolmen." Paddling Light. www.paddlinglight.com/articles/trip-reports/boundary-waters-route-the-hunt-for-the-viking-dolmen (post dated November 10, 2009; accessed September 28, 2012).

Haughton, Brian, *Hidden History*. Pompton Plains, N.J.: New Page Books, 2007.

Hawkes, Jacquitta. *Man Before History*. Upper Saddle River, N.J.: Prentice-Hall, Inc., 1964.

Hawkins, Gerald S. "Prehistoric Astronomy: Archaeo-Astronomy, the Unwritten Evidence," Science and Man in the Americas, Science and Public Affairs. *Bulletin of the Atomic Scientists* 29, no. 8 (October 1973).

Heindel, Max, and Augusta Foss. *The Message of the Stars*. 7th ed., London: L. N. Fowler & Co.,1927.

Helferich, Gerard. *Humboldt's Cosmos*. New York: Gotham Books, 2005.

Henneberg, Bernhard. "Über die Bedeutung der Ohrmuschel." *Zeitschrift für Anatomie und Entwicklungsgeschichte,* Bd 111, H2 (1941): 22.

Herouni, Paris. *Armenians and Old Armenia: Archaeo-astronomy, Linguistics, Oldest History*. Yerevan, Armenia: Tigran Mets, 2004.

Heureux, John L. *The Shrine jat Altamira*. New York: Grove Press, 1999.

Heyerdahl, Thor. *The Maldive Mystery*. Chevy Chase, Md.: Adler & Adler, 1986.

Heywang, Walter, Karl Lubitz, and Wolfram Wersing. *Piezoelectricity: Evolution and Future of a Technology*. New York: Springer, 2008.

Hides, Jack. "Megalithic Madness," *Australian Geographer* 2, no. 8 (1935), 19 through 24.

Hibben, Frank C. *Prehistoric Man in Europe*. Norman: Oklahoma University Press, 1968.

Hirst, K. Kris. "Megafauna Extinctions." About.com Archaeology. http://archaeology.about.com/od/mterms/g/megaextinct.htm (undated article; accessed September 27, 2012).

———. "The Solutrean-Clovis Connection: A Theory for the Peopling of America," About.com. Archaeology. http://archaeology.about.com/od/skthroughsp/qt/solutrean_clovi.htm (undated article; accessed September 25, 2012).

Howells, William. *Mankind in the Making*. New York: Doubleday & Co., 1957.

James, Henry. *Henry James: Autobiography*. Princeton, N.J.: Princeton University Press, 1983.

James, Kate. "New Human Ancestor Will Rewrite Evolution." Gather.com Technology. http://technology.gather.com/viewArticle.action?articleId=281474980232031 (article dated September 10, 2011; accessed October 2, 2012).

Jasch, Mary. "The Tripod Rock Caper." Skylands Visitor: Northwest NJ Tourism Site. www.njskylands.com/odhiketripod.htm (undated page; accessed September 28, 2012).

Jones, Frederic Wood. *Man's Place among the Mammals.* London: E. Arnold & Co., 1929.

Joseph, Frank. *The Atlantis Encyclopedia.* Pompton Plains, N.J.: New Page Books, 2005.

———. *The Lost Civilization of Lemuria.* Rochester, Vt.: Bear and Company, 2006.

———. *Sacred Sites: A Guidebook to Sacred Centers and Mysterious Places in the United States.* Woodbury, Minn: Llewellyn Publications, 1992.

Keith, Sandra. *Pinnacles National Monument.* Tucson, Ariz.: Western National Parks Association, 2005.

Khorenatsi, Movses. *History of Armenia.* Edited by Gagik Kh. Sargsyan. Annotated translation and commentary by Stepan Malkhasyants. Yerevan, Armenia: Hayastan Publishing, 1997.

Knappert, Jan. *Pacific Mythology: An Encyclopedia of Myth and Legend.* London: Diamond Books, 1995.

Knight, Christopher, and Alan Butler. *Before the Pyramids: Cracking Archaeology's Greatest Mystery.* London: Watkins, 2011.

Kramer, Noah. *The Sumerians.* Chicago: University of Chicago Press, 1969.

Krieger, Herbert William. *Design Areas in Oceania Based on Specimens in the United States National Museum.* Washington, D.C.: Smithsonian Institution, 1932.

Krupp, E. C. *Echoes of the Ancient Skies: The Astronomy of Lost Civilizations.* Mineola, N.Y.: Dover Publications, 2003.

Lanpo, Jia. *Early Man in China.* San Francisco: China Books and Periodicals, 1980.

Langdon, J. H. "Umbrella Hypotheses and Parsimony in Human Evolution: A Critique of the Aquatic Ape Hypothesis." *Journal of Human Evolution* 33, no. 4 (1997): 479–94.

Lawson, Alastair. "Rare British India Documents Surface." *BBC News,* January 3, 2007. http://news.bbc.co.uk/2/hi/6176805.stm (accessed October 3, 2012).

Lawson, Andrew J., *Painted Caves: Palaeolithic Rock Art in Western Europe.* New York: Oxford University Press, 2012.

Leakey, Richard. *Origins.* New York: E.P. Dutton, 1977.

Leighton, Robert. *The Whole Works of Robert Leighton.* Ann Arbor: University of Michigan Library, 1832.

Lemesurier, Peter. *Decoding the Great Pyramid.* Rockport, Mass.: Element Books, Ltd., 2000.

Leonard, R. Cedric. *The Quest for Atlantis.* New York: Manor Books, 1979.

Le Plongeon, Augustus. *Sacred Mysteries Among the Mayas and Quiches, 11,500 Years Ago.* New York: Macoy Publishing, 1886.

Lieberman, Philip. *On the Origins of Language: An Introduction to the Evolution of Human Speech.* New York: Macmillan, 1975.

Lilley, Ian, ed. *Archaeoogy of Oceania: Australia and the Pacific Islands.* Hoboken, N.J.: Wiley-Blackwell, 2006.

Lippel, Philip. "Shell Beads from South African Cave Show Modern Human Behavior 75,000 years ago." National Science Foundation. www.eurekalert .org/pub_releases/2004-04/nsf-sbf041304.php (article dated April 15, 2004; accessed September 24, 2012).

Lynch, David K., and William Livingston. *Color and Light in Nature.* Cambridge, Mass.: Cambridge University Press, 2001.

MacKie, Euan Wallace. *The Megalith Builders.* London: Phaidon Press, 1977.

Malville, J. McKim, R. Schild, F. Wendorf, and R. Brenmer. "Astronomy of Nabta Playa." *African Sky*, 2007.

Manilius. *Astronomica.* Translated by G. P. Goold. Loeb Classical Library No. 469. Cambridge, Mass.: Harvard University Press, 1977.

Marshack, Alexander. *The Roots of Civilization.* New York: McGraw-Hill Book Co., 1972.

McKusick, Victor A. *Mendelian Inheritance in Man: A Catalog of Human Genes and Genetic Disorders.* 12th ed. Baltimore, Md.: The Johns Hopkins University Press, 1998.

Melville, Leinani. *Children of the Rainbow: The Religion, Legends and Gods of Pre-Christian Hawaii.* Wheaton, Ill.: Quest Books, Theosophical Publishing House, 1969.

Mercatante, Anthony S. *Who's Who in Egyptian Mythology.* New York: Clarkson N. Potter, Inc., 1978.

Mercer, John. *Fuerteventura and the Canary Islands.* Mechanicsburg, Pa.: Stackpole Books, 1973.

Miller, Frederic P., ed. *Göbekli Tepe.* Mauritius: Alphascript Publishing, 2011.

Moorehead, Warren King. *The Stone Age In North America.* Whitefish, Mont.: Kessinger Publishing, LLC, 2009.

Morgan, Elaine. *The Aquatic Ape.* New York: Stein & Day Publishing, 1982.

———."Aquatic Ape Theory." Primitivism. www.primitivism.com/aquatic-ape.htm (undated article; accessed September 21, 2012).

Morris, Desmond. "Desmond Morris on the Aquatic Ape Hypothesis." YouTube video. www.youtube.com/watch?v=mFRYtPQfyCk (undated video; accessed September 21, 2012).

Morse, Edward Sylvester. "Dolmens in Japan." *Popular Science Monthly* 16 (March 1880).

Moskowitz, Clara. "Neanderthal Brains Grew Like Ours." *Live Science.* www .livescience.com/2856-neanderthal-brains-grew.html (article dated September 8, 2008; accessed September 25, 2012).

Murdock, D. M. "World's Oldest Observatory Found?" *Examiner.* www.examiner .com/article/world-s-oldest-observatory-found (article dated October 12, 2010; accessed September 27, 2012).

Murray, George Read. "Red Paint People and Red Ochre People, Link or Legend." *Ancient American* 1, no 1 (July/August 1993).

Muzquiz Perez-Seoane, Matilde. *The Cave of Altamira.* New York: Harry N. Abrams, 1999.

Napier, William M."Evidence for Cometary Bombardment Episodes." Cardiff Centre for Astrobiology, Cardiff University, October 2005. www.stat.berkeley .edu/~aldous/157/Papers/napier.pdf (accessed September 27, 2012).

Napier, W. M. "Paleolithic extinctions at the Taurid Complex," Cardiff Centre for Astrobiology, Cardiff University, January 23, 2010.

"South American Prehistory Parameters Challenged," National Academy of Sciences. *Memoirs Of The National Academy Of Sciences.* Charleston, S.C.: Nabu Press, 2010.

*National Geographic* 147, no. 4 (1975): 12 (article on Tierra del Fuego).

Nietzsche, Friedrich. *Twilight of the Idols.* Oxford, England: Oxford University Press, 2009.

Niskanen, Markku. "The Origin of the Baltic-Finns from the Physical Anthropological Point of View." *Mankind Quarterly* 43, no. 2 (winter 2002): 121–53.

Nogués-Bravo, D., R. Ohlemüller, P. Batra, and M. B. Araújo. "Climate Predictors of Late Quaternary Extinctions." *Evolution*, 2010.

Noorbergen, Rene. *Secrets of Lost Races.* New York: Barnes and Noble Publishers, 1977.

Norbu, Namkhai. *Drung, Deu and Boen, Narrations, Symbolic Languages and the*

*Boen Tradition in Ancient Tibet.* Translated by Adriano Clemente and Andrew Lukianowicz. New York: Library of Tibetan Works and Archives, 1988.

Odent, M. "Birth Under Water." *Lancet* (1983): 1476–77.

Olsen, Brad. *Sacred Places North America.* San Francisco: CCC Publishing, 2008.

Oppenheimer, Stephen. *Eden in the East, The Drowned Continent of Southeast Asia.* London: Weidenfeld and Nicolson, 1999.

Osborne, W. H., and R. S. Laughlin. *Human Variation and Origins.* New York: W.H. Freeman and Company, 1967.

Owen, James. "Stone Age Adults Couldn't Stomach Milk, Gene Study Shows." *National Geographic News.* http://news.nationalgeographic.com/news/2007/02/070226-europe-milk.html (article dated February 26, 2007; accessed September 24, 2012).

Palmer, Trevor, and Mark E. Bailey, eds. *Natural Catastrophes During Bronze Age Civilizations: Archaeological, Geological, Astronomical and Cultural Perspectives.* Oxford, England: Archaeo Press, 1998.

Patrick, John M., Vernon Reynolds, Machteld Roede, and Jan Wind, eds. *The Aquatic Ape: Fact or Fiction?* London: Souvenir Press, 1991.

Pepper, Elizabeth, and John Wilcock. *Magical and Mystical Sites: Europe and the British Isles.* Grand Rapids, Mich.: Phanes Press, 2000.

Pfeiffer, John E. *The Emergence of Man.* New York: Harper & Row, 1969.

Plato. *The Republic.* Translated by G. M. A. Grube. Indianapolis, Ind.: Hackett Publishing Company, 1992.

———. *The Timaeus and the Kritias.* Translated by Desmond Lee. London: Penguin Books, 1977.

Preston, Richard. *The Wild Trees.* New York: Random House, 2007.

Price, Theron Douglas. *Europe's First Farmers.* Cambridge, Mass.: Cambridge University Press, 2000.

Pringle, Heather. "Did Humans Colonize the World by Boat?" *Discover,* June 2008. http://discovermagazine.com/2008/jun/20-did-humans-colonize-the-world-by-boat (article dated May 20, 2008; accessed September 25, 2012).

Pulinets, Sergey, and Kyrill Boyarchuk. *Ionospheric Precursors of Earthquakes.* New York: Springer, 2010.

Rainey, Froelich G. "Mystery of the Arctic." *Natural History* 46, no. 12 (1941).

Rock, Barbara Holley. "Pendejo Cave." *Ancient American* 2, no. 7 (September/October 1994).

Rothenberg, Marc, ed. *The Papers of Joseph Henry,* vol. 10 (January 1858–December 1865). Sagamore Beach, Mass.: Science History Publications, 2004.

Rydholm, Fred. "Michigan's Dolmen: A Stone Age Presence in America?" *Ancient American* 1, no. 1 (July/August 1993).

Saletan, William. "The Mismeasure of Stephen Jay Gould." *Discover,* January–February Special Issue. http://discovermagazine.com/2012/jan-feb/59 (article dated January 3, 2012; accessed September 25, 2012).

Scarre, Chris. *Monuments and Landscape in Atlantic Europe: Perception and Society During the Neolithic and Early Bronze Age.* New York: Routledge, 2002.

Scherz, James P. "The Stone Face at Mummy Mountain." *Ancient American* 5, no. 32 (April 2000).

*Science Newsletter.* "Nature, Not Man, Made Mummies in Island Cave." *Science Newsletter* 29, no. 370 (1936).

Service, Alastair, and Jean Bradbery. *Megaliths and Their Mysteries.* London: Weidenfeld and Nicolson, 1979.

Settegast, Mary. *Plato, Prehistorian: 10,000 To 5000 B.C. in Myth and Archaeology.* Cambridge, Mass.: Rotenberg Press, 1987.

Smith, Philip E. L. "Stone Age Man on the Nile." *Scientific American* 235, no. 2 (August 1976).

Spence, Lewis. *The History of Atlantis.* New York: Bell Books 1968. Reprint of the 1926 original.

Squier, E. G. "Americana Antiqua." *The Popular Science Monthly* 41 (May–October 1892), 19–44.

Stanhope, Philip Dormer [Lord Chesterfield]. *Lord Chesterfield's Letters.* Oxford, England: Oxford University Press, 2008.

Steiger, Brad. *Worlds Before Our Own.* New York: Anomalist Books, 2007. Reprint of the 1978 original.

Steel, Duncan, in Palmer and Bailey, *Natural Catastrophes During Bronze Age Civilizations:Archaeological, Geological, Astronomical and Cultural Perspectives.*

Steen-McIntyre, Virginia. "A Quarter-Million-Year-Old Human Habitation Site found in Mexico." *Ancient American* 19/20 (July/August–September/October 1998).

Streep, Peg. *Sanctuaries of the Goddess.* New York: Little, Brown and Company, 1994.

Sturluson, Snorri. *The Prose Edda.* New York: Penguin Classics, 2006.

Swan, James A., ed. *The Power of Place.* Wheaton, Ill.: Quest Books, 1991.

Sweeney, Emmet. *Atlantis: The Evidence of Science.* New York: Algora Publishing, 2010.

*The Great Soviet Encyclopedia.* 3rd edition. Farmington Hills, Mich.: The Gale Group, Inc., 1979.

Thom, Alexander. *Megalithic Remains in Britain and Brittany.* Oxford, England: Oxford University Press, 1978.

———. *Megalithic Sites in Britain.* Oxford, England: Oxford University Press, 1979.

Temple, Robert. *The Sphinx Mystery.* Rochester, Vt.: Inner Traditions, 2009.

Thompson, Gunnar. *American Discovery, the Real Story.* Seattle, Wash.: Argonauts Misty Isles Press, 1994.

Thorpe, S. K., R. L. Holder, and R. H. Crompton. "Origin of Human Bipedalism as an Adaptation for Locomotion on Flexible Branches." *Science* 316 (2007): 1328–31.

Vieira, James. "Search for the Mysterious Stone Builders of New England" pt. 1. *Ancient American* 15, no. 92.

Wakefield, Jay Stuart, and Reinoud M. de Jonge. *Rocks & Rows.* n.p., Wash.: MCS, Inc., 2010.

Wallace, Alfred Russell. "The Antiquity of Man in North America." *The Nineteenth Century Magazine* 12, no. 4 (November 1887).

Washburn, Sherwood L. "Tools and Human Evolution." in Osborne and Laughlin, *Human Variation and Origins.*

Weber, Bob. "Alberta Sun Temple has 5,000-year-old Calendar." *The Canadian Press.* www.thestar.com/News/Canada/article/579301 (article dated January 29, 2009; accessed September 28, 2012).

Wells, Sherill Brown. *Jean Monnet: Unconventional Statesman.* Boulder: Lynne Rienner Publishers, 2011.

Wells, Spencer. *Pandora's Seed: The Unforeseen Cost of Civilization.* New York: Random House, 2010.

Westenhöfer, Max. *Der Eigenweg des Menschen: Dargestellt auf Grund von vergleichend morphologischen Untersuchungen über die Artenbildung und Menschwerdung* [The singular way to mankind, depicted on the basis of comparative morphological studies on the formation of species and the origin of humanity]. Berlin, Germany: Mannstaedt Verlag, 1942.

———. "Die Grundlagen meiner Theorie vom Eigenweg des Menschen" [The basics of my theory of man's unique path]. Heidelberg, Germany: Carl Winter University, 1948.

———. *Das Problem der Menschwerdung* [The problem of human origin]. Berlin: Nornen-Verlag, 1935.

Westerdahl, Christer. "A Circumpolar Reappraisal: The Legacy of Gutorm Gjessing

(1906–1979)." Proceedings of an International Conference held in Trondheim, Norway. *British Archaeological Reports*. London: The Museum of Natural History, 2010.

Whitmore, Frank C. Jr., K. O. Emery, H. B. S. Cooke, and Donald J. P. Swift. "Elephant Teeth from the Atlantic Continental Shelf." *Science* 156 (1967): 1477–81.

Whittall, James Jr. "2995 B.P. +/-180." *NEARA Newsletter* 4, no. 3 (September 1969).

Wiley, Keith. *Assignment New Guinea*. Milton, Australia: The Jacaranda Press, 1974.

Willard, Emma Hart. "Rocked in the Cradle of the Deep." Poem available at http://womenshistory.about.com/library/etext/poem1/blp_willard_cradle_deep.htm (accessed September 22, 2012).

Wilford, John Noble. "Old, for Sure, but Human?" *New York Times,* December 13, 2005. www.nytimes.com/2005/12/13/science/13find.html (accessed October 2, 2012).

Wilson, Roy I. *Medicine Wheels: Ancient Teachings for Modern Times*. New York: The Crossroad Publishing Company, 1994.

Wind, Jan. "Human Drowning: Phylogenetic Origins." *Journal of Human Evolution* 5, no. 4 (July 1976): 349–63. Reproduced by Science Direct, http://dx.doi.org/10.1016/0047-2484(76)90040-3 (accessed September 21, 2012).

Wray, Alison, ed. *The Transition to Language*. Oxford, England: Oxford University Press, 2002.

Wyse, Elizabeth. *Past Worlds, the Times Atlas of Archaeology*. New York: Crescent Books, 1995.

Zeller, Eduard Gottlob. *Über die Anachronismen in den platonischen Gesprächen*. Berlin, Germany: Akademie der Wissenschaften, 1873.

Zhirov, Nikolay Atlantis. *Atlantis: Atlantology, Basic Problems*. Honolulu, Hawaii: University Press of the Pacific, 2001.

Zink, David D. *The Ancient Stones Speak*. Ontario, Canada: Musson Book Company, 1979.

# About the Author

Frank Joseph has published more books (nine) about Atlantis than any other writer in history. These have been released in thirty-five foreign-language editions around the world. He was the editor in chief of *Ancient American* magazine for fourteen years from its inception in 1993. A scuba diver since 1962, he has participated in underwater expeditions from the Bahamas and waters off Yucatan to the Canary Islands, the Eastern Mediterranean, and Polynesia.

His dozens of media appearances include interviews with Shirley MacLaine (seven between 2001 to 2010), Art Bell, Whitley Strieber, Linda Moulton-Howe, Jeff Rense, and many others. During 2000, the Savant Society of Japan, where Joseph has repeatedly lectured and appeared on national television, nominated him Professor of World Archaeology. In the United States, he received the Victor Moseley Award (1995) and Burrows Cave Society Award (1999) from Ohio's Midwest Epigraphic Society (Columbus), and his work has been granted official recognition by the Ancient American Artifact Preservation Society (Michigan).

Joseph lives today with his wife, Laura, and Norwegian Forest cat, Sammy, in the Upper Mississippi Valley.

# Index

Page numbers in *italics* refer to illustrations.